lonely planet

NEW YORK CITY

TOP SIGHTS, AUTHENTIC EXPERIENCES

Lorna Parkes, Hugh McNaughtan,
Regis St Louis

Contents

Central **⑨** @Guggenheim Museum
Park @Metropolitan Museum of Art

Upper East Side
High-end boutiques,
sophisticated man-
sions and Museum
Mile – one of the
most cultured strips
in the world.
(Map p254)

⑨ LaGuardia
Airport

Roosevelt
Island

Museum of Modern Art
⑨
@Rockefeller Center

@Grand Central Terminal

Empire State Building

**Union Square, Flatiron
District & Gramercy**
A bustling, vibrant park
binds surrounding areas
filled with good eats.
(Map p250)

East River

**East Village &
Lower East Side**
Two of the city's hot-
test 'hoods that lure
students, bankers and
scruffier types alike.
(Map p246)

wer East Side
enement Museum

n Bridge

yn Bridge Park

**Lower Manhattan &
the Financial District**
Iconic monuments,
riverfront access and
Wall St mingle at the
island's southern end.
(Map p244)

John F Kennedy
International **⑨** (5mi)
→

t

⑨ Prospect
Park

Coney Island
(6mi)

Welcome to New York City

Epicenter of the arts. Dining and shopping capital. Center of international commerce. Trendsetter in fashion and design. One of the world's greatest cities, New York wears many crowns, and spreads an irresistible feast for all.

Few other destinations can compete with NYC – or even Manhattan alone – for its breadth of world-class attractions and genuine icons. Around 65 million visitors a year flock here to feel like they're on a movie set by scaling the Empire State, passing through Grand Central Terminal, strolling Central Park or catching the ferry to Lady Liberty. There's the Met, MoMA and the Guggenheim – just the beginning of a dizzying list of art-world icons. Then when the sun sinks slowly beyond the Hudson and luminous skyscrapers light up the night, New York transforms into one grand stage. Got time for more? Well you're in for a treat.

If you can dream it up, it's probably happening somewhere in New York. With its compact size and streets packed with eye candy of all sorts – architectural treasures, retro diners, atmospheric booksellers – NYC is a wanderer's delight. Crossing continents is as easy as walking a few avenues in this jumbled city of 200-plus nationalities.

You can lose yourself in the crowds of Chinatown amid bright Buddhist temples and steaming noodle shops, then stroll up to Nolita for fancy boutiques and coffee-tasting. Every neighborhood offers a dramatically different version of the city, from the 100-year-old Jewish delis of the Upper West Side to the meandering cobblestone lanes of Greenwich Village. It should come as no surprise that such diversity makes New York one of the world's best places to eat, drink and play.

With eye candy of all sorts ... NYC is a wanderer's delight

42nd Street, Manhattan
PRASIT PHOTO/GETTY IMAGES ©

★ NEW YORK CITY ★

Upper West Side & Central Park
Home to the premier performing arts center and the park that helps define the city.
(Map p254)

Midtown
Times Square, Broadway theaters, canyons of skyscrapers, and bustling crowds that rarely thin.
(Map p250)

Lincoln Center

Broadway
Times Square ◎
Pennsylvania (Penn) Station

Greenwich Village, Chelsea & Meatpacking District
Quaint, intimate streets plus trendy nightlife, shopping and art galleries galore. *(Map p246)*

High Line ❶ ❶ Chelsea
Whitney Museum ◎ Market
of American Art 🏛

Hudson River

One World Trade Center
◎
🏛

National September 11 Memorial & Museum

◎ Brookl
❶ Brook

Liberty State Park

◎ Ellis Island

Upper New York Bay

Governors Island

SoHo & Chinatown
Soup dumpling parlors and hawkers selling bric-a-brac next door to cobblestone streets and stores with the biggest name brands in the world.
(Map p246)

❶
Statue of Liberty

Brooklyn
These days, the name is shorthand for 'artsy cool' the world over, b there's far more here than hipster stereotypes. *(Map p256)*

Ⓝ 0 _____ 2 km
0 _____ 1 mile

Plan Your Trip
This Year in New York City

New York City

This is New York, baby, and you can expect something to be happening every day of the year – music and arts festivals, holiday markets, celebratory parades, sports tournaments, gourmet gatherings and more. Make sure to plan ahead for the bigger events.

Clockwise from left: Village Halloween Parade (p15); SummerStage (p10); Independence Day (p12); Tribeca Film Festival (p9)

★ Top Festivals & Events

Tribeca Film Festival, Apr (p9)

SummerStage, May–Oct (p10)

Shakespeare in the Park, Jun–Aug (p11)

Independence Day, Jul 4 (p12)

Village Halloween Parade, Oct 31 (p15)

Plan Your Trip
This Year in New York City

January

01

The winter doldrums arrive following the build-up of Christmas and New Year's Eve. Despite the long nights, New Yorkers take advantage of the frosty weather, with outdoor ice skating and weekend ski trips to the Catskills.

🎽 New Year's Day Swim   Jan 1
What better way to greet the new year than with an icy dip in the Atlantic? Join the Coney Island Polar Bear Club for this annual brrrr fest (pictured above).

🎽 No Pants Subway Ride   Jan 12
On the second Sunday in January, some 4000 New Yorkers spice things up with a bit of leg nudity on public transit. Anyone can join in, and there's usually an after-party for the cheeky participants. Check www.improveverywhere.com for meeting times and details.

☆ Winter Jazzfest   mid-Jan
This weeklong music fest (www.winter jazzfest.com) brings over 100 acts playing at nearly a dozen venues around the city. Most of the action happens around the West Village.

🎋 Lunar (Chinese) New Year Festival   Jan 25
One of the biggest Lunar New Year celebrations in the country, this display of fireworks and dancing dragons draws mobs of thrill seekers into the streets of Chinatown.

☆ Broadway Week   mid-Jan–early Feb
For about 2½ weeks from mid-January into early February (and again in September), you can buy two-for-one tickets for top-notch Broadway musicals and plays, often including new productions (www.nycgo. com/broadway-week). In 2019, *Book of Mormon*, *King Kong* and *Mean Girls* all took part.

✗ Restaurant Week   late Jan–early Feb
Celebrate the dreary weather with slash-cut meal deals at some of the city's finest eating establishments during New York's Winter Restaurant Week (www.nycgo.com/ nyc-restaurant-week), which actually runs for about two weeks. A two-course lunch costs around $26 ($42 for a three-course dinner).

February

The odd blizzard and below-freezing temperatures make February a good time to stay indoors nursing a drink or a warm meal at a cozy bar or bistro.

☆ Westminster Kennel Club Dog Show
Feb 8–11

New York goes to the dogs each February at this canine competition (www.westminsterkennelclub.org), where some 3000 dogs come from around the world to vie for top honors. The 'best in show' judging is held in Madison Square Garden.

☉ New York Fashion Week
mid-Feb

The infamous New York Fashion Week (pictured above; www.nyfw.com) is sadly not open to the public. But whether you're invited or not, being in the city could provide a vicarious thrill, especially if you can find the after-parties.

☆ Mardi Gras
Feb 25

New Yorkers let their hair down for New Orleans-inspired 'Fat Tuesday' celebrations

☆ Off-Broadway Week
mid-Feb–late Feb

In the second half of February (and again in September/October), get two-for-one tickets to various Off-Broadway shows around town, often including long-running productions like Avenue Q and Stomp (www.nycgo.com/off-broadway-week).

the day before Ash Wednesday. It's a good excuse to hit up a jazz performance or two, go to a carnival-crazy knees-up, or try some Cajun cuisine.

8

BLFMR/SHUTTERSTOCK ©

Plan Your Trip

This Year in New York City

March

After months of freezing temperatures and thick winter coats, the odd warm spring day appears and everyone rejoices – though it's usually followed by a week of subzero drear as winter lingers on.

☆ Big East Basketball Tournament early Mar
Part of NYC's 'March Madness' for college basketball, this major tournament (www.bigeast.com) has been held at Madison Square Garden for over 30 years. Ten eastern school teams compete for the title and a chance to play in the NCAA tournament later in the month.

🎋 St Patrick's Day Parade Mar 17
A massive audience, rowdy and wobbly from cups of green beer, lines Fifth Ave for this popular parade (www.nycstpatricksparade.org) of bagpipe blowers, floats and clusters of Irish-lovin' politicians. The parade, which was first held here in 1762, is the city's oldest and largest.

☆ Armory Show mid-Mar
New York's biggest contemporary art fair (www.thearmoryshow.com) sweeps into the city for one weekend in March, showcasing the works of thousands of artists from around the world on three piers (Piers 90, 92 and 94) that jut into the Hudson River.

☆ BAAD!Ass Women Festival mid-Mar
Expect bags of energy and inspiration from this annual fringe festival (www.baadbronx.org) put on by the Bronx Academy of Arts & Dance. Its lineup of music, dance, comedy and more is driven by LGBTQ+ performers, Latinx culture and women of color.

◉ Macy's Flower Show late Mar–early Apr
For two weeks in spring, Macy's department store is turned into a floral wonderland. The Herald Square flagship store (pictured above) hosts elaborate displays of blooms, lush mini-landscapes and clever blends of the natural and human-made environment.

April

Spring finally appears: optimistic alfresco joints have a sprinkling of street-side chairs as the city squares overflow with bright tulips and blossom-covered trees.

☆ **Brooklyn Folk Festival**   early Apr
Pack your banjo for one of the jam sessions and the banjo toss contest at this grass-roots community festival (www.brooklyn folkfest.com), attracting thousands of music lovers. It lasts for three days, hosts more than 30 bands, and includes music workshops and even a family-friendly square dance.

☆ **Easter Bonnet Parade**   Apr 12
Dating back to the 1870s, this parade (pictured above) features scores of nattily dressed, bonnet- wearing participants who show off their finery along Fifth Ave in Midtown (from 49th to 57th Sts). Bring your wildest hat and join in the action. It usually kicks off at 10am.

☆ **Tribeca Film Festival**   Apr
Created in response to the tragic events of September 11, Robert De Niro's downtown

🍷 **NYC Craft Beer Festival**   early Apr
This craft suds festival (www.nyccraft beerfest.com) pulls together the best of New York's indie brewers, with 75 participating breweries and around 150 seasonal – hic – local beers being poured over two days. In 2019 it moved to a sparkly new venue right by the High Line.

film festival (www.tribecafilm.com) has quickly become a star in the indie movie circuit. You'll have to make some tough choices: over 150 films are screened during the 10-day fest.

🏃 **Earth Day**   Apr 22
New York hosts a packed day of events at Union Square, with live music, presenta-tions on sustainability and hands-on activ-ities for kids (www.earthdayinitiative.org). There's also a '5K Green Tour,' exploring NYC businesses and attractions that are flying the green flag.

Plan Your Trip
This Year in New York City

QUIGGYT4/SHUTTERSTOCK ©

May

April showers bring May flowers in the form of brilliant bursts of blossoms adorning trees all around the city. The weather is warm and mild without the unpleasant humidity of summer.

☉ Cherry Blossom Festival   early May
This annual tradition (pictured) held over one weekend celebrates the magnificent flowering of cherry trees in the Brooklyn Botanic Garden. It's complete with entertainment and activities, plus refreshments and, of course, beautiful blossoms.

☘ TD Bank Five Boro Bike Tour   early May
Bike Month features two-wheelin' tours, parties and other events for pedal-pushing New Yorkers. TD Bank Five Boro Bike Tour (www.bike.nyc/events/td-five-boro-bike-tour), the main event, sees thousands of cyclists hit the pavement for a 40-mile ride, much of it on roads closed to traffic or on waterfront paths.

☉ Memorial Day   May 25
This day remembers Americans who have died in combat. Each borough hosts a

❀ Governors Ball   late May–early Jun
This big-ticket contemporary music fest (www.governorsballmusicfestival.com) rocks out over three days on Randall's Island. Roving street artists, life-size board games and some of NYC's best food trucks add extra flair.

parade featuring marching bands and flag-waving veterans; the biggest is Queens' Little Neck–Douglaston Memorial Day Parade (www.lndmemorialday.org).

☆ SummerStage   May–Oct
Central Park's SummerStage (www.cityparksfoundation.org) features a great lineup of music and dance, and most events are free. There's also a Summer-Stage Kids program.

☆ Fleet Week   late May
Manhattan resembles a 1940s movie set for one week (www.fleetweeknewyork.com) as clusters of fresh-faced, uniformed sailors go 'on the town' to look for adventures. You can hop aboard the ships they leave behind, docked in the Hudson River, for tours.

June

When summer arrives locals crawl out of their office cubicles to relax in the city's green spaces. Parades roll down the busiest streets, and portable movie screens are strung up in several parks.

☆ Bryant Park Summer Film Festival   Jun–Aug

Bryant Park hosts free Monday-night outdoor screenings (www.bryantpark.org) of classic Hollywood films. Arrive early (the lawn area opens at 5pm and folks line up by 4pm); films begin at sunset.

⊙ Puerto Rican Day Parade   Jun 14

The second Sunday in June attracts thousands of flag-waving revelers for the annual Puerto Rican Day Parade. Now in its sixth decade, it runs up Fifth Ave from 44th to 86th Sts.

⊙ Mermaid Parade   Jun 20

On the Saturday closest to the summer solstice, this quirky afternoon parade (www.coneyisland.com) celebrates sand, sea and summer. It's a flash of glitter and glamour, as elaborately costumed folks display their fishy finery along the Coney Island boardwalk. All in costume are welcome.

🎉 NYC Pride   Jun 28

Gay Pride Month culminates in a major march down Fifth Ave on the last Sunday of the month. NYC Pride (pictured) is a five-hour spectacle of dancers, drag queens, gay police officers, leathermen, lesbian soccer moms and representatives of every other LGBT+ scene under the rainbow.

☆ Shakespeare in the Park   Jun–Aug

Shakespeare in the Park (www.centralpark.com) pays tribute to the Bard, with free performances in Central Park. The catch? You'll have to wait hours to score tickets, or win them in the lottery. Tickets are given out at noon; arrive no later than 10am.

☆ Museum Mile Festival   mid-Jun

For one evening, Fifth Ave from 82nd to 105th Sts is transformed into one big traffic-free block party (www.museummilefestival.org), celebrating the thoroughfare's museums. Some give free entry or host special talks and events, there are also street performers, activities for kids and live music.

This Year in New York City

ELZBIETA SEKOWSKA/SHUTTERSTOCK ©

07

July

As the city swelters, locals flee to beachside escapes on Long Island. It's a busy month for tourism, however, as holidaying North Americans and Europeans fill the city.

✿ Independence Day   Jul 4

America's Independence Day is celebrated on the 4th of July with dramatic fireworks over the East River, starting at 9pm. Good viewing spots include the waterfronts of the Lower East Side and Williamsburg, Brooklyn, or any high rooftop or east-facing Manhattan apartment.

✕ Nathan's Famous
Hot Dog Eating Contest   Jul 4

This bizarre celebration (pictured above) of gluttony (www.nathansfamous.com) brings world-champion food inhalers to Coney Island each July 4. Eleven-time winner Joey Chestnut holds the men's record, having scoffed 74 hot dogs (including buns!) in just 10 gut-busting minutes. (Five-time women's champion Miki Sudo's record stands at 41.)

☆ MoMA PS1 Warm Up   Jul–Sep

Hang with the cool crowd on Saturdays from July through early September at this outdoor party at MoMA PS1

(www.momaps1.org/warmup) in Queens, which features a stellar lineup of DJs, bands and experimental musicians, all playing tunes under the summer sky.

☆ Lincoln Center
Out of Doors   late Jul–mid-Aug

New York City's performing arts power-house stages a celebratory program of concerts and dance parties at outdoor stages in the Lincoln Center complex (www.lcoutofdoors.org). Afrobeat, Latin jazz and country are all part of the lineup, and there are special events for families.

✿ Harlem Week   late Jul–mid-Aug

Lasting way longer than a week, this culture appreciation fest (www.harlemweek.com) hosts more than 100 events honoring the rich history of this storied upper Manhattan neighborhood. Expect park parties, a 5K race, restaurant specials and, of course, music.

August

Thick waves of summer heat slide between skyscrapers as everyone heads to the seashore or gulps cool blasts of air-conditioning. Myriad outdoor events and attractions add life to the languid urban heat.

☆ Hong Kong Dragon Boat Festival   mid-Aug
This Queens festival (www.hkdbf-ny.org) celebrates the fifth month of the Chinese lunar calendar with international music and dance, martial arts demonstrations, crafts and food – and the main event of 200 dragon boat teams racing across the lake in Flushing Meadows–Corona Park.

🎷 Blues BBQ Festival   mid-Aug
Blues hounds congregate on a pier in Hudson River Park for this annual celebration (www.hudsonriverpark.org) of one of America's defining sounds. The packed lineup is accompanied by, you've guessed it, finger-licking Southern-style barbecue.

☆ US Open   late Aug–early Sep
Queens' Arthur Ashe Stadium takes center stage as the world's top tennis players

☆ Jazz Age Lawn Party   late Aug
Be the cat's pajamas in summery 1920s attire at this Governors Island party (pictured), a full day of big band jazz, Charleston dancing and pre-Prohibition cocktails (www.jazzagelawnparty.com). Buy your tickets as early as possible – this event always sells out. Also happens in June.

compete in the final Grand Slam tournament of the year (www.usopen.org). If you can't find tickets, you can watch the matches screened in sports bars all around town.

☆ Charlie Parker Jazz Festival   late Aug
This open-air two-day fest (www.cityparks foundation.org) is a great day out for music fans. Incredible jazz talents take to the stage in Marcus Garvey Park in Harlem and in Tompkins Square Park in the East Village.

This Year in New York City

JOE TABACCA/SHUTTERSTOCK ©

September

Labor Day officially marks the end of the Hamptons' share-house season as the blistering heat of summer fades to more tolerable levels. As locals return to work, the cultural calendar ramps up.

☉ West Indian American Day Carnival — Sep 2

This exuberant parade and carnival (www.wiadcacarnival.org) down Eastern Pkwy every September celebrates Caribbean culture and the West Indian community of Crown Heights in Brooklyn, with reggae music, steel-drum bands and glittering, feathered-and-beaded costumes of every color in the rainbow.

☆ Electric Zoo — Sep 5–6

Celebrated over the Labor Day weekend, Electric Zoo (www.electriczoo.com) is New York's electronic music festival held in sprawling Randall's Island Park. Past headliners have included Moby, Afrojack, Tiësto, Martin Solveig and The Chemical Brothers.

☆ Feast of San Gennaro — mid-Sep

Rowdy, loyal crowds descend on the narrow streets of Little Italy for carnival games, a meatball-eating contest and more Italian treats than you can stomach in one evening. The San Gennaro Festival (www.sangennaro.nyc; pictured above) has been going for over 90 years.

✗ Vendy Awards — mid-Sep

This street food awards showdown (www.vendyawards.streetvendor.org) is the biggest event on the calendar for NYC's sidewalk chefs. Twenty-five publicly nominated food trucks pitch up on Governors Island for a ticketed, one-day event with all-you-can-eat food, beer and wine. Public ballots determine the overall winner.

✶ Atlantic Antic — late Sep

New York's best street festival offers live music, a cornucopia of food and drink, and numerous craft and clothing vendors. Climb aboard some vintage buses at the New York Transit Museum's display. It runs along Brooklyn's Atlantic Ave (www.atlanticave.org) between Fourth Ave and the waterfront, usually on the fourth Sunday in September.

10

October

Brilliant bursts of color fill the trees as temperatures cool and alfresco cafes finally shutter their windows. Along with May, October is one of the most pleasant and scenic months to visit NYC.

☆ BAM's Next Wave Festival   Oct–Dec
Celebrated for over 30 years, the Brooklyn Academy of Music's Next Wave Festival (www.bam.org), which runs October through December, showcases world-class avant-garde theater, music and dance.

☆ Comic Con   early Oct
Enthusiasts gather at this annual beacon of fandom (www.newyorkcomiccon.com; pictured above) to dress up as their favorite characters. Tickets sell out months in advance.

☆ Open House New York   mid-Oct
The country's largest architecture and design event, Open House New York (www. ohny.org) weekend features special architect-led tours, plus lectures, design workshops, studio visits and site-specific performances all over the city.

✵ Blessing of the Animals   Oct 4
In honor of the Feast Day of St Francis, pet owners flock to the grand Cathedral Church of St John the Divine for the annual Blessing of the Animals (pictured above right) with their sidekicks – poodles, lizards, parrots, llamas, you name it.

◉ Village Halloween Parade   Oct 31
On Halloween, New Yorkers don their wildest costumes for a night of revelry. See the most outrageous displays at the Village Halloween Parade (www.halloween-nyc. com) that runs up Sixth Ave in the West Village. It's fun to watch, but even better to join in.

Plan Your Trip
This Year in New York City

November

As the leaves tumble, light jackets are replaced by wool and down. A headliner marathon is tucked into the final days of prehibernation weather, then families gather to give thanks.

☆ New York Comedy Festival
early Nov

Funny-makers take the city by storm during this weeklong festival (www.nycomedy festival.com), with stand-up sessions, improv nights and big-ticket shows hosted by the likes of Rosie O'Donnell and Ricky Gervais.

🏃 New York City Marathon
early Nov

This annual 26-mile run (www.tcsnyc marathon.org) draws thousands of athletes from around the world, and many more fans line the streets to cheer the runners on.

☉ Thanksgiving Day Parade
Nov 26

Massive helium-filled balloons soar overhead, high-school marching bands rattle their snares and millions of onlookers bundle up with scarves and coats to celebrate Thanksgiving with Macy's world-famous 2.5-mile-long parade (pictured above).

☆ Radio City Christmas Spectacular
Nov–Dec

Expect queues every day of the week for this Christmas extravaganza (www.rockettes.com/christmas) featuring New York's high-kicking Rockettes, which runs daily throughout the holiday season. There are plenty of tickets, and it's a kitsch, razzle-dazzle tradition (dating back to 1933) that kids and adults love.

🏃 Ice Skating
Nov–Mar

New Yorkers make the most of the winter on outdoor rinks across the city. These open in November and run until late March; top choices include Central Park, Bryant Park, Prospect Park and Rockefeller Center.

12

December

Winter's definitely here, but there's plenty of holiday cheer to warm the spirit. Fifth Ave department stores (as well as Macy's) create elaborate worlds within their storefront windows, and Manhattan transforms into one of the best places in the world to see Christmas decorations.

🔒 Holiday Markets   Dec 1–24

In December New York becomes a wonderland of holiday markets, selling crafts, jewelry, clothing and accessories, ceramics, toys and more. Get a steaming cup of hot chocolate and stroll the aisles. The biggest markets can be found at Union Square, Bryant Park and Grand Central Terminal.

🏃 New York Road Runners Midnight Run   Dec 31

Not a drinker? How about joining other runners on a 4-mile dash through Central Park to ring in the new year (the festivities and fireworks kick off beforehand). Sign up with New York Road Runners (www. nyrr.org).

☆ Christmas Tree Lighting Ceremony   late Nov/early Dec

The flick of a switch ignites the massive Christmas tree (www.rockefellercenter. com) in Rockefeller Plaza, officially ushering in the holiday season. Bedecked with over 25,000 lights, it is NYC's unofficial Yuletide headquarters and a must-see for anyone visiting the city during December.

☆ Holiday Train Show   mid-Nov–mid-Jan

Kids go wild for this Christmas tradition at the New York Botanical Gardens (www.nybg. org) in the Bronx, where model trains weave through elaborately built recreations of NYC landmarks – all constructed out of plants.

🎊 New Year's Eve   Dec 31

Times Square (pictured) swarms with millions who come swig booze, freeze in subarctic temperatures, witness the annual dropping of the ball and chant the '10...9...8...' countdown in perfect unison.

Plan Your Trip
Hot Spots For...

CULTURE VULTURES

◉ **MoMA** NYC's darling museum has brilliantly curated spaces boasting the best of the world's modern art. (p70)

◉ **Metropolitan Museum of Art** The most encyclopedic museum in the Americas. (pictured above; p48)

✗ **Cookshop** Great indoor-outdoor dining spot near the heart of Chelsea's gallery scene. (p130)

♟ **La Compagnie des Vins Surna-turels** A sophisticated wine bar in Noli-ta, with hundreds of vintages. (p168)

☆ **Brooklyn Academy of Music** This hallowed theater hosts cutting-edge works, particularly during its celebrated Next Wave Festival. (p189)

GLITZ & GLAMOUR

☆ **Broadway** Book seats to an award-winning show starring some of the best actors in show business (p56; pictured below).

◉ **Frick Collection** This mansion has Vermeers, El Grecos and Goyas and a stunning courtyard fountain. (p51)

🛍 **Barneys** The fashionista's closet comes with a hefty price tag. (p156)

✗ **Eleven Madison Park** Arresting, cutting-edge cuisine laced with unexpected whimsy. (p133)

♟ **Raines Law Room** Curtained booths at this Prohibition-style cocktail lounge evoke the Jazz Age. (p171)

HISTORY BUFFS

⊙ **Lower East Side Tenement Museum** Gain fascinating insight into the lives of 19th- and early-20th century immigrants on a tour of a preserved tenement. (p94)

⊙ **Ellis Island** The gateway to freedom and opportunity for so many of America's immigrants. (p42)

☆ **Hamilton** An American history lesson set to urban rhythms.(p59)

✕ **Chumley's** A former speakeasy with Prohibition-era decor and a first-rate seasonal menu. (p133)

♟ **Old Town Bar & Restaurant** Classic tin-roofed boozer that has welcomed New Yorkers since 1892. (p171)

MUSIC LOVERS

⊙ **Metropolitan Opera** Dress to the nines and have a fancy night out at Lincoln Center. (p110)

⊙ **Empire State Building** Ascend this New York icon for live sax Thursday to Saturday nights from 9pm. (p66)

☆ **Birdland** Book bargain tickets for the intimate 'Big Band' show at this Midtown jazz club on Fridays. (p187)

☆ **Smalls** Tiny West Village basement bar with nightly jazz and weekend afternoon jam sessions. (p183)

✕ **Sylvia's** Brunch on waffles and fried chicken with a side of gospel music in Harlem. (pictured above; p139)

FRESH AIR

⊙ **The High Line** Wild plants and towering weeds steal the show. (p52)

⊙ **Prospect Park** Escape the crowds at Brooklyn's gorgeous park, with trails, hills, a canal, lake and meadows. (p98)

⚓ **Loeb Boathouse** Maroon yourself on a boat in the middle of Central Park. (pictured above; p199)

🛒 **Union Square Greenmarket** Assemble a picnic from the lovely produce and gourmet goodies at this outdoor market. (p127)

✕ **Smorgasburg** Hunt out this roving, alfresco street food market in Brooklyn. (p140)

Plan Your Trip
Top Days in New York City

Lower Manhattan & Brooklyn

Leave behind the concrete canyons for a day of broad horizons and river views, not to mention a stroll over an iconic bridge. Be sure to book advance tickets for the Statue of Liberty and Ellis Island, and One World Trade Center.

❶ Statue of Liberty & Ellis Island (p40)

Book tickets in advance and arrive for your ferry early. Ellis Island will likely occupy most of the morning. Food options are poor on the islands, so bring snacks.

● Statue Cruises ferry dock to Tiny's

S Take the 1 line from South Ferry Station to Chambers St Station. Walk two blocks north on Broadway.

❷ Lunch at Tiny's & the Bar Upstairs (p123)

This Tribeca townhouse with antique furnishings is a comfy spot for a classy modern American lunch.

● Tiny's to One World Trade Center

🏃 Walk half a mile south on Broadway, then turn west onto Vesey St for One World Trade Center.

❸ One World Trade Center (p90)

Step into NYC's tallest building and ride up to the One World Observatory for

AGATHA KADAR/SHUTTERSTOCK ©

astounding views over NYC. Reserve tickets in advance.

➡ One World Trade Center to the National September 11 Memorial & Museum

🚶 Walk south to the memorial, located next to the building.

❹ National September 11 Memorial & Museum (p86)

One of New York's most powerful sites, this memorial pays moving tribute to the victims of the 2001 terrorist attack. Visit the adjoining museum to learn more about that day's tragic events.

➡ National September 11 Memorial & Museum to Brooklyn Bridge

🚶 Walk east on Vesey St, cross Broadway, and then continue up Park Row. The walkway entrance is across from City Hall Park.

❺ Brooklyn Bridge (p46)

Join the hordes of other visitors making this magical pilgrimage over one of the city's most beautiful landmarks.

➡ Brooklyn Bridge to Empire Fulton Ferry State Park

🚶 Walk over the bridge from Manhattan to Brooklyn. Take the stairs and turn left at the bottom. Walk downhill to the waterfront.

❻ Empire Fulton Ferry State Park (p47)

This lovely park has staggering views of Manhattan and the Brooklyn Bridge, and a fully restored 1922 carousel. Dumbo's atmospheric brick streets are sprinkled with cafes, shops and 19th-century warehouses.

➡ Empire Fulton Ferry State Park to Juliana's

🚶 Walk west on Water St to Old Fulton St; turn left and walk east toward Front St.

❼ Dinner at Juliana's (p141)

Enjoy pizza maestro Patsy Grimaldi's legendary thin-crust pies – the classic margherita is one of NYC's best.

From left: Statue of Liberty & Ellis Island (p40); Brooklyn Bridge (p46)

Plan Your Trip
Top Days in New York City

DIEGO GRANDY/SHUTTERSTOCK ©

Upper East Side & Midtown

Landmarks, highlights, big-ticket items: on this itinerary you'll experience the NYC of everyone's collective imagination, including the city's most famous museum and park. Take in the mythic landscape of Midtown's skyscrapers from amid the clouds at Rockefeller Center.

❶ Breakfast at the Guggenheim (p78)

Get in early at the Guggenheim before crowds form. If you visit on the weekend, start your day with brunch at the museum's art-worthy modernist Wright restaurant.

◐ Guggenheim to Metropolitan Museum of Art

✦ Walk six blocks south along Fifth Ave.

❷ Metropolitan Museum of Art (p48)

Head to this world-class museum and delve into the sprawling Ancient Greek and Roman collections. Check out the Egyptian Wing (which includes an ancient temple), then take in works by European masters on the 2nd floor. Head up to the Cantor Roof Garden in season for park views.

◐ Metropolitan Museum of Art to Central Park

✦ Walk into Central Park at the 79th St entrance.

OSCITY/SHUTTERSTOCK ©

❸ Central Park (p36)

Get some fresh air in Central Park, the city's spectacular public backyard. Walk south to Bethesda Terrace, where there's a restaurant-bar and boating on the lake.

⟳ Central Park to Times Square

🚶 Exit the park on Fifth Ave however far south you'd like, and grab a cab for Times Square.

❹ Times Square (p62)

Soak up the bright lights and crowded streets of Times Square from the TKTS Booth's stadium seating at the northern end, where you can take in the dazzling tableau. Get discounted tickets for a show that night.

⟳ Times Square to Rockefeller Center

🚶 Walk west to Sixth Ave and then north to 49th St.

❺ Top of the Rock (p82)

Buy a ticket for the open-air observation deck at Rockefeller Center's Top of the Rock – this is where you'll get the best view of the neighboring Empire State Building.

⟳ Rockefeller Center to Grand Central Terminal

🚶 It's half a mile south from Rockefeller Plaza to Grand Central's 42nd St entrance.

❻ Dinner at Grand Central Terminal (p76)

New York's *grande dame* of the rails has brilliant options for an early pre-show dinner – slurp seafood at the atmospheric Grand Central Oyster Bar, go casual at the Great Northern Food Hall, or book a table at Michelin-starred Agern.

⟳ Grand Central Terminal to a Broadway show

🚕 Your feet will be exhausted by now; take a taxi to Theater Land.

❼ Broadway Show (p56)

Enjoy a blockbuster musical for an only-in-New-York spectacle. Afterwards, book a table for cocktail swigging up in the gods at Bar SixtyFive.

From left: Metropolitan Museum of Art (p48); Manhattan skyline with a view of the Empire State Building (p66)

Plan Your Trip
Top Days in New York City

Chelsea & Upper West Side

The best in American art, a famed elevated green space, market adventures and some spectacular dinosaurs set the stage for a fun day's ramble on the West Side. Cap off the day at Lincoln Center, one of the country's top performance spaces.

Day

03

❶ Whitney Museum of American Art (p84)

Start your day perusing the spacious galleries here, with great American artists such as O'Keeffe, Rothko and Hopper.

⊙ Whitney Museum of American Art to the High Line

🚶 Enter the High Line at its southern end on Gansevoort St, just outside the museum.

❷ The High Line (p52)

The stroll-worthy High Line is an abandoned railway 30ft above the street and one of New York's favorite downtown destinations. Enter at the southern end and meander north for views of the Hudson River and the city streets below.

⊙ The High Line to Chelsea Market

🚶 Exit at the 16th St stairway for the Tenth Ave entrance of Chelsea Market.

❸ Lunch at Chelsea Market (p130)

The main concourse of this former cookie factory is packed with food stalls slinging

everything from spicy Korean noodle soups to Aussie-style sausage rolls.

🔵 Chelsea Market to American Museum of Natural History

Ⓢ Grab an uptown C train at Eighth Ave and 14th St and take it to 86th and Central Park West.

❹ American Museum of Natural History (p111)

No matter what your age, you'll experience childlike wonder at the dinosaur fossils at the exceptional American Museum of Natural History. Don't miss the Rose Center for Earth & Space, a unique architectural gem.

🔵 American Museum of Natural History to Boulud Sud

🚌 Take the bus down Columbus Ave, walk or grab a cab the 0.8 miles south to W 64th.

❺ Dinner at Boulud Sud (p138)

Celebrity chef Daniel Boulud presents his take on Mediterranean cuisines in a mid-century modern setting. The pre-theater prix-fixe meal is a bargain.

🔵 Boulud Sud to Lincoln Center

🚶 Cross Broadway and Columbus Ave to Lincoln Center.

❻ Show at Lincoln Center (p108)

Head across to Lincoln Center for opera at the Metropolitan Opera House (the largest in the world), a symphony in Avery Fisher Hall, or ballet or a play at one of its two theaters – all great shows in architecturally mesmerizing settings.

🔵 Lincoln Center to Manhattan Cricket Club

Ⓢ Take the 1 train two stops to 79th St and walk half a block east.

❼ Manhattan Cricket Club (p174)

This swanky spot is accessed through a hidden staircase inside the Burke & Wills restaurant (ask the host for access). While away the night on a Chesterfield with cocktail in hand.

From left: The High Line (p52); Lincoln Center (p108)

Plan Your Trip
Top Days in New York City

Lower East Side, SoHo & the East Village

Gain insight into immigrant history, grab ethnic eats, check out cutting-edge art and theater (as well as cheap booze and live music), and walk up and down tiny blocks to peek into stylish boutiques. As a general rule, the further east you go the looser things get.

Day

04

Lower East Side Tenement Museum (p94)

Gain fantastic insight into the shockingly cramped living conditions of 19th- and early-20th-century immigrants at this brilliantly curated museum.

⊙ Lower East Side Tenement Museum to Little Italy

🚶 Walk west on Delancey St through Sara D Roosevelt Park to Mulberry St.

❶ Little Italy (p128)

There's little of the old authentic Italian flavor left in this eclectic 'hood known for shopping, eating and drinking. Stroll up Mulberry to the boutiques and hip little cafes of Nolita.

⊙ Little Italy to The Butcher's Daughter

🚶 Walk two blocks north along Mulberry and turn right onto Kenmare St; it's another two blocks further.

❷ Lunch at The Butcher's Daughter (p126)

Grab a bite at this delightful earth-friendly eatery in Nolita. The vegetarian cafe serves

MICHAL STIPEK/GETTY IMAGES ©

up creative, healthy dishes that also happen to be delicious. Wash them down with a craft beer or bespoke mimosa.

➜ The Butcher's Daughter to the New Museum of Contemporary Art

🚶 Walk several blocks east to Bowery and turn north.

3 New Museum of Contemporary Art (p97)

Symbolic of the once-gritty Bowery's transformation, this ultramodern museum has a steady menu of edgy works in new forms.

➜ New Museum of Contemporary Art to Chinatown

🚶 Turn right on Delancey St and then left on Mott St and continue until you reach Canal St.

4 Chinatown (p74)

Take an afternoon stroll through one of New York's most vibrant districts. Chinatown's teeming streets are lined with dumpling houses, bakeries, fish markets, vegetable stands, massage parlors and colorful shops selling everything under the sun.

➜ Chinatown to Ivan Ramen

🚶 It's about a mile northeast to Clinton & Stanton Sts; walk if you can, as taxi traffic is terrible around Chinatown.

5 Dinner at Ivan Ramen (p128)

Long Islander Ivan Orkin brought his ramen know-how back from Tokyo, and his small East Village shop is the holy grail for New York ramen lovers – you may have to wait for a counter seat.

➜ Ivan Ramen to Rue B

🚶 About half a mile straight up Clinton St brings you to Rue B.

6 Rue B (p169)

In the midst of the East Village bar scene, this basement live-music bar has walls plastered with jazz greats and a lively crowd that will help you celebrate the end of your night in musical style.

From left: The Butcher's Daughter (p126); Chinatown (p74)

Plan Your Trip

Need to Know

Daily Costs

Budget:
Less than $200

- Dorm bed: $40–70
- Slice of pizza: around $4
- Food-truck taco: from $3
- Happy hour glass of wine: $10
- Bus or subway ride: $3

Midrange:
$200–500

- Double room in a midrange hotel: from around $200
- Empire State Building dual observatories ticket: $58
- Dinner for two at a midrange eatery: $150
- Craft cocktail at a lounge: $15–19
- Discount TKTS ticket to a Broadway show: $80

Top End:
More than $500

- Luxury stay at the NoMad Hotel: $400–850
- Tasting menu at a top-end restaurant: $90–315
- A 1½-hour massage at the Great Jones Spa: $200
- Metropolitan Opera orchestra seats: $100–390

Advance Planning

Two months before Book hotel reservations as soon as possible – prices increase the closer you get to your arrival date. Snag tickets to the Broadway blockbuster of your choice.

One month before Most high-end restaurants release bookings four weeks ahead; now is the time to reserve your table for that blow-out meal.

One week before Surf the web and scan blogs and Twitter for the latest restaurant and bar openings, plus upcoming art exhibitions.

Useful Websites

NYC: The Official Guide (www.nycgo.com) New York City's official tourism portal.

Explore Brooklyn (www.explorebk.com) Brooklyn-specific events and listings.

New York Magazine (www.nymag.com) Comprehensive, current listings for bars, restaurants, entertainment and shopping.

New York Times (www.nytimes.com) Excellent local news coverage and theater listings.

Lonely Planet (www.lonelyplanet.com/usa/new-york-city) Destination information, hotel bookings, traveler forum and more.

Currency
US dollar (US$)

Language
English

Visas

The US Visa Waiver Program allows nationals of 38 countries to enter the US without a visa, but you must fill out an ESTA application before departing.

Money

ATMs widely available; credit cards accepted at most hotels, stores and restaurants. Farmers markets, food trucks and some restaurants and bars are cash-only.

Cell Phones

International travelers can use local SIM cards in a smartphone provided it is unlocked. Alternatively, you can buy a cheap US phone and load it with prepaid minutes. Some phone carriers also offer free international data roaming so check your package before leaving home.

Time

Eastern Standard Time (GMT/UTC minus five hours)

For more, see the **Survival Guide** (p227)

When to Go

Spring or fall offer the best weather to explore. Summer (June to August) can be scorching. Winter is cold and sometimes snowy; festive fun draws crowds.

New York City

°C/°F Temp
Rainfall inches/mm

Arriving in New York City

John F Kennedy International Airport The AirTrain ($5) links to the subway ($2.75), which makes the one-hour journey into Manhattan. Express buses to Grand Central or Port Authority cost $19. Taxis cost a flat $52, excluding tolls, tip and rush-hour surcharge.

LaGuardia Airport The closest airport to Manhattan but the least accessible by public transportation: take the Q70 express bus from the airport to the 74th St–Broadway subway station. Express buses to Midtown cost $16. Taxis range from $34 to $53, excluding tolls and tip.

Newark Liberty International Airport Take the AirTrain ($5.50) to Newark Airport train station, and board any train bound for New York's Penn Station ($13). Taxis range from $60 to $80 (plus $15 toll and tip). Allow 45 minutes to one hour of travel time.

Getting Around

Check the Metropolitan Transportation Authority website (www.mta.info) for public transportation information (buses and subway).

Subway Inexpensive, somewhat efficient and operates around the clock, though navigating lines can be confusing. A single ride is $2.75 with a MetroCard.

Buses Convenient during off hours – especially when transferring between the city's eastern and western sides (most subway lines run north to south). Uses the MetroCard; same price as the subway.

Taxi Meters start at $2.50 and increase roughly $5 for every 20 blocks. See www.nyc.gov/taxi.

Bicycle The popular bike-share program Citi Bike (www.citibike nyc.com) provides excellent access to most of Manhattan.

Inter-borough ferries The New York City Ferry (www.ferry. nyc) provides handy transport between waterside stops in Manhattan, Brooklyn and Queens.

Top Tips

o MetroCards are valid on subways, buses, ferries and the tramway to Roosevelt Island. If staying a few days, buy a 7-Day Unlimited Pass.

o Pay attention to 'Downtown' vs 'Uptown' subway station entrances. Sometimes there are separate entrances (usually across the street from one another) depending on which direction the train is going.

o Subway lines run both local and express trains. Local trains stop at all stations, express trains do not.

o If the number on a taxi's top light is lit, it's available. Note that green Boro taxis can't make pick-ups south of W 110th St and E 96th St.

o When giving an address, always include the nearest cross street/s (eg 700 Sixth Ave at 22nd St).

Plan Your Trip
What's New

CBD

Said to reduce anxiety and inflammation, NYC venues like Mamacha (p125) and Butcher's Daughter (p126) have started dropping shots of CBD – cannabidiol, a non-psychotic (completely legal) substance derived from the cannabis plant – into matchas, lattes and cocktails.

Hudson Yards Redevelopment

At the northern end of the High Line, a $4.5 billion engineered neighborhood is emerging with the highest open-air observatory in the Western Hemisphere and the Vessel – an astounding Escher-like steel structure of interlocking walkways and staircases for climbing.

Russ & Daughters Moves Uptown

The Lower East Side's legendary Jewish deli has expanded uptown, with a new artsy outpost in the Jewish Museum (p81) on Fifth Ave and Shabbat brunches on Saturdays.

Affordable Digs with Class

The 2018 opening of retro-inspired Free-hand New York (https://freehandhotels.com/new-york) has upped the hotel game in Manhattan by offering stylish digs with perks for budget travelers.

Grand Central Noshing

In a surprising twist of fate, Grand Central Terminal has become home to a Nordic food hall (p76) and Michelin-starred New Nordic restaurant Agern (p136), both under the direction of Noma co-founder Claus Meyer.

Cultural Upgrade

The MoMA (p70) is undergoing a major redesign that will add 40,000 sq ft of new gallery space. The museum will stay open during construction, which is due for completion in late October 2019.

Above: Vessel

Plan Your Trip
For Free

Museums

The following are free or pay-what-you-wish:

Frick Collection (p51) 2pm to 6pm Wednesday and 6pm to 9pm first Friday of month (excluding January and September)

National September 11 Memorial Museum (p86) 5pm to 8pm Tuesday

MoMA (p70) 4pm to 8pm Friday

Guggenheim Museum (p78) 5pm to 7:45pm Saturday

Whitney Museum of American Art (p84) 7pm to 10pm Friday

New Museum of Contemporary Art (p97) 7pm to 9pm Thursday

And these are free 365 days a year:

National Museum of the American Indian (p45)

American Folk Art Museum (p39)

Tours & Activities

The Staten Island Ferry (p199) provides magical views of the Statue of Liberty, and you can enjoy it with a cold beer (available on the boat). For a bit more adventure, take out a kayak, available at the Downtown Boathouse (p199) and Manhattan Community Boathouse (p199). Reserve in advance for a tour of a neighborhood of your choice with Big Apple Greeter (p201), which works with locals keen to show off their city (and can tailor-make accessible tours).

Summer Sessions

From May through early October, SummerStage (p10) features over 100 free concerts at parks around the city. You'll have to be tenacious to get tickets to Shakespeare in the Park (p11), held in Central Park, but it's well worth the effort. Top actors such as Meryl Streep and Al Pacino have taken the stage in the past.

Prospect Park has the Celebrate Brooklyn! (www.bricartsmedia.org) summer series of live music, dance and theater. Summertime also brings the Bryant Park Summer Film Festival (p11) – all you need to do is show up with a picnic blanket.

Resources

Find free and discounted events through **Club Free Time** (www.clubfreetime. com) and **The Skint** (www. theskint.com), with daily listings of free (or cheap) tours, concerts, talks, workshops, art openings, book readings and more.

Above: National Museum of the American Indian (p45)

Plan Your Trip
Family Travel

ANDREA IZZOTTI/SHUTTERSTOCK ©

Need to Know

Entry fees Many attractions offer free admission to young kids, from under six (eg, Empire State) up to 16 (eg, MoMA).

Eating out You won't find many kids in Manhattan restaurants past 7pm; high chairs are easy to come by.

Resources Check out Time Out New York Kids (www.timeout.com/new-york-kids) and Mommy Poppins (www.mommypoppins.com).

City Trails: New York If you're traveling with kids aged eight and up, Lonely Planet has a guide aimed directly at this age group.

Sights & Activities

Nearly every big museum – including the **Metropolitan Museum of Art** (p48), the **Museum of Modern Art** (p70), **Guggenheim Museum** (p78), **Museum of the City of New York** (www.mcny.org) and **Cooper Hewitt Smithsonian Design Museum** (p81) – has a kids' program, but NYC is also crammed with museums aimed specifically at kids.

The **American Museum of Natural History** (p111), star of the *Night at the Museum* movies, is always a hit, with its dinosaurs, marine world, planetarium and IMAX films. Bigger kids can clamber on vintage subway cars at the **New York Transit Museum** (www.mta.info/mta/museum) or slide down a pole at the **New York City Fire Museum** (www.nycfiremuseum.org). Budding fans of planes, submarines and space will love the excellent **Intrepid Sea, Air & Space Museum** (p61) of military relics docked at a Midtown pier.

If you need some downtime with tots aged one to five, hit the **Children's Museum of the Arts** (www.cmany.org) in West SoHo or the **Brooklyn Children's Museum** (www.brooklynkids.org) in Crown Heights. Both have story times, art classes, craft hours and painting sessions.

The city has several zoos, but the best by far is the **Bronx Zoo** (www.bronxzoo.com), which is known for its well-designed habitats. If you're pressed for time, **Central Park Zoo** (www.centralparkzoo.com) is

ULU_BIRD/GETTY IMAGES ©

great for a short visit – and for reliving
Madagascar movie moments.

The boat ride to the **Statue of
Liberty** (p40) offers the opportunity to
chug around New York Harbor and get to
know an icon that most kids only know
from textbooks. Kids will also love the free
Staten Island Ferry (p199).

Recite tall tales about a giant ape running amok at the **Empire State Building**
(p66). A movie screen embedded in the
roof of the elevator will keep kids enthralled
as you speed to the top for stupendous
views and free telescopes.

Hot dogs. Ice cream. Amusement-park
rides. **Coney Island** (p114) is just the ticket
if you're in need of some lowbrow summertime entertainment.

Transportation

A startling number of subway stations
lack elevators and will have you lugging
strollers up and down flights of stairs (you
can avoid the turnstile by getting buzzed

★ Best Outdoors Entertainment

Central Park (p225)
Prospect Park (p98)
Brooklyn Bridge Park (p102)
The High Line (p52)
Wollman Skating Rink (p198)

through an easy-access gate); visit http://
web.mta.info/accessibility/stations.htm for
a guide to stations with elevators. Anyone
over 44 inches is supposed to pay full fare,
but the rule is rarely enforced. Strollers are
not allowed on public buses unless folded.
If you'd rather hop in a cab, know that
children under seven can ride on an adult's
lap in a taxi. Ridesharing services may have
available car seats.

From left: American Museum of Natural History (p111);
Riegelmann Boardwalk, Coney Island (p114)

TOP EXPERIENCES

The very best to see and do

Central Park

Lush lawns, cool forests, flowering gardens, glassy bodies of water and meandering, wooded paths provide a dose of serene nature amid the urban rush of New York City. Today, this 'people's park' is still one of the city's most popular attractions.

Great For...

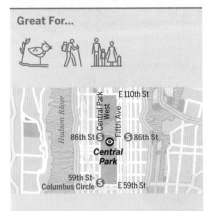

ℹ Need to Know

Map p254; www.centralparknyc.org; 59th to 110th Sts, btwn Central Park West & Fifth Ave; ⊙6am-1am; ♿

★ **Top Tip**

To escape the crowds, try the North Meadow (north of 97th St) or the Harlem Meer.

Like the city's subway system, the vast and majestic Central Park, an 843-acre rectangle of open space in the middle of Manhattan, is a great class leveler – which is exactly what it was envisioned to be. Created in the 1860s and '70s by Frederick Law Olmsted and Calvert Vaux on the marshy northern fringe of the city, the immense park was designed as a leisure space for all New Yorkers, regardless of color, class or creed.

Throughout the year, visitors find free outdoor concerts at the Great Lawn, precious animals at the Central Park Wildlife Center and top-notch drama at the annual Shakespeare in the Park productions, held each summer at the open-air Delacorte Theater. Some other recommended stops include the ornate Bethesda Fountain, which edges the Lake, and its Loeb Boathouse, where you can rent rowboats;

the Shakespeare Garden (west side between 79th and 80th Sts), which has lush plantings and excellent skyline views; and the Ramble (mid-park from 73rd to 79th Sts), a wooded thicket that's popular with bird-watchers. While parts of the park swarm with joggers, musicians and tourists on warm weekends, it's quieter on weekday afternoons and in winter.

Folks flock to the park even in winter, when snowstorms can inspire cross-country skiing and sledding or a simple stroll through the white wonderland, and crowds turn out every New Year's Eve for a midnight run.

Strawberry Fields

This tear-shaped garden serves as a memorial to former Beatle John Lennon, who lived directly across the street with Yoko Ono in the Dakota apartment building

Bethesda Terrace

and was fatally shot there. It is composed of a grove of stately elms and a tiled mosaic that reads, simply, 'Imagine.' Visitors can listen to an audio guide to Strawberry Fields, narrated by Yoko, at centralparknyc.org/imagine. Find the garden at the level of 72nd St on the park's west side.

Bethesda Terrace & Mall

The arched walkways of Bethesda Terrace, crowned by the magnificent Bethesda Fountain, have long been a gathering area for New Yorkers of all flavors. To the south is the Mall (featured in countless movies), a promenade shrouded in mature North American elms. The southern stretch, known as Literary Walk, is flanked by statues of famous authors.

☑ Don't Miss

Free or inexpensive tours with the **Central Park Conservancy** (www.centralparknyc.org/tours), including ones that focus on public art, wildlife, and places of interest to kids.

SEAN PAVONE/SHUTTERSTOCK ©

Conservatory Water & Around

North of the zoo at the level of 74th St is the Conservatory Water, where model sailboats drift lazily and kids scramble about on a statue of Alice in Wonderland. There are Saturday story hours at the Hans Christian Andersen statue to the west of the water (at 11am from June to September).

Great Lawn & Around

The Great Lawn is a massive emerald carpet at the center of the park – between 79th and 86th Sts. It's surrounded by ball fields and London plane trees. Immediately to the southeast is the Delacorte Theater, home to the annual Shakespeare in the Park festival, as well as Belvedere Castle (p200).

What's Nearby?

American Folk Art Museum Museum

(Map p254; ☎212-595-9533; www.folkartmuseum.org; 2 Lincoln Sq, Columbus Ave, btwn 65th & 66th Sts; 🕒11:30am-7pm Tue-Thu & Sat, noon-7:30pm Fri, noon-6pm Sun; [S]1 to 66th St-Lincoln Center) [FREE] This tiny institution offers rotating exhibitions in three small galleries. Past exhibits have included quilts made by 19th-century soldiers and sculptures by a celebrated Ghanaian coffin-maker of forts through which slaves were trafficked. There's free music on Wednesdays (at 2pm) and Fridays (5:30pm).

🍴 Take a Break

Class things up with an afternoon martini at the **Loeb Boathouse** (Map p254; ☎212-517-2233; www.thecentralparkboathouse.com; Central Park Lake, Central Park, near E 74th St; mains lunch $26-38, dinner $29-45; 🕒restaurant noon-4pm Mon-Fri, from 9:30am Sat & Sun year-round, 5:30-9:30pm Mon-Fri, from 6pm Sat & Sun Apr-Nov; [S]B, C to 72nd St; 6 to 77th St).

MARK AND ANNA PHOTOGRAPHY/SHUTTERSTOCK ©

Statue of Liberty & Ellis Island

Stellar skyline views, a scenic ferry ride, a lookout from Lady Liberty's crown, and a moving tribute to America's immigrants at Ellis Island – unmissable is an understatement.

Great For...

☑ Don't Miss

The breathtaking views from Lady Liberty's crown (remember to reserve tickets well in advance).

Statue of Liberty

A Powerful Symbol

Lady Liberty has been gazing sternly toward 'unenlightened Europe' since 1886. Dubbed the 'Mother of Exiles,' she's often interpreted as a symbolic admonishment to an unjust old world. Emma Lazarus' 1883 poem 'The New Colossus' articulates this challenge: 'Give me your tired, your poor, your huddled masses yearning to breathe free, the wretched refuse of your teeming shore.'

History of the Statue

Conceived as early as 1865 by French intellectual Édouard Laboulaye as a monument to the republican principles shared by France and the USA, the Statue of Liberty is still a symbol of the ideals of opportunity and

GARY LATHAM/LONELY PLANET ©

Upper
New York
Bay

Ellis Island ⊚

Governors
Island

⊚ **Statue of Liberty**

❶ Need to Know

📞212-363-3200, tickets 877-523-9849; www. nps.gov/stli; Liberty Island; adult/child incl Ellis Island $18.50/9, incl crown $21.50/12; ⊙8:30am-5:30pm, hours vary by season; 🚢to Liberty Island, **S**1 to South Ferry, 4/5 to Bowling Green, then ferry

✕ Take a Break

Pack a picnic or chow beforehand at one of the upmarket food courts in Brookfield Place (p122).

★ Top Tip

All ferry tickets to Liberty Island include access to guided ranger tours and self-guided audio tours.

freedom. French sculptor Frédéric-Auguste Bartholdi traveled to New York in 1871 to select the site, then spent more than 10 years in Paris designing and making the 151ft-tall figure known in full as *Liberty Enlightening the World*. It was then shipped to New York, erected on a small island in the harbor (then known as Bedloe's Island) and unveiled in 1886. Structurally, it consists of an iron skeleton (designed by Gustave Eiffel) with a copper skin attached to it by stiff but flexible metal bars.

The robed statue represents Libertas, the Roman goddess of freedom.

Visiting the Statue

Access to the crown is extremely limited and the only way in is to reserve your spot in advance; the further ahead you can do it, the better (a six-month lead time is

allowed; book through www.statuecruises. com). Children must be at least 4ft tall to be admitted. Pedestal tickets are slightly easier to bag but should still be booked in advance (for one thing, advance booking will guarantee a specific time slot to visit and cut down on long wait times.) Keep in mind, there's no elevator and the climb from the base is equal to a 22-story building. The free audio guide (available upon arrival to the island) provides historical details and little-known facts about the statue.

Liberty Island is usually visited in conjunction with nearby Ellis Island. **Ferries** (Map p244; 📞877-523-9849; www.statuecruises. com; Battery Park, Lower Manhattan; adult/ child from $18.50/9; ⊙departures 8:30am-5pm, shorter hours winter; **S**4/5 to Bowling Green, R/W to Whitehall St, 1 to South Ferry) leave from Battery Park; South Ferry and Bowling Green are the closest subway stations. (Ferry tickets include admission to both sights.)

Ellis Island

Ellis Island (☎212-363-3200, tickets 877-523-9849; www.nps.gov/elis; Ellis Island; ferry incl Liberty Island adult/child $18.50/9; ⏰8:30am-6pm, hours vary by season; ⛴to Ellis Island, [S]1 to South Ferry, 4/5 to Bowling Green, then ferry) is America's most famous and historically important gateway – the very spot where old-world despair met new-world promise. Between 1892 and 1924, more than 12 million immigrants passed through this processing station, their dreams in tow. An estimated 40% of Americans today descend from those millions, making this island central to the story of modern America. It is now a National Monument.

Main Building Architecture

With their Main Building, architects Edward Lippincott Tilton and William A Boring created a suitably impressive and imposing 'prologue' to America. The designing duo won the contract after the original wooden building burnt down in 1897. Having attended the Ecole des Beaux Arts in Paris, it's not surprising that they opted for a beaux-arts aesthetic for the project. The building evokes a grand train station, with majestic triple-arched entrances, decorative Flemish bond brickwork, and granite quoins (cornerstones) and belvederes. It reopened to the public as the Ellis Island Immigration Museum in 1990, after a long and expensive restoration.

Inside, it's the 2nd-floor, 338ft-long Registry Room (also known as the Great Hall)

Main Building

that takes the breath away. It was under its beautiful vaulted ceiling that the newly arrived lined up to have their documents checked, and that the polygamists, paupers, criminals and anarchists were turned back. Among the immigrants to pass through here were Hungarian Erik Weisz (Harry Houdini), Italian Rodolfo Guglielmi (Rudolph Valentino) and Brit Archibald Alexander Leach (Cary Grant).

The original plaster ceiling was severely damaged by an explosion of munitions barges at nearby Black Tom Wharf. It was something of a blessing in disguise: the

★ **Top Tip**

If you're seeing the Statue of Liberty first, the last ferry you can get to Ellis Island leaves at 3:40pm (arrives 4pm); from there the last boat back to Manhattan is at 5:15pm.

AWL IMAGES/GETTY IMAGES ©

rebuilt version was adorned with striking, herringbone-patterned tiles by Rafael Guastavino. The Catalan-born engineer was also responsible for the beautiful tiled ceiling at the Grand Central Oyster Bar & Restaurant at Grand Central Terminal.

Immigration Museum Exhibits

The museum's interactive exhibits are spread over three levels. To get the most out of your visit, opt for the 50-minute self-guided audio tour (free with ferry ticket, available from the museum lobby). Featuring narratives from a number of sources, including historians, architects and the immigrants themselves, the tour brings to life the museum's hefty collection of personal objects, official documents, photographs and film footage. It's an evocative experience to witness personal memories – both good and bad – in the very halls and corridors in which they occurred.

The collection is divided into a number of permanent and temporary exhibitions. *Journeys: The Peopling of America 1550–1890* on the 1st floor is interesting, but the real focus begins on the 2nd floor, where you'll find the two most fascinating exhibitions. *Through America's Gate* examines the step-by-step process faced by the newly arrived (including the chalk-marking of those suspected of illness, a wince-inducing eye examination, and 29 questions) in the beautiful, vaulted Great Hall, while *Peak Immigration Years* explores the motives behind the immigrants' journeys and the challenges they faced once free to begin their new American lives. Particularly interesting is the collection of old photographs, which

★ **Mayor in the House**

One of NYC's most famous mayors worked at Ellis Island before going into politics. Fluent in Italian, Croatian and Yiddish, Fiorello LaGuardia worked as a translator while attending NYU law school at night.

offers intimate glimpses into the daily lives of these courageous new Americans.

If you don't feel like listening to the audio tour, you can pick up one of the phones in each display area and hear the recorded, affecting memories of real Ellis Island immigrants, taped in the 1980s. Another option is the free 45-minute guided tour with a park ranger. If booked three weeks in advance by phone, the tour is also available in American Sign Language.

American Immigrant Wall of Honor & Fort Gibson Ruins

Accessible from the 1st-floor *Journeys: The Peopling of America 1550–1890* exhibit is the outdoor American Immigrant Wall of Honor, inscribed with the names of more than 700,000 immigrants. Believed to be the world's longest wall of names, it's a fund-raising project, allowing any American to have an immigrant relative's name recorded in return for a donation. Construction of the wall in the 1990s uncovered the remains of the island's original structure, Fort Gibson – you can see the ruins at the southwestern corner of the memorial. Built in 1808, the fortification was part of a harbor-defense system against the British that also included Castle Clinton in Battery Park and Castle Williams on Governors Island. During this time, Ellis Island measured a modest 3.3 acres of sand and slush.

What's Nearby?

Ferries depart from Battery Park. Nearby attractions include the following museums.

Museum of Jewish Heritage   Museum (Map p244; ☏646-437-4202; www.mjhnyc.org; 36 Battery Pl, Financial District; adult/child $12/ free, 4-8pm Wed free; ⏱10am-6pm Sun-Tue, to 8pm Wed & Thu, to 5pm Fri mid-Mar–mid-Nov, to 3pm Fri rest of year; ⛶; Ⓢ4/5 to Bowling Green, R/W to Whitehall St) This evocative waterfront museum explores all aspects of modern Jewish identity and culture, from religious traditions to artistic accomplishments. The museum's core exhibition covers three themed floors: *Jewish Life a Century Ago*,

Jewish Renewal and *The War Against the Jews* – a detailed exploration of the Holocaust through thousands of personal artifacts, photographs, documentary films and survivor testimony. Also commemorating Holocaust victims is the external installation **Garden of Stones**, a narrow pathway of 18 boulders supporting living trees.

The building itself consists of six sides, symbolizing the Star of David and the six million Jews who perished in WWII. Exhibitions aside, the venue also hosts films, music concerts, lecture series and special holiday performances. Frequent, free workshops for families with children are also on offer, while on-site LOX at Café Bergson serves light food, including lox (smoked salmon) in intriguing flavors such as grapefruit and gin and pastrami spice (mains $13 to $16).

American Immigrant Wall of Honor

The museum is closed on Saturday and major Jewish holidays, so check the website's holiday schedule before visiting.

National Museum of the American Indian   Museum

(Map p244; ☎212-514-3700; www.nmai.si.edu; 1 Bowling Green, Financial District; ☺10am-5pm Fri-Wed, to 8pm Thu; 🚼; Ⓢ4/5 to Bowling Green, R/W to Whitehall St) **FREE** An affiliate of the Smithsonian Institution, this elegant tribute to Native American culture occupies Cass Gilbert's spectacular 1907 **Custom House**, one of NYC's finest beaux-arts buildings. Beyond a vast elliptical rotunda capped by a 140-ton skylight, sleek galleries play host to changing exhibitions featuring Native American art, culture, life and beliefs. The museum's permanent collection includes stunning decorative arts, textiles and ceremonial objects that document the diverse native cultures across the Americas, while the imagiNATIONS Activity Center explores their technologies.

The four giant female sculptures outside the building are the work of **Daniel Chester French**, who would go on to sculpt the seated Abraham Lincoln at Lincoln Memorial in Washington, DC. Representing (from left to right) Asia, North America, Europe and Africa, the figures offer a revealing look at America's worldview at the beginning of the 20th century.

The museum also hosts a range of cultural programs, including dance and music performances, readings for children, craft demonstrations, films and workshops. The museum shop is well stocked with Native American jewelry, books, CDs and crafts.

SOPA COLLECTION/SHUTTERSTOCK ©

Brooklyn Bridge

Even before its completion, the world's first suspension bridge inspired poet Walt Whitman, and later Jack Kerouac too. This rainbow of steel across the East River is one of NYC's most photographed sights.

A New York icon, the Brooklyn Bridge was the world's first steel suspension bridge, and, at 1596ft, the longest when it opened in 1883. Although construction was fraught with disaster, the bridge became a magnificent example of urban design. Its suspended bicycle/pedestrian walkway delivers soul-stirring views of Manhattan, the East River and the Brooklyn waterfront.

Construction

Sadly, one man deprived of this view was the bridge's designer, John Roebling. The Prussian-born engineer's foot was crushed in an accident on Fulton Landing in June 1869; he died of tetanus poisoning a few weeks later, before construction even began. His son, Washington Roebling, took over the work, which lasted 14 years and managed to survive budget overruns and

Great For...

☑ **Don't Miss**

An early morning stroll over the bridge – a magical time to take in the view.

ⓘ Need to Know

Map p244; Ⓢ4/5/6 to Brooklyn Bridge-City Hall, J/Z to Chambers St, R/W to City Hall, Ⓢ2/3 to Clark St, A/F to High St-Brooklyn Bridge Station)

✕ Take a Break

For classic and specialty coal-fired thin-crust pizzas, head to Juliana's (p141).

★ Top Tip

Crowds can be thick. Don't try riding a bike across unless going in the early morning or at night.

cyclists. The bridge walk is 1.3 miles (2km). Structural repairs that began in 2010 are expected to continue until 2022 – though they're a hassle and can make bridge entrances harder to spot, it's still possible to cross.

What's Nearby?

Just north of the Manhattan-side access to the bridge lies **Chinatown.** On the Brooklyn side, you're a short stroll from Dumbo and Brooklyn Bridge Park (p102).

Dumbo

Dumbo's nickname is an acronym for its location: 'Down Under the Manhattan Bridge Overpass,' and while this north Brooklyn slice of waterfront used to be strictly for industry, it's now the domain of high-end condos, furniture shops, cafes and art galleries. Several highly regarded performing-arts spaces are located in the cobblestone streets and the **Empire Fulton Ferry State Park** hugs the waterfront and offers picture-postcard Manhattan views.

the deaths of an estimated 27 workers. The younger Roebling himself suffered from the bends (decompression sickness) while helping to excavate the riverbed for the bridge's western tower and remained bedridden within sight of the bridge for much of the project. His wife, Emily, oversaw construction in his stead. There was one final tragedy to come in June 1883, when the bridge opened to pedestrian traffic: someone in the crowd (falsely) shouted that the bridge was collapsing and the mad rush that ensued killed 12 people.

Crossing the Bridge

Walking across the grand Brooklyn Bridge is a rite of passage for New Yorkers and visitors alike – with this in mind, walk no more than two abreast or else you're in danger of colliding with runners and speeding

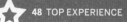

Metropolitan Museum of Art

This museum of encyclopedic proportions has more than two million objects in its permanent collection, and many of its treasures are showcased in no less than 17 acres' worth of galleries. You could spend weeks exploring the Met and still not see it all.

This sprawling museum, founded in 1870, houses one of the world's largest and most important art collections, with everything from Egyptian temples to European Renaissance masterpieces. 'The Met' attracts over six million visitors a year to its never-ending galleries, making it the largest single-site attraction in NYC. In other words: plan on spending some time here.

Great For...

☑ Don't Miss

The hieroglyphic-covered Temple of Dendur, complete with reflecting pond and Central Park views.

Egyptian Art

The museum has an unrivaled collection of ancient Egyptian art, some of which dates back to the Paleolithic era. Located to the north of the Great Hall, the 39 Egyptian galleries open dramatically with one of the Met's prized pieces: the **Tomb of Perneb** (c 2300 BC), an Old Kingdom burial chamber crafted from limestone. From here, a web of rooms is cluttered with funerary

Temple of Dendur

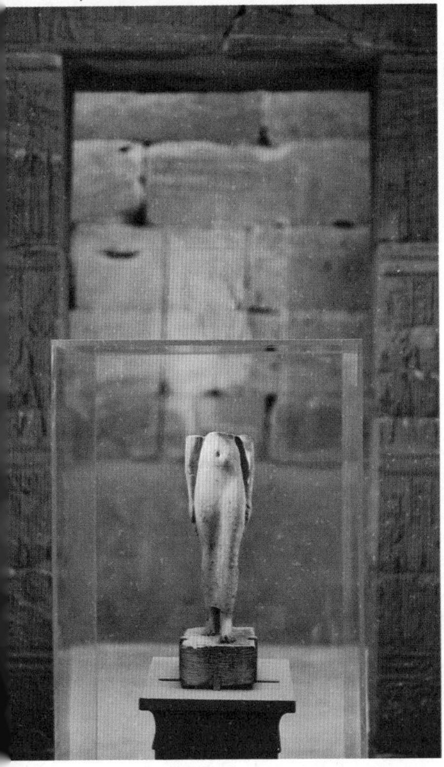

T PHOTOGRAPHY/SHUTTERSTOCK ©

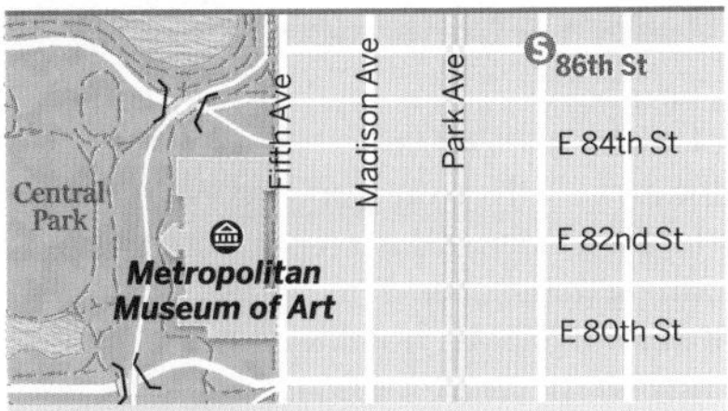

Need to Know

Map p254; ☎212-535-7710; www.metmuseum.org; 1000 Fifth Ave, at E 82nd St; 3-day pass adult/senior/child $25/$17/free; pay-as-you-wish for NY State residents; ⏰10am-5:30pm Sun-Thu, to 9pm Fri & Sat; 👪; [S]4/5/6, Q to 86th St; 6 to 77th St)

Take a Break

The casual Petrie Court cafe serves good lunch and drink options in a pretty setting.

★ Top Tip

Docents offer free guided tours of specific galleries, and the Met smartphone app is free to download – it includes plenty of excerpts from the $7 audio guide available in the museum.

stelae, carved reliefs and fragments of pyramids. Don't miss the intriguing models from the **Tomb of Meketre**, clay figurines meant to help in the afterlife, in Gallery 105. These eventually lead to the **Temple of Dendur** (Gallery 131), a sandstone temple to the goddess Isis given to the US by Egypt in 1965. It resides in a sunny atrium gallery with a reflecting pool – a must-see for the first-time visitor.

Greek & Roman Art

The 27 galleries devoted to classical antiquity are another Met doozy. From the Great Hall, a passageway takes you through a barrel-vaulted room flanked by the chiseled torsos of Greek figures. This spills right into one of the Met's loveliest spaces: the airy **Greek and Roman sculpture court** (Gallery 162), full of marble carvings of gods and historical figures. The statue of a bearded Hercules from AD 68–98 is particularly awe-inspiring.

Art of the Arab Lands

In the southeastern corner of the 2nd floor you'll find the Islamic galleries, with 15 incredible rooms showcasing the museum's extensive collection of art from the Middle East, and Central and South Asia. In addition to garments, secular decorative objects and manuscripts, you'll find a magnificent 14th-century mihrab (prayer niche) from Iran, lined with elaborately patterned blue, white and yellow tile work (Gallery 455). There's also a superb array of Ottoman textiles (Gallery 459), a medieval-style **Moroccan court** (Gallery 456) and the 18th-century **Damascus Room** (Gallery 461).

Modern & Contemporary Art

The rooms in the far southwestern corner of the 1st and 2nd floors feature art from the early 20th century onward. All the rock stars of modern art are represented here, putting this section of the gallery right up there with MoMA. Notable names include Spanish masters Picasso (whose 'high' cubist *Still Life with a Bottle of Rum* hangs in Gallery 905), Dalí and Miró, as well as American painters Georgia O'Keeffe and Edward Hopper. Thomas Hart Benton's magnificent 1930s 10-panel mural *America Today* takes up an entire room in Gallery 909.

American Wing

In the northwestern corner, the two-floor American Wing showcases a wide variety of decorative and fine art from throughout US history. These include everything from colonial portraiture to Hudson River School art – not to mention Emanuel Leutze's massive canvas of *Washington Crossing the Delaware* (Gallery 760). What the permanent collection lacks, though, is a serious body of Native American art. In 2018/19, a landmark exhibition showcased 116 works of sculpture, painting, textiles and regalia from more than 50 indigenous North American cultures. The works were gifts, donations and loans from the Diker Collection, considered to be the most significant private collection of Native American art in the US.

The Roof Garden

One of the best spots in the entire museum is the roof garden, which features rotating sculpture installations by contemporary and 20th-century artists. (Jeff Koons, Andy Goldsworthy and Imran Qureshi have all

American Wing

shown here.) Best of all are the views it offers of the city and Central Park. It's also home to the Cantor Roof Garden Bar (p173), an ideal spot for a drink – especially at sunset. It's open from April to October.

What's Nearby?

The Met has two satellite museums, both of which are included in the price of your ticket and well worth a look. The closest is Met Breuer, an outlandish concrete behemoth on Madison Ave specializing in 20th and 21st century works; Met Cloisters in Upper Manhattan houses the Met's medieval treasures.

★ For Kids

The Met hosts plenty of youth-centric events (see the website) and distributes a museum brochure and map made specially for kids.

ALEXANDER PROKOPENKO/SHUTTERSTOCK ©

Frick Collection   Gallery
(Map p254; ☎212-288-0700; www.frick.org; 1 E 70th St, at Fifth Ave; adult/student $22/12, pay-what-you-wish 2-6pm Wed, 1st Fri of month excl Jan & Sep 6-9pm free; ⏱10am-6pm Tue-Sat, 11am-5pm Sun; Ⓢ6 to 68th St-Hunter College) This spectacular art collection sits in a mansion built by steel magnate Henry Clay Frick, one of the many such residences lining the section of Fifth Ave that was once called 'Millionaires' Row.' The museum has over a dozen splendid rooms displaying masterpieces by Titian, Vermeer, Gilbert Stuart, El Greco, Joshua Reynolds, Van Dyck and Rembrandt. Sculpture, ceramics, antique furniture and clocks are also on display. Fans of classical music will enjoy the frequent piano and violin concerts (p188) on Sunday evenings.

Neue Galerie   Museum
(Map p254; ☎212-628-6200; www.neuegalerie. org; 1048 Fifth Ave, at E 86th St; adult/student $22/12, 6-9pm 1st Fri of month free; ⏱11am-6pm Thu-Mon; Ⓢ4/5/6, Q to 86th St) This restored Carrère and Hastings mansion from 1914 is a resplendent showcase for Austrian and German art, featuring works by Paul Klee and Ernst Ludwig Kirchner, and incredible collections of Gustav Klimt and Egon Schiele drawings. In pride of place on the 2nd floor is Klimt's golden 1907 *Portrait of Adele Bloch-Bauer I* – acquired for the museum by cosmetics magnate Ronald Lauder for a whopping $135 million. The fascinating story of the painting's history is told in the 2015 film *Woman in Gold*.

★ The Met's Mascot

In Gallery 111 you'll find a small, blue-glazed faience hippopotamus that was sealed into an Egyptian tomb 3900 years ago to guard its owner in the afterlife. Nicknamed 'William,' he's the Met's unofficial mascot. If you'd like your own guardian hippo, head to the **museum shop** on the 1st floor, where he's available in many forms.

The High Line

A resounding triumph of urban renewal, the High Line is a remarkable public park built along a disused elevated rail line. Each year, this aerial greenway attracts millions of visitors who come for art installations, native-inspired landscaping and a unique perspective on the streets below.

Great For...

ⓘ Need to Know

Map p246; ☏212-500-6035; www.thehigh line.org; Gansevoort St, Meatpacking District; ⏱7am-11pm Jun-Sep, to 10pm Apr, May, Oct & Nov, to 7pm Dec-Mar; 🚌M14 crosstown along 14th St, M23 along 23rd St, ⓢA/C/E, L to 8th Ave-14th St, 1, C/E to 23rd St, 7 to 34th St-Hudson Yards

★ **Top Tip**

Stairs up to the High Line are every two to four blocks from 14th to 34th Sts. Beat the crowds by starting early at 30th St or 34th St, wandering south and exiting at 14th St for Chelsea Market and the West Village.

History

Long before the High Line was a beacon for eager tourists, happy-snapping families and New Yorkers seeking respite from the street-level grind, it was an unglamorous freight line running through neighborhoods of industry and slaughterhouses. Commissioned in the 1930s as the 'West Side Elevated Line,' the idea was to eliminate the rail accidents that claimed over 500 lives along 'Death Ave' (Tenth Ave).

The project cost more than $150 million (equivalent to around $2 billion by today's dime) and took roughly five years to complete. After two decades of effective service, a rise in truck transportation led to an eventual decrease in use of the line; finally, in the 1980s, the rails became obsolete, quickly growing thick with wild foliage.

Locals signed petitions to remove the eyesore the tracks had become, but in 1999 a committee called Friends of the High Line – founded by Joshua David and Robert Hammond – was formed to save the rusting iron and transform the tracks into a unique elevated green space. The park opened to the public, full of blooming flowers and broad-leaved trees, in 2009. Later phases of development have added to its length, so that it now links the Meatpacking District with Midtown.

Along the Way

The attractions are numerous, and include stunning vistas of the Hudson River, public art installations commissioned especially for the park, wide lounge chairs for soaking up some sun, willowy stretches of native-inspired landscaping (including a

mini sumac forest), food and drink vendors (in the warmer months), and a thoroughly unique perspective on the neighborhood streets below – especially at various overlooks, where bleacher-like seating faces huge panes of glass that frame the traffic, buildings and pedestrians below as living works of art. There's also André Balazs' luxury hotel, the Standard (p171), which straddles the park, as well as the sparkling Whitney Museum (p91), which anchors the southern end.

Information, Tours, Events & Eats

The High Line is becoming less 'just' an unusual park and more an inspiring meeting point for families and friends. As you walk its length you'll find staffers wearing the signature double-H logo who can point you in the right direction or offer you additional information about the converted rails. There are also myriad people behind the scenes organizing public art exhibitions and activity sessions, especially in summer. Special tours and events explore a variety of topics: history, horticulture, design, art, food and stargazing. Check the schedule at www.thehighline.org for the latest.

☑ Don't Miss

The amphitheater-style viewing platforms at 17th and 26th Sts.

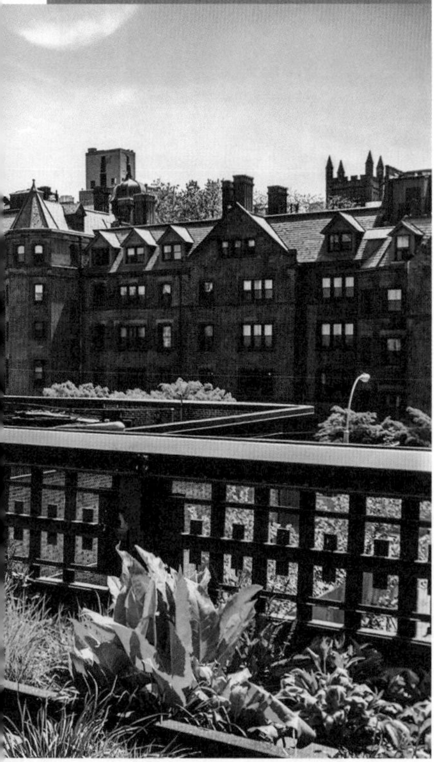

ALBACHIARAA/SHUTTERSTOCK ©

What's Nearby?

Chelsea Galleries

Chelsea is home to the highest concentration of art galleries in NYC. Most lie between 20th and 26th Sts, on the blocks between Tenth and Eleventh Aves, and show launches are typically held on Thursday evenings. Highlights include David Zwirner and Pace Gallery. Most galleries are open Tuesday through Sunday, but double-check opening hours. Visit www.chelseagalleries.nyc for a map of locations and details on current and upcoming exhibitions.

David Zwirner Gallery

(☎212-517-8677; www.davidzwirner.com; 537 W 20th St, btwn Tenth & Eleventh Aves, Chelsea; 🕐10am-6pm Tue-Sat; [S]1, C/E to 23rd St)

David Zwirner operates several galleries around Chelsea, including this five-story LEED-certified building with 30,000 sq ft of exhibition space. He stages some of New York's best gallery shows, including the work of such artists as Sigmar Polke, Yayoi Kusama and Donald Judd. Long lines can be a hassle.

🍴 Take a Break

You'll find a wonderland of food vendors behind the brick walls of the Chelsea Market (p130), at the 14th St exit.

Broadway

Broadway is NYC's dream factory – a place where romance, betrayal, murder and triumph come with dazzling costumes, toe-tapping tunes and stirring scores. The lineup is truly staggering here, with a wide range of musicals, dramas and comedies – and plenty of blurring between genres. Reserve well ahead for the best seats.

Great For...

☑ Don't Miss

On the edge of the Theater District stands the gorgeous 1930s Radio City Music Hall (p72), home to the legendary Rockettes and one of the few theaters to run regular tours.

★ **Top Tip**

The TKTS Booth at Times Sq is an attraction in its own right, with its illuminated roof of 27 ruby-red steps rising a panoramic 16ft 1in above the 47th St sidewalk.

Broadway Beginnings

The neighborhood's first playhouse was the long-gone Empire, opened in 1893 and located on Broadway between 40th and 41st Sts. Two years later, cigar manufacturer and part-time comedy scribe Oscar Hammerstein opened the Olympia, also on Broadway, before opening the Republic – now children's theater **New Victory** (Map p252; ☎646-223-3010; www.newvictory.org; 209 W 42nd St, btwn Seventh & Eighth Aves; 🚹; Ⓢ N/Q/R/W, S, 1/2/3, 7 to Times Sq-42nd St; A/C/E to 42nd St-Port Authority Bus Terminal) – in 1900. This led to a string of new venues, among them the still-beating **New Amsterdam Theatre** (Aladdin; Map p250; ☎866-870-2717; www.newamsterdamtheatre.com; 214 W 42nd St, btwn Seventh & Eighth Aves; ⊗box office 9am-8pm Mon-Fri, from 10am Sat, 10am-6:30pm Sun; 🚹; Ⓢ N/Q/R/W, S, 1/2/3, 7 to Times Sq-42nd St;

A/C/E to 42nd St-Port Authority Bus Terminal) and **Lyceum Theatre** (Map p252; www.shubert.nyc/theatres/lyceum; 149 W 45th St, btwn Sixth & Seventh Aves; Ⓢ N/R/W to 49th St).

The Broadway of the 1920s was well-known for its lighthearted musicals, commonly fusing vaudeville and music-hall traditions, and producing classic tunes like Cole Porter's *Let's Misbehave*. At the same time, Midtown's theater district was evolving as a platform for new American dramatists. One of the greatest was Eugene O'Neill. Born in Times Square at the long-gone Barrett Hotel (1500 Broadway) in 1888, the playwright debuted many of his works here, including Pulitzer Prize winners *Beyond the Horizon* and *Anna Christie*. O'Neill's success on Broadway paved the way for other American greats like Tennessee Williams, Arthur Miller and

New Victory children's theater

Edward Albee – a surge of serious talent that led to the establishment of the annual Tony Awards in 1947.

These days, New York's Theater District covers an area stretching roughly from 40th St to 54th St between Sixth and Eighth Aves, with dozens of Broadway and Off-Broadway theaters spanning blockbuster musicals to new and classic drama.

★ **Did You Know?**

The term 'Off-Broadway' is not a geographical one – it simply refers to theaters that are smaller in size (200 to 500 seats) and usually have less of a glitzy production budget than the Broadway big hitters.

Getting a Ticket

Broadway is expensive – more so than London's West End. Unless there's a specific show you're after, the best – and cheapest – way to score tickets in the area is at the **TKTS Booth** (www.tdf.org/tkts; Broadway, at W 47th St; ☺3-8pm Mon & Fri, 2-8pm Tue, 10am-2pm & 3-8pm Wed & Sat, 10am-2pm Thu, 11am-7pm Sun; ⓢN/Q/R/W, S, 1/2/3, 7 to Times Sq-42nd St), where you can line up and get same-day discounted tickets for top Broadway and Off-Broadway shows. Smartphone users can download the free TKTS app, which offers rundowns of both Broadway and Off-Broadway shows, as well as real-time updates of what's available on that day. Always have a back-up choice in case your first preference sells out, and never buy from scalpers on the street.

Some shows also offer discounted, day-of 'rush' tickets, available when the box office opens (expect queues). But several popular NYC shows including Hamilton, Book of Mormon, Kinky Boots and Mean Girls now run an online lottery for bargain seats. Check www.luckyseat.com for options the day ahead of when you want to go.

What's On?

Musicals rule the marquees on Broadway, with the hottest shows of the day blending song and dance in lavish, star-studded productions.

Hamilton

Lin-Manuel Miranda's acclaimed new musical is Broadway's hottest ticket, using contemporary hip-hop beats to recount the story of America's founding father, Alexander Hamilton. Inspired by Ron Chernow's

★ **Tony Awards**

The annual Tony Awards are the Oscars of the theater world, bestowing awards across a host of categories (best direction, musical, costume design, etc). Check out the latest winners on www.tonyawards.com.

biography *Alexander Hamilton*, the musical has won a swath of awards, including top honors at the Drama Desk Awards and New York Drama Critics' Circle Awards and a whopping 11 Tony Awards.

Harry Potter and the Cursed Child

As Broadway's highest grossing play of all time, Harry Potter and the Cursed Child has broken new ground. It's a marathon two-part play requiring two separate tickets, each part designed to be seen in order or on consecutive nights, that follows Harry Potter into his adult life as an employee at the Ministry of Magic. It won six Tony Awards, including Best Play, in 2018.

Book of Mormon

Subversive, obscene and ridiculously hilarious, this cutting musical satire is the work of *South Park* creators Trey Parker and Matt Stone and *Avenue Q* composer Robert Lopez. Winner of nine Tony Awards, it tells the story of two naive Mormons on a mission to 'save' a Ugandan village.

Kinky Boots

Adapted from a 2005 British indie film, Harvey Fierstein and Cyndi Lauper's smash hit tells the story of a doomed English shoe factory unexpectedly saved by Lola, a business-savvy drag queen. Its solid characters and electrifying energy have not been lost on critics, and the musical won six Tony Awards – including Best Musical – in 2013.

Chicago

A little easier to score tickets to than some of the newer Broadway musicals, this beloved Bob Fosse/Kander & Ebb classic tells the story of showgirl Velma Kelly, wannabe Roxie Hart, lawyer Billy Flynn and the fabulously sordid goings-on of the Chicago underworld. Revived by director Walter Bobbie, its sassy, infectious energy more than makes up for the theater's tight-squeeze seating.

Wicked

An extravagant prequel to *The Wizard of Oz*, this long-running, pop-rock musical gives the story's witches a turn to tell the tale. The musical is based on Gregory Maguire's 1995 novel.

Aladdin

This witty dervish of a musical recounts the tale of a street urchin who falls in love with the daughter of a sultan. Based on the 1992 Disney animation, the stage version includes songs from the film and numerous numbers which didn't make the final cut, as well as new material written specifically for the live production.

Enterprise space shuttle, Intrepid Sea, Air & Space Museum

What's Nearby?

Intrepid Sea, Air & Space Museum

Museum

(☎877-957-7447; www.intrepidmuseum.org; Pier 86, Twelfth Ave at W 46th St; adult/child $33/24, discounted for NYC residents; ⏰10am-5pm Mon-Fri, to 6pm Sat & Sun Apr-Oct, 10am-5pm Mon-Sun Nov-Mar; 👪; 🚌westbound M42, M50 to 12th Ave, [S]A/C/E to 42nd St-Port Authority Bus Terminal) In WWII, the USS *Intrepid* survived both a bomb and kamikaze attacks. Now this hulking aircraft carrier plays host to an impressive, multimillion-dollar interactive military museum that tells its fascinating tale through videos, historical artifacts and frozen-in-time living quarters. The flight deck features fighter planes and military helicopters, which might inspire you to try the museum's high-tech flight simulators. Topical rotating exhibits add to the fun.

The hands-on exhibits include a number of simulators, such as the G Force Encounter, allowing you to experience the virtual thrill of flying a supersonic jet plane, and headsets in the Space Shuttle Pavilion – a vast hangar housing the *Enterprise*, NASA's first space shuttle orbiter from the 1970s – that enable you to experience the life of an astronaut in space. The museum is also home to the guided-missile submarine *Growler* (not for the claustrophobic) and a decommissioned Concorde plane.

🍴 Take a Break

Take a pre-theater drink with a side of nostalgia at the **Chatwal New York** (www.thechatwalny.com) hotel bar, an art deco jewel that has been faithfully revived.

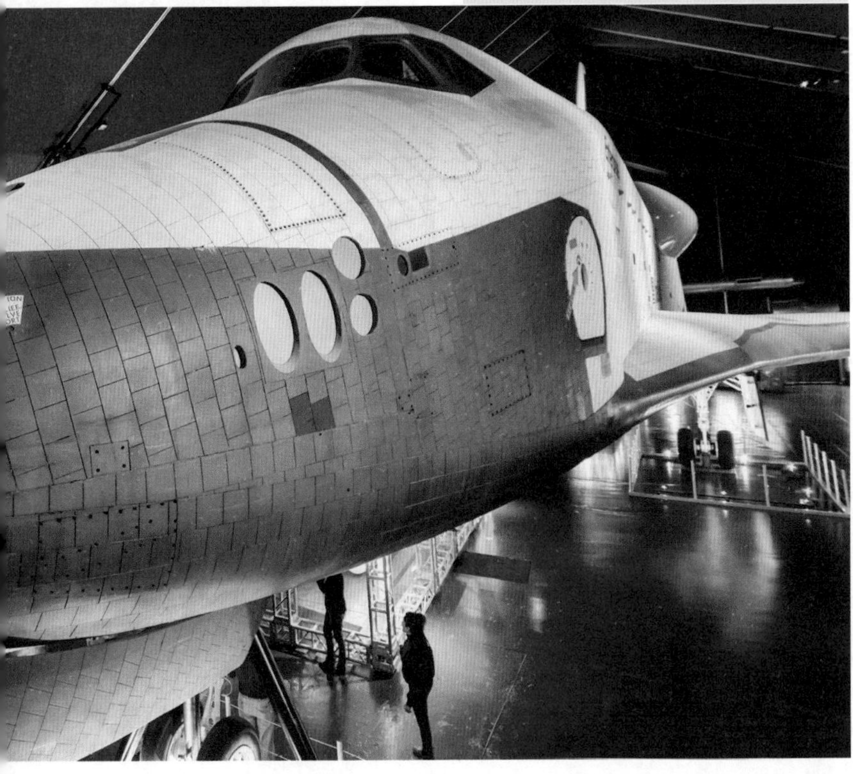

ALARAX/SHUTTERSTOCK ©

Times Square

Love it or hate it, the intersection of Broadway and Seventh Ave, better known as Times Square, is New York City's hyperactive heart: a restless, hypnotic torrent of glittering lights, bombastic billboards and raw urban energy.

Great For...

ℹ Need to Know

Map p252; www.timessquarenyc.org; Broadway, at Seventh Ave; Ⓢ N/Q/R/W, S, 1/2/3, 7 to Times Sq-42nd St

★ Top Tip

Times Square's neon-lit fame has made it NYC's biggest tourist trap. Don't come here to shop, and definitely don't come here to eat.

NYC Icons

Times Square is not hip, fashionable or in-the-know, and it couldn't care less. It's too busy pumping out iconic, mass-marketed NYC – yellow cabs, golden arches, soaring skyscrapers and razzle-dazzle Broadway marquees. This is the New York of collective fantasies – the place where Al Jolson 'makes it' in the 1927 film *The Jazz Singer*, where photojournalist Alfred Eisenstaedt famously captured a lip-locked sailor and nurse on VJ Day in 1945, and where Alicia Keys waxed lyrically about the concrete jungle.

For several decades, the dream here was a sordid one. The economic crash of the early 1970s led to a mass exodus of corporations from Times Square. Billboard niches went dark, stores shut and once-grand hotels were converted into SRO (single-room occupancy) dives. While the

adjoining Theater District survived, its respectable playhouses shared the streets with porn cinemas and strip clubs. That all changed with tough-talking former mayor Rudolph Giuliani, who, in the 1990s, boosted police numbers and lured a wave of 'respectable' retail chains, restaurants and attractions. By the new millennium, Times Square had gone from 'X-rated' to 'G-rated,' drawing almost 40 million visitors annually.

How the New York Times Made New Year's Eve

At the turn of the 20th century, Times Square was an unremarkable intersection known as Longacre Sq. This would change with a deal made between subway pioneer August Belmont and *New York Times* publisher Adolph Ochs. Heading construction of the city's first subway line (from Lower

Diamond District

Manhattan to Harlem), Belmont astutely realized that a Midtown business hub would encourage use of the line (and maximize profit). Belmont persuaded Ochs to move to Broadway and 42nd St and convinced mayor George B McClellan Jr to rename the square in honor of the broadsheet. In the winter of 1904–05, both the subway station and the *Times'* new HQ made their debut.

In honor of the move, the *Times* hosted a New Year's Eve party in 1904, setting off fireworks from its skyscraper rooftop. By 1907, the square had become so built-up that fireworks were deemed a safety hazard, forcing the newspaper to come up with an alternative crowd-puller. It came in the form of a 700lb wood-and-iron ball, lowered from the roof of One Times Square to herald the arrival of 1908. Around one million people still gather in Times Square every New Year's Eve to watch a Waterford crystal ball descend from the building at midnight.

What's Nearby?

Museum of Arts & Design Museum

(MAD; Map p254; ☎212-299-7777; www.madmuseum.org; 2 Columbus Circle, btwn Eighth Ave & Broadway; adult/child under 19 $16/free, by donation 6-9pm Thu; ◷10am-6pm Tue-Sun, to 9pm Thu; ⛗; ⓢA/C, B/D, 1 to 59th St-Columbus Circle) MAD offers four floors of superlative design and handicrafts, from blown glass and carved wood to elaborate metal jewelry. Its temporary exhibitions are innovative: one past show rendered fake news into art. The 6th floor houses resident artists' studios where you can interact with designers. The museum gift shop sells fantastic contemporary jewelry, while the 9th-floor restaurant/bar **Robert** is perfect for cocktails with a view.

Diamond District Area

(Map p252; www.diamonddistrict.org; W 47th St, btwn Fifth & Sixth Aves; ⓢB/D/F/M to 47th-50th Sts-Rockefeller Center) Like Diagon Alley in *Harry Potter,* the Diamond District is a world unto itself. Best experienced on weekdays, it's an industrious whirl of Hasidic Jewish traders, pesky hawkers and love-struck couples looking for the perfect rock. It's home to more than 2600 businesses cutting, polishing, appraising or showcasing all manner of diamonds. Giant diamond-shaped street lamps on silver plinths demarcate the road at either end.

CHRISTIAN MUELLER/SHUTTERSTOCK ©

> **☑ Don't Miss**
>
> For a panoramic overview, order a drink at the Renaissance Hotel's **R Lounge** (www.rloungetimessquare.com), which offers floor-to-ceiling glass windows onto the neon-lit spectacle below.

> **✕ Take a Break**
>
> A 10-minute walk from the neon glow, teeny Totto Ramen (p135) is hands-down the most exquisite noodle broth you're going to find this side of Japan.

Empire State Building

The Chrysler Building may be prettier, and One World Trade Center may be taller, but the queen bee of the New York skyline remains the Empire State Building. NYC's tallest star has enjoyed close-ups in around 100 films, from King Kong to Independence Day.

Great For...

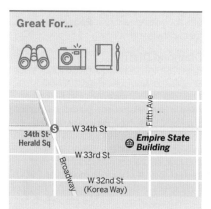

❶ Need to Know

Map p250; www.esbnyc.com; 350 Fifth Ave, at W 34th St; 86th-fl observation deck adult/child $38/32, incl 102nd-fl observation deck $58/52; ⊙8am-2am, last elevators up 1:15am; S6 to 33rd St, B/D/F/M, N/Q/R/W to 34th St-Herald Sq

★ **Top Tip**

To beat the queues, buy tickets online (well worth the extra $2 convenience fee) and head up for 8am when the Empire State opens its doors.

Observation Decks

There are two observation decks. The open-air 86th-floor lookout offers an alfresco experience on a broad deck. Further up, the enclosed (and rather pokey) 102nd-floor deck is New York's second-highest observation deck, trumped only by the one at One World Trade Center. Getting up to the 102nd floor used to involve a ride in a manually operated heritage elevator, but it was finally removed in 2017. Now that it's gone, it's debatable whether it's worth the extra bucks to visit this observatory.

Needless to say, the views over the city's five boroughs from both decks are quite simply exquisite. If you want a closer look at the metropolis in action or more information on what you can see, download the Empire State's app or use the (now free!) telescopes on both decks. The Chrysler is best viewed from the north side of the building.

By the Numbers

Before ascending to the 86th floor, your visit starts at the 'Dare to Dream' exhibition about the building's construction, featuring archive photos, architectural drawings and correspondences. The statistics are astounding: 10 million bricks, 60,000 tons of steel, 6400 windows and 328,000 sq ft of marble. Built on the original site of the Waldorf-Astoria, construction took a record-setting 410 days, using seven million hours of labor and costing $41 million. It might sound like a lot, but it fell well below its $50 million budget (just as well, given it went up during the Great Depression). Coming in at 102 stories and 1454ft from top to bottom, the limestone

New York Public Library

phallus opened for business on May 1, 1931. Generations later, Deborah Kerr's words to Cary Grant in *An Affair to Remember* still ring true: 'It's the nearest thing to heaven we have in New York.'

Language of Light

Since 1976, the building's top 30 floors have been floodlit in a spectrum of colors each night, reflecting seasonal and holiday hues. Famous combos include orange, white and green for St Patrick's Day; blue and white for Hanukkah; white, red and green for Christmas; and the rainbow colors for Gay Pride weekend in June. For a full rundown of the color schemes, check the website.

☑ Don't Miss

Live jazz on the 86th floor, held on Thursday to Saturday nights from 9pm to 1am.

PERCYALBAN/SHUTTERSTOCK ©

What's Nearby?

New York Public Library Historic Building

(Stephen A Schwarzman Building; Map p250; ☎917-275-6975; www.nypl.org; 476 Fifth Ave, at W 42nd St; 🕐10am-6pm Mon & Thu-Sat, to 8pm Tue & Wed, 1-5pm Sun, guided tours 11am & 2pm Mon-Sat, 2pm Sun; [S]B/D/F/M to 42nd St-Bryant Park, 7 to 5th Ave) [FREE] Loyally guarded by 'Patience' and 'Fortitude' (the marble lions overlooking Fifth Ave), this beaux-arts show-off is one of NYC's best free attractions. When dedicated in 1911, New York's flagship library ranked as the largest marble structure ever built in the US, and to this day its recently restored **Rose Main Reading Room** steals the breath away with its lavish coffered ceiling. It's only one of several glories inside, among them the **DeWitt Wallace Periodical Room** (1st floor).

Madison Square Park Park

(Map p250; ☎212-520-7600; www.madisonsquarepark.org; E 23rd to 26th Sts, btwn Fifth & Madison Aves, Flatiron District; 🕐6am-11pm; 👪; [S]R/W, F/M, 6 to 23rd St) This park defined the northern reaches of Manhattan until the island's population exploded after the Civil War. These days it's a welcome oasis from Manhattan's relentless pace, with a popular children's playground, dog-run area and **Shake Shack** burger joint. It's also one of the city's most cultured parks, with specially commissioned art installations and (in the warmer months) activities ranging from literary discussions to live music gigs. See the website for more information.

🍴 Take a Break

Feast on dumplings, barbecue and kimchi in nearby restaurant-lined Koreatown (32nd St between Fifth & Sixth Aves).

1000 WORDS/SHUTTERSTOCK ©

Museum of Modern Art

Quite possibly the greatest hoarder of modern masterpieces on earth, the Museum of Modern Art (MoMA) is a cultural promised land. The MoMA is a thrilling crash course in all that is beautiful and addictive about art.

Great For...

ⓘ Need to Know

MoMA; Map p252; ☎212-708-9400; www.moma.org; enter at 18 W 54th St, btwn Fifth & Sixth Aves; adult/child under 17 $25/free, 4-8pm Fri free; ⏲10:30am-5:30pm Sat-Thu, to 8pm Fri; 👪; [S]E/M to 5th Ave-53rd St; F to 57th St

Since its founding in 1929, MoMA has amassed almost 200,000 artworks, documenting the creativity of the late 19th century through to today. For art buffs, it's Valhalla.

Visiting MoMA

It's easy to get lost in the museum's vast collection, so it makes sense to download MoMA's free app and plan your visit before you go.

MoMA's permanent collection spans four levels but the museum is just emerging from a drive to add another 40,000 sq ft, equating to 30% more gallery space. As part of this reincarnation, museum directors are snatching the opportunity to rehang MoMA's works by chronological periods rather than by discipline, mixing painting, photography and other media

OSCITY/SHUTTERSTOCK ©

☑ **Don't Miss**

The outdoor sculpture garden makes a fine retreat when you have gallery fatigue (note it's closed during inclement weather).

★ **Top Tip**

To maximize your time and create a plan of attack, download the museum's free smartphone app from the website beforehand. It's available in a number of different languages.

like never before. It is hoped the move will help increase diversity in the galleries. A state-of-the-art performance space is also being developed to show more experimental art.

Works are on rotation so it's hard to say exactly what you'll find on display, but Van Gogh's phenomenally popular *The Starry Night* is usually a sure bet – mobbed by a circle of star-struck fans wielding cameras. Other highlights of the collection include Picasso's *Les Demoiselles d'Avignon* and Henri Rousseau's *The Sleeping Gypsy*, not to mention iconic American works like Warhol's *Campbell's Soup Cans* and *Gold Marilyn Monroe*, Lichtenstein's equally poptastic *Girl with Ball*, and Hopper's haunting *House by the Railroad*.

Abstract Expressionism

One of the greatest strengths of MoMA's collections is abstract expressionism, a radical movement that emerged in New York in the 1940s and boomed a decade later. Defined by its penchant for irreverent individualism and monumentally scaled works, this so-called New York School helped turn the metropolis into *the* epicenter of Western contemporary art. Among the stars are Rothko's *Magenta, Black, Green on Orange,* Pollock's *One (Number 31, 1950)* and De Kooning's *Painting.*

Lunchtime Talks

To delve a little deeper into MoMA's collection, join one of the museum's lunchtime talks and readings, which see writers, artists, curators and designers offering expert insight into specific works and exhibitions on view. The talks take place daily at 11:30am and 1:30pm. To check upcoming topics, click the 'Exhibitions & Events' link on the MoMA website.

Sculpture Garden

With architect Yoshio Taniguchi's reconstruction of the museum in 2004 came the restoration of the Sculpture Garden to the original, larger vision of Philip Johnson's 1953 design. Johnson described the space as a 'sort of outdoor room,' and on warm, sunny days, it's hard not to think of it as a soothing alfresco lounge. One resident that can't seem to get enough of it is Aristide Maillol's *The River*, a larger-than-life female sculpture that featured in Johnson's original garden. She's in fine company too, with fellow works from greats including Matisse, Miró and Picasso.

Film Screenings

Not only a palace of visual art, MoMA screens an incredibly well-rounded selection of celluloid gems from its col-

lection of over 22,000 films, including the works of the Maysles Brothers and every Pixar animation film ever produced. Expect anything from Academy Award–nominated documentary shorts and Hollywood classics, to experimental works and international retrospectives. Best of all, your museum ticket will get you in for free (though you'll still need to get a ticket for the film you want to see).

What's Nearby
Radio City Music Hall
Historic Building

(Map p252; www.radiocity.com; 1260 Sixth Ave, at W 51st St; tours adult/child $27/20; ⊙tours 9:30am-5pm; ♿; SB/D/F/M to 47th-50th Sts-Rockefeller Center) This spectacular Moderne movie palace was the brainchild of vaudeville producer Samuel Lionel 'Roxy'

Radio City Music Hall

Rothafel. Never one for understatement, Roxy launched his venue on December 23, 1932 with an over-the-top extravaganza that included camp dance troupe the Roxyettes (mercifully renamed the Rockettes). Guided tours (75 minutes) of the sumptuous interiors include the glorious auditorium, Witold Gordon's classically inspired mural *History of Cosmetics* in the Women's Downstairs Lounge, and the VIP Roxy Suite, where luminaries such as Elton John and Alfred Hitchcock have been entertained.

✕ Take a Break

For a really special meal plan your MoMA visit around a reservation at its Michelin-starred restaurant Modern (p136), which overlooks the sculpture garden.

LITTLENY/GETTY IMAGES ©

As far as catching a show here goes, be warned: the vibe doesn't quite match the theater's glamour these days. That said, there are often some fabulous talents in the lineup, with past performers including Lauryn Hill, Rufus Wainwright, Aretha Franklin and Dolly Parton. And while the word 'Rockettes' provokes eye rolling from most New Yorkers, fans of glitz and kitsch might just get a thrill from the troupe's annual **Christmas Spectacular**.

Same-day tickets are available at the box office inside the Sixth Ave entrance. Whether you book here or in advance online, expect horrendous queues to get into the show; it's hugely popular. Tour tickets are usually easy enough to book on the day, and tours depart from the entrance around the corner on W 52st St.

St Patrick's Cathedral   Cathedral

(Map p252; 212-753-2261; www.saintpatricks cathedral.org; Fifth Ave, btwn E 50th & 51st Sts; 6:30am-8:45pm; SB/D/F/M to 47th-50th Sts-Rockefeller Center, E/M to 5th Ave-53rd St) Still shining after a $200 million restoration in 2015, America's largest Catholic cathedral graces Fifth Ave with Gothic Revival splendor. Built at a cost of nearly $2 million during the Civil War, the building did not originally include the two front spires; those were added in 1888. Step inside to appreciate the Louis Tiffany–designed altar, gleaming below a 7000-pipe church organ, and Charles Connick's stunning Rose Window above the Fifth Ave entrance. Walk-in guided tours are available; check the website for details.

A **basement crypt** behind the altar contains the coffins of every New York cardinal and the remains of Pierre Toussaint, a champion of the poor and the first African American up for sainthood.

★ Top Tip

Keep your museum ticket handy, as it also provides free entry to film screenings and MoMA PS1 (p12).

Walking Tour: Inside Chinatown

The storied lanes of Chinatown are pure sensory overload amid fast-talking street vendors, neon-lit noodle parlors and colorful storefronts packed with eye candy from the Far East.

Start Chatham Sq
Distance 1 mile
Duration 1½ hours

7 The Chinese-American experience is expertly told at the **Museum of Chinese in America** (www.mocanyc.org).

3 In the early 1900s crooked **Doyers Street** was so popular with feuding *tongs* (secret societies) that it gained the nickname Bloody Angle.

2 Chinatown's unofficial living room, **Columbus Park** was NYC's notorious Five Points slum in the 19th century.

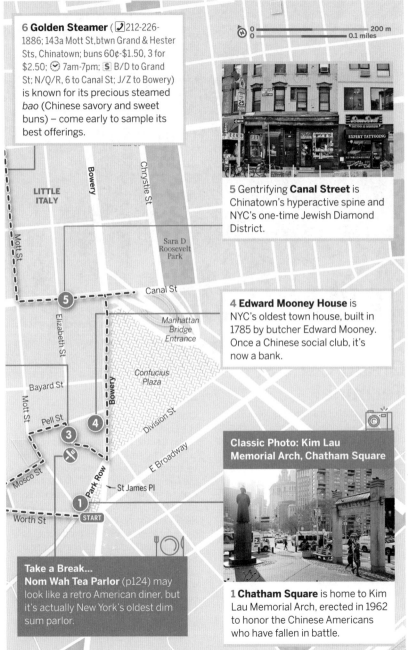

6 Golden Steamer (212-226-1886; 143a Mott St, btwn Grand & Hester Sts, Chinatown; buns 60¢-$1.50, 3 for $2.50; 7am-7pm; B/D to Grand St; N/Q/R, 6 to Canal St; J/Z to Bowery) is known for its precious steamed *bao* (Chinese savory and sweet buns) – come early to sample its best offerings.

5 Gentrifying **Canal Street** is Chinatown's hyperactive spine and NYC's one-time Jewish Diamond District.

4 Edward Mooney House is NYC's oldest town house, built in 1785 by butcher Edward Mooney. Once a Chinese social club, it's now a bank.

Classic Photo: Kim Lau Memorial Arch, Chatham Square

Take a Break...
Nom Wah Tea Parlor (p124) may look like a retro American diner, but it's actually New York's oldest dim sum parlor.

1 Chatham Square is home to Kim Lau Memorial Arch, erected in 1962 to honor the Chinese Americans who have fallen in battle.

1 PATTI MCCONVILLE/ALAMY STOCK PHOTO © 3 MASSIMO BORCHI/ATLANTIDE PHOTOTRAVEL/GETTY IMAGES © 5 PHOTO KIT/SHUTTERSTOCK ©

ALARAX/SHUTTERSTOCK ©

Grand Central Terminal

This cathedral of transport is New York's most breathtaking beaux-arts building. Its chandeliers, marble and historic bars and restaurants are from an era when train travel and romance went hand in hand.

Great For...

☑ Don't Miss

The **Great Northern Food Hall** (www. greatnorthernfood.com; sandwiches $7-12; ⏱7am-11pm Mon-Fri, 8am-8pm Sat & Sun; 🛜) inside the beaux-arts Vanderbilt Hall, where commuters graze on gourmet Nordic morsels.

42nd St Facade

Clad in Connecticut Stony Creek granite at its base and Indiana limestone on top, Grand Central's showpiece facade is crowned by America's greatest monumental sculpture, *Transportation*. Designed by the French sculptor Jules-Félix Coutan and rising 48ft, the piece was executed in Long Island City by local carvers Donnelly and Ricci. Once completed, it was hoisted up, piece by piece, in 1914. Its protagonist is a wing-capped Mercury, the Roman god of travel and commerce. To the left is Hercules, while looking down on the mayhem of 42nd St is Minerva. The clock beneath Mercury's foot contains the largest example of Tiffany glass in the world.

ℹ️ Need to Know

Map p252; www.grandcentralterminal.com; 89 E 42nd St, at Park Ave; ⏰5:30am-2am; Ⓢ S, 4/5/6, 7 to Grand Central-42nd St, Ⓡ Metro North to Grand Central

✕ Take a Break

Stop by The Campbell (p172) for a top-shelf cocktail in swanky surrounds.

★ Top Tip

Come back at night, when the calmness gives the hallways an almost sacred vibe.

Main Concourse

Grand Central's trump card is more akin to a glorious ballroom than a thoroughfare. The marble floors are Tennessee pink, while the vintage ticket counters are Italian Botticino marble. The vaulted ceiling is heavenly, its turquoise and gold-leaf mural depicting eight constellations...backwards. A mistake? Apparently not. Its French designer, painter Paul César Helleu, wished to depict the stars from God's point of view – from the out, looking in. The original, frescoed execution of Helleu's design was by New York–based artists J Monroe Hewlett and Charles Basing. Moisture damage saw it faithfully repainted (alas, not in fresco form) by Charles Gulbrandsen in 1944. By the 1990s, however, the mural was in ruins again. Enter renovation architects Beyer Blinder Belle, who restored the work,

but left a small rectangular patch of soot as testament to just what a fine job they did.

What's Nearby?

Chrysler Building   Historic Building

(Map p252; 405 Lexington Ave, at E 42nd St; ⏰lobby 7am-6.30pm Mon-Fri; Ⓢ S, 4/5/6, 7 to Grand Central-42nd St) Designed by William Van Alen and completed in 1930, the 77-floor Chrysler Building is the pin-up for New York's purest art-deco architecture, guarded by stylized eagles of chromium nickel and topped by a beautiful seven-tiered spire reminiscent of the rising sun. The building was constructed as the headquarters for Walter P Chrysler and his automobile empire; unable to compete on the production line with bigger rivals Ford and General Motors, Chrysler trumped them on the skyline. And while the Chrysler Building might not offer a restaurant or observation deck, its lobby, where dark African wood and marble contrast against the brash steel of industrial America, makes for a lavish consolation prize.

Guggenheim Museum

A sculpture in its own right, architect Frank Lloyd Wright's swirling white building is one of New York's most photogenic museums. It stages exceptional shows by some of the greatest artists of the 20th and 21st centuries.

Great For...

ℹ Need to Know

Map p254; ☏212-423-3500; www.guggen heim.org; 1071 Fifth Ave, at E 89th St; adult/child $25/free, cash-only pay-what-you-wish 5-7:45pm Sat; ⊙10am-5:30pm Wed-Fri, Sun & Mon, to 8pm Tue & Sat; 👪; Ⓢ4/5/6, Q to 86th St

★ **Top Tip**

Entrance lines can be brutal; save time by purchasing tickets online in advance, or come for opening time.

Frank Lloyd Wright's elegant curvilinear building almost overshadows the collection of 20th-century art that it houses. Completed in 1959, the inverted ziggurat structure was derided by some critics but hailed by others, who welcomed it as a beloved architectural icon.

Abstract Roots

The Guggenheim came out of the collection of Solomon R Guggenheim, a New York mining magnate who began acquiring abstract art in his 60s at the behest of his art adviser, an eccentric German baroness named Hilla Rebay. In 1939, with Rebay serving as director, Guggenheim opened a temporary museum on 54th St titled the Museum of Non-Objective Painting. (Incredibly, it had grey velour walls, piped-in classical music and burning incense.) Four years later, the pair commissioned Wright to construct a permanent home for the collection.

Years in the Making

Like most developments in New York City, the project took forever to come to fruition. Construction was delayed for almost 13 years due to budget constraints, the outbreak of WWII and outraged neighbors who weren't all that excited to see a giant concrete spaceship land in their midst. Construction was finally completed in 1959 – after both Wright and Guggenheim had passed away.

When the Guggenheim finally opened its doors in October 1959, the ticket price was 50¢ and the works on view included pieces by Kandinsky, Alexander Calder and abstract expressionists Franz Kline and Willem de Kooning.

Visiting Today

A renovation in the early 1990s added an eight-story tower to the east, which provided an extra 50,000 sq ft of exhibition space. These galleries feature rotating exhibitions from the collection, while the ramps of the rotunda show temporary exhibits.

The museum's holdings include works by Kandinsky, Picasso and Jackson Pollock. Over time, other key additions have included paintings by Monet, Van Gogh and Degas, photographs by Robert Mapplethorpe, and key surrealist works donated by Guggenheim's niece Peggy.

☑ Don't Miss

The onsite Guggenheim Store is a must for fans of art and design, with unusual books, modernist posters, gifts and homewares.

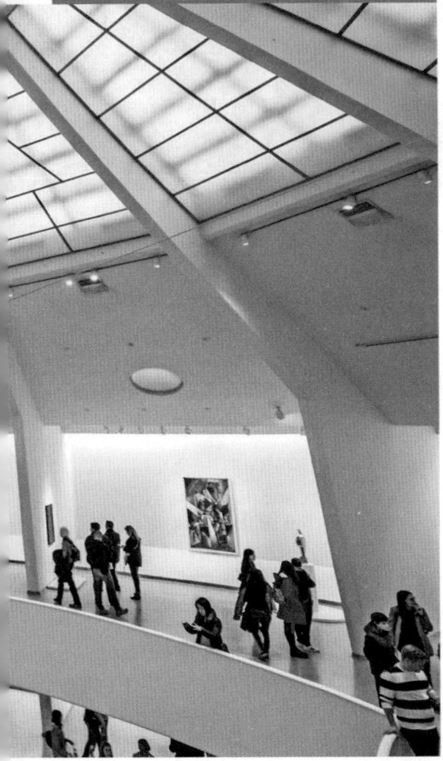

ITZAVU/SHUTTERSTOCK © SOLOMON R GUGGENHEIM MUSEUM, NEW YORK

What's Nearby?

Jewish Museum Museum

(Map p254; ☎212-423-3200; www.thejewishmuseum.org; 1109 Fifth Ave, btwn E 92nd & 93rd Sts; adult/child $18/free, Sat free, pay-what-you-wish 5-8pm Thu; 🕐11am-5:45pm Sat-Tue, to 8pm Thu, to 4pm/5pm Fri winter/summer; 👪; [S]6, Q to 96th St) This gem occupies a French-Gothic mansion from 1908, housing 30,000 items of Judaica including torah shields and Hanukkah lamps, as well as sculpture, painting and decorative arts. It does not, however, include any historical exhibitions relating to the Jewish community in New York. Temporary exhibits are often excellent, featuring retrospectives on influential figures such as Art Spiegelman, as well as world-class shows on luminaries like Marc Chagall and Modigliani. The landmark Lower East Side deli Russ & Daughters has a restaurant in the basement.

Cooper Hewitt Smithsonian Design Museum Museum

(Map p254; ☎212-849-2950; www.cooperhewitt.org; 2 E 91st St, at Fifth Ave; adult/child $18/free, pay-what-you-wish 6-9pm Sat; 🕐10am-6pm Sun-Fri, to 9pm Sat; [S]4/5/6 to 86th St) Part of the Smithsonian Institution in Washington DC, this is the only US museum dedicated to both historic and contemporary design. Housed in the 64-room mansion built by billionaire Andrew Carnegie in 1901, the 210,000-piece collection offers artful displays spanning 3000 years. Free tours are at 11:30am and 1:30pm on weekdays, and at 1pm and 3pm on weekends.

🍴 Take a Break

Guggenheim's **Wright** (Map p254; ☎212-423-3665; www.guggenheim.org; Guggenheim Museum, 1071 Fifth Ave, at E 89th St; mains $23-28; 🕐11:30am-3:30pm Mon-Fri, from 11am Sat & Sun; 📶; [S]4/5/6, Q to 86th St) restaurant is a modernist beauty serving brunch, seasonal dishes and cocktails.

S4SVISUALS/SHUTTERSTOCK ©

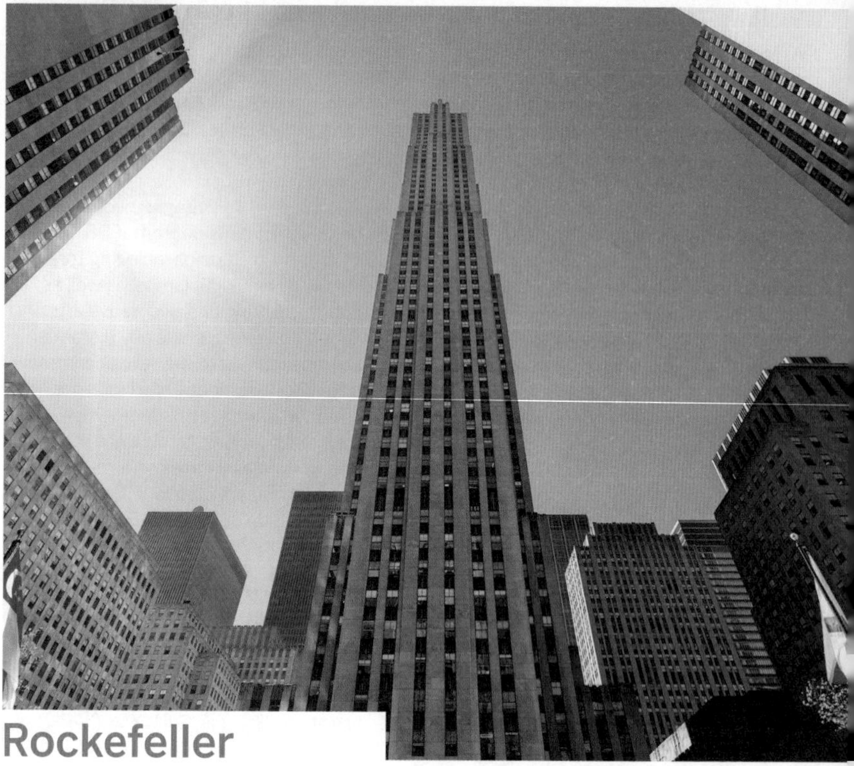

Rockefeller Center

An art-deco behemoth and historic landmark, Rockefeller Center remains a hive of activity with some of NYC's best shops, a sky-high viewing platform, a famed ice rink in winter and the city's number-one Christmas tree each December.

Great For...

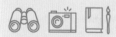

☑ Don't Miss

New York's legendary toy shop FAO Schwarz (p156) has been reborn inside the Rockefeller Center, and it's pretty magical.

This 22-acre 'city within a city' debuted at the height of the Great Depression. Taking nine years to build, it was America's first multi-use retail, entertainment and office space – a modernist sprawl of buildings (14 of which are the original art-deco structures), outdoor plazas and big-name tenants, interspersed with public artworks.

Top of the Rock

There are views, and then there's *the* view from the **Top of the Rock** (Map p252; ☎212-698-2000, toll-free 877-692-7625; www.topoftherocknyc.com; 30 Rockefeller Plaza, entrance on W 50th St, btwn Fifth & Sixth Aves; adult/child $36/30, sunrise/sunset combo $54/43; 🕐8am-midnight, last elevator at 11pm; [S]B/D/F/M to 47th-50th Sts-Rockefeller Center). Crowning the GE Building, 70 stories above Midtown, its blockbuster vista includes one icon that

JEFF WHYTE/SHUTTERSTOCK ©

❶ Need to Know

Map p252; ☏212-588-8601; www.rocke
fellercenter.com; Fifth to Sixth Aves, btwn
W 48th & 51st Sts; Ⓢ B/D/F/M to 47th-50th
Sts-Rockefeller Center

✕ Take a Break

Grab a bite at Burger Joint (p135), well
concealed inside Le Parker Meridien
Hotel.

★ Top Tip

To beat the wintertime ice-skating
crowds and avoid a long wait, come at
the first skating period (8:30am).

you won't see from atop the Empire State
Building – *the* Empire State Building. If
possible, head up just before sunset to see
the city transform from day to glittering
night (if you're already in the area and the
queues aren't long, purchase your tickets
in advance to avoid the late-afternoon
rush). If you don't have under-21s in tow,
the Rockefeller's 65th-floor cocktail bar, Bar
SixtyFive (p172), has similar views without
the admission price, but don't expect to get
anywhere near the windows unless you've
reserved a table.

Public Artworks

Rockefeller Center features the work of
30 great artists, commissioned around
the theme 'Man at the Crossroads Looks
Uncertainly but Hopefully at the Future.'
Paul Manship contributed the 18ft *Pro-
metheus,* overlooking the sunken plaza,
while Lee Lawrie made the 24ft-tall bronze
Atlas, in front of the International Building
(630 Fifth Ave). Isamu Noguchi's *News* sits
above the entrance to the Associated Press
Building (50 Rockefeller Plaza), and José
Maria Sert's oil *American Progress* awaits
in the lobby of the GE Building. The latter
work replaced Mexican artist Diego Rivera's
original painting, rejected by the Rockefel-
lers for containing 'communist imagery'
and destroyed.

Rockefeller Plaza

Come the festive season, Rockefeller
Plaza is where you'll find New York's most
famous Christmas tree. Ceremoniously lit
just after Thanksgiving, it's a tradition that
dates back to the 1930s, when construction workers set up a small tree on the site.
In its shadow, Rink at Rockefeller Center
(p198) is the city's most famous ice-skating
rink. Although magical, it's also undeniably
small and crowded. Come summer, the rink
becomes a cafe.

Whitney Museum of American Art

Even in the midst of Chelsea and the Meatpacking District's plenitude of galleries, the Whitney's collection of American art is exceptional. As is the contemporary landmark building it now resides in.

Great For...

☑ Don't Miss

Free expert tours of parts of the collection are offered every day; reservations aren't needed, but check the schedule online.

The Building

Designed by Italian architect Renzo Piano (also responsible for Paris's Pompidou Centre) the Whitney's asymmetrical, glass-cloaked home quickly became a major landmark in the southern reaches of the Meatpacking District, housing myriad galleries, theaters, classrooms and outdoor spaces over 63,000 sq ft, and anchoring the first-opened section of the High Line.

The cleverly designed indoor- and outdoor-exhibition space is the perfect showcase for the world's foremost collection of 20th-century and contemporary American art, much of it the work of living artists. One gallery in particular is noteworthy – a vast, 18,000 sq ft space that is New York's largest column-free exhibition space. Once the decision was made to move from the Whitney's original, Marcel Breuer–designed

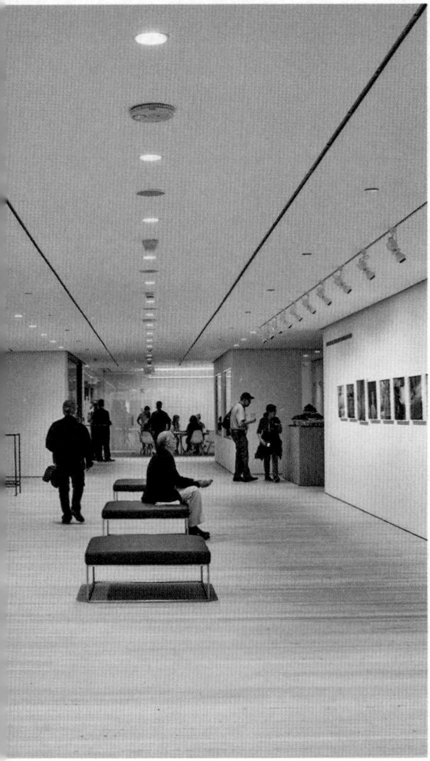

JACKIE WEISBERG/ALAMY STOCK PHOTO ©

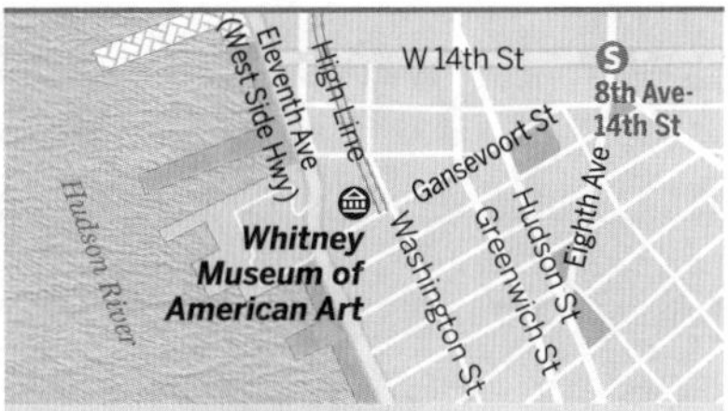

ℹ Need to Know

Map p246; ☎212-570-3600; www.whitney.org; 99 Gansevoort St, at Washington St, Meatpacking District; adult/child $25/free, 7-10pm Fri pay-what-you-wish; 🕒10:30am-6pm Mon, Wed, Thu & Sun, to 10pm Fri & Sat; [S]A/C/E, L to 8th Ave-14th St

🍴 Take a Break

Sink a sundowner at **Top of the Standard** (Map p246; ☎212-645-7600; www.standardhotels.com; Standard, 848 Washington St, at W 13th St, Meatpacking District; 🕒4pm-midnight Sun-Tue, to 9pm Wed-Sat; [S]A/C/E, L to 8th Ave-14th St), the cocktail bar atop the stylish Standard Hotel just north of the museum.

★ Top Tip

Buying tickets in advance online avoids any frustrating queues; entry is 'pay-what-you-wish' from 7pm to 10pm each Friday.

home on Madison Ave, something on the scale of this nine-story cultural colossus was always likely. Commenced in 2010, it cost $422 million to build, and opened to great acclaim in 2015.

The Collection

The Whitney's collection of over 23,000 works by 3,000-plus American artists assumes greater significance when you consider it's all 20th- and 21st-century work, much of it by still-practicing artists. Works from the permanent collection you might expect to encounter include Sol LeWitt's *Five Towers* (1986), looking like the load-bearing frame of an abandoned building; several of Andy Warhol's ten luridly colored *Mao Tse-Tung* prints (1972); Alice Neel's *Andy Warhol* (1970), for which the pop-art legend sat while recovering from a near-fatal shooting; Jasper Johns' *Three Flags* (1958); Marsden Hartley's early-modernist *Painting, Number 5* (1914–15); and plenty of comparable treasures.

The Founder

Gertrude Vanderbilt Whitney, of New York's wealthy Vanderbilt family, was an accomplished sculptor in her own right. But her greatest talent may have been for using her clout as an heiress to nourish American art. When the New York Metropolitan Museum of Art churlishly refused her collection of American works, she took matters into her own hands, donating both the collection and money to kick-start the museum in 1931.

Reflecting pools, National September 11 Memorial

National September 11 Memorial & Museum

An evocative museum and North America's largest artificial waterfalls are as much a symbol of hope and renewal as they are a tribute to the victims of terrorism.

Great For...

☑ Don't Miss

Santiago Calatrava's dramatic white Oculus, the WTC Transportation Hub next to the museum, was inspired by dove wings.

The National September 11 Memorial and Museum is a dignified tribute to the victims of the worst terrorist attack on American soil. Titled *Reflecting Absence,* the memorial's two massive reflecting pools are a symbol of renewal and commemorate the thousands who lost their lives. Beside them stands the Memorial Museum, a striking, solemn space documenting that horrific fall day in 2001.

Reflecting Pools

Surrounded by a plaza planted with more than 400 swamp white oak trees, the September 11 Memorial's reflecting pools occupy the original footprints of the ill-fated Twin Towers. From their rim, a steady cascade of water pours 30ft down toward a central void. The flow of the water is richly symbolic, beginning as thousands

Memorial Museum

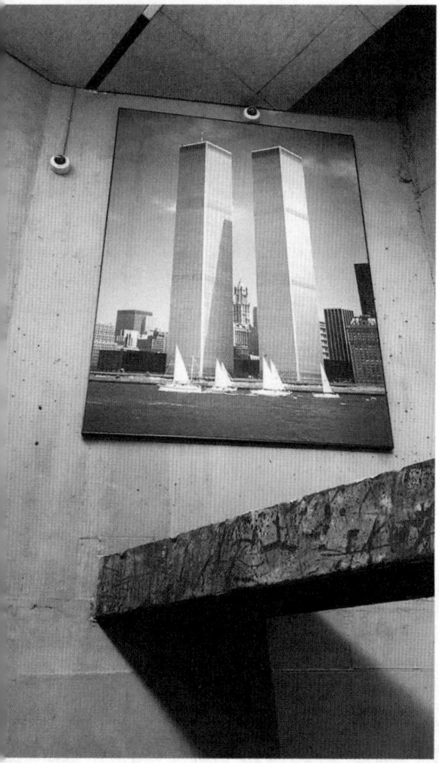

LOUIS.ROTH/SHUTTERSTOCK ©

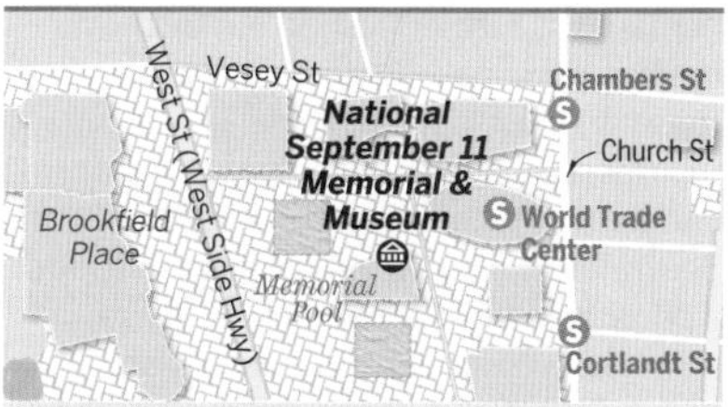

Need to Know

Map p244; ☎212-312-8800; www.911memorial.org/museum; 180 Greenwich St, Lower Manhattan; memorial free, museum adult/child $24/15, 5-8pm Tue free; 🕘9am-8pm Sun-Thu, to 9pm Fri & Sat, last entry 2hr before close; [S]E to World Trade Center, 2/3 to Park Pl, R/W to Cortlandt St

Take a Break

Head up to Tribeca for great dining options such as Locanda Verde (p123).

★ Top Tip

To minimize queuing, purchase tickets online or at one of the machines outside the museum; last entry is two hours before closing time.

of smaller streams, merging into a massive torrent of collective confusion, and ending with a slow journey toward an abyss. Bronze panels frame the pools, inscribed with the names of those who died in the terrorist attacks of September 11, 2001, and in the World Trade Center car bombing on February 26, 1993. Designed by Michael Arad and Peter Walker, the pools are both striking and deeply poignant.

Memorial Museum

The contemplative energy of the monument is further enhanced by the National September 11 Memorial Museum. Standing between the reflective pools, the museum's glass entrance pavilion eerily evokes a toppled tower. Inside the entrance, an escalator leads down to the museum's subterranean main lobby. On the descent, visitors stand in the shadow of two steel tridents, originally embedded in the bedrock at the base of the North Tower. Each over 80ft tall and weighing 50 tons, they once provided the structural support that allowed the towers to soar over 1360ft into the sky. They remained standing in the subsequent sea of rubble, becoming immediate symbols of resilience.

The tridents are two of more than 10,300 objects in the museum's collection. Among these are the Vesey Street Stairs. Dubbed the 'Survivors Stairs,' they allowed hundreds of workers to flee the WTC site on the morning of September 11. At the bottom of these stairs is the moving In Memoriam gallery, its walls lined with the photographs and names of those who perished. Interactive touch screens and a central reflection room shed light on the victims' lives. Their humanity is further fleshed out by the numerous personal effects on display. Among these is a dust-covered wallet belonging to Robert Joseph Gschaar, an insurance underwriter who worked on level 92 of the South Tower. The wallet's contents include a photograph of Gschaar's wife, Myrta, and a $2 bill: when he proposed, Gschaar gave a $2 bill to Myrta as a symbol of their second chance at happiness (theirs was a second marriage for both of them); he kept another with him.

Around the corner from the In Memoriam gallery is the NYC Fire Department's Engine Company 21. One of the largest artifacts on display, its burnt-out cab is testament to the inferno faced by those at the scene.

The fire engine stands at the entrance to the museum's main Historical Exhibi-

tion. Divided into three sections – *Events of the Day, Before 9/11* and *After 9/11* – its collection of videos, real-time audio recordings, images, objects and testimonies provide a rich, meditative exploration of the tragedy, the events that preceded it (including the WTC bombing of 1993), and the stories of grief, resilience and hope that followed.

The *Historical Exhibition* spills into the monumental Foundation Hall, flanked by a massive section of the original slurry wall, built to hold back the waters of the Hudson River during the towers' construction. It's also home to the last steel column removed during the clean-up, adorned with the messages and mementos of recovery workers, first responders and loved ones of the victims.

Memorial Museum

What's Nearby?

Trinity Church — Church

(Map p244; ☎212-602-0800; www.trinitywallstreet.org; 75 Broadway, at Wall St, Lower Manhattan; ⏰7am-6pm, churchyard closes dusk; Ⓢ1, R/W to Rector St, 2/3, 4/5 to Wall St) New York City's tallest building upon completion in 1846, Trinity Church features a 280ft-high bell tower and a richly colored stained-glass window over the altar. Famous residents of its serene cemetery include Founding Father Alexander Hamilton, while its excellent music series includes Concerts at One (1pm Thursdays) and magnificent choir concerts, including an annual December rendition of Handel's *Messiah*.

★ Angel of 9/11

One of the Memorial Museum's most curious (and famous) artifacts is the so-called 'Angel of 9/11,' the eerie outline of a woman's anguished face on a twisted girder believed to originate from the point where American Airlines Flight 11 slammed into the North Tower. (Experts have a more prosaic explanation: natural corrosion and sheer coincidence.)

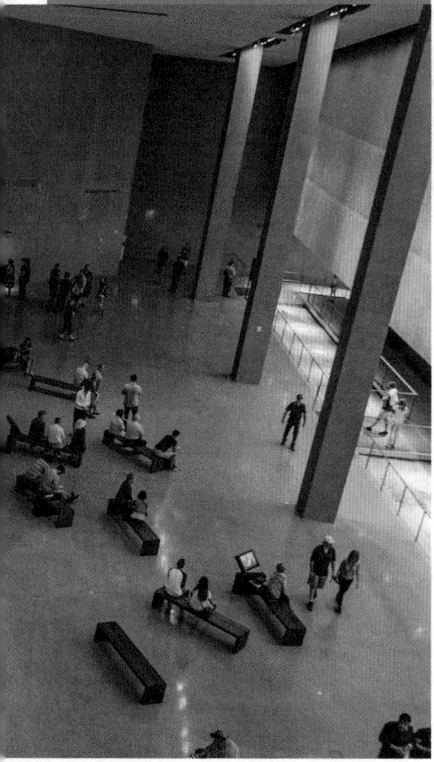

PIT STOCK/SHUTTERSTOCK ©

St Paul's Chapel — Church

(Map p244; ☎212-602-0800; www.trinitywallstreet.org; 209 Broadway, at Fulton St, Lower Manhattan; ⏰10am-6pm Mon-Sat, from 7am Sun, churchyard closes dusk; ⓈA/C, J/Z, 2/3, 4/5 to Fulton St, R/W to Cortlandt St) After his inauguration in 1789, George Washington worshipped at this classic revival brownstone chapel, which found new fame in the aftermath of September 11. With the World Trade Center destruction occurring just a block away, the mighty structure became a spiritual support and volunteer center, movingly documented in its exhibition 'Unwavering Spirit: Hope & Healing at Ground Zero.'

African Burial Ground National Monument — Memorial

(Map p246; ☎212-637-2019; www.nps.gov/afbg; 290 Broadway, btwn Duane & Reade Sts, Lower Manhattan; ⏰10am-4pm Tue-Sat; ⓈJ/Z to Chambers St, R/W to City Hall, 4/5/6 to Brooklyn Bridge-City Hall) FREE In 1991, construction workers here uncovered more than 400 stacked wooden caskets. The boxes contained the remains of both enslaved and free African Americans from the 17th and 18th centuries (nearby Trinity Church would not allow them to be buried in its graveyard). Today, a poignant **memorial site** and a **visitor center** with educational displays honor the estimated 15,000 men, women and children buried here.

As the visitor center is located inside a federal building, you'll need to go through an airport-like security screening.

Take a Break

There's a dearth of good food options in the Financial District, but Brookfield Place (p122) has a string of chef-driven food courts.

One World Trade Center

Soaring above the city skyline is this shimmering tower, a symbol of Lower Manhattan's rebirth. Its observation decks offer mesmerizing views over the vast metropolis (and surrounding states).

Filling what was a sore and glaring gap in the Lower Manhattan skyline, One World Trade Center symbolizes rebirth, determination and resilience. More than just another super-tall skyscraper, it's a richly symbolic giant, well aware of the past yet firmly focused on the future. It's also the hot new stop for dizzying, unforgettable urban views.

The Building

Leaping from the northwestern corner of the World Trade Center site, the 104-floor tower is architect David M Childs' redesign of Daniel Libeskind's original 2002 concept. Not only the loftiest building in America, this tapered giant is currently the tallest building in the Western Hemisphere – not to mention the fourth tallest in the world by pinnacle height. The tower soars skywards

Great For...

☑ Don't Miss

The staggering view from the base of the tower looking skyward.

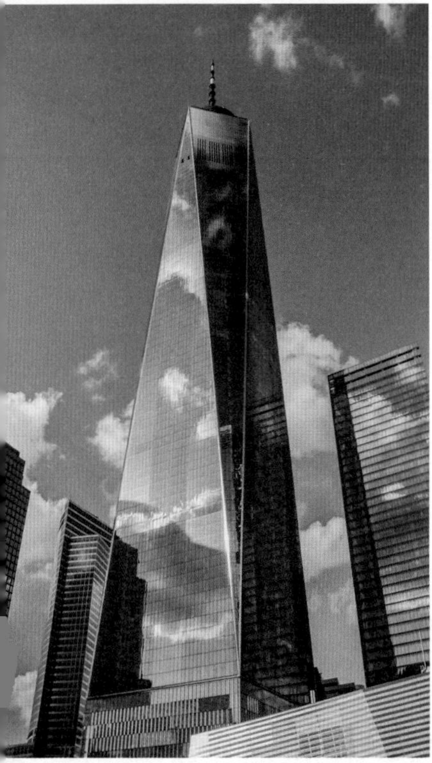

GREGORIO KOJI/SHUTTERSTOCK ©

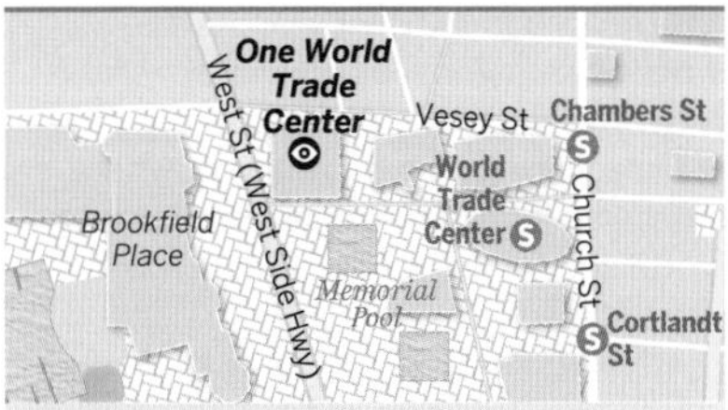
One World Trade Center
West St (West Side Hwy)
Vesey St
Chambers St
World Trade Center
Brookfield Place
Memorial Pool
Church St
Cortlandt St

ⓘ Need to Know

One WTC; Map p244; www.onewtc.com; cnr West & Vesey Sts; [S]E to World Trade Center, 2/3 to Park Pl, A/C, J/Z, 4/5 to Fulton St, R/W to Cortlandt St

🍴 Take a Break

Head a block west to Brookfield Place (p122) for fancy food courts Hudson Eats and Le District.

★ Top Tip

Prepurchase your tickets online (www.oneworldobservatory.com/tickets) to avoid the longest queues. Sunset is the busiest time.

with chamfered edges, resulting in a series of isosceles triangles that, seen from the building's base, reach to infinity. Crowning the structure is a 408ft cable-stayed spire. Co-designed by sculptor Kenneth Snelson, it brings the building's total height to 1776ft, a symbolic reference to the year of American independence.

Indeed, symbolism feeds several aspects of the building: the tower's footprint is equal to those of the original Twin Towers, while the observation decks match the heights of those in the old complex. Unlike the original towers, however, One WTC was built with a whole new level of safety in mind, its precautionary features including a 200ft-high blast-resistant base (clad in more than 2000 pieces of glimmering prismatic glass) and 39.4in-thick concrete walls encasing all elevators, stairwells, and communication and safety systems. One thing not foreseen by the architects and engineers, though, was the antenna's noisy disposition: the strong winds that race through its lattice design produce a haunting, howling sound known to keep some locals up at night.

One World Observatory

Not one to downplay its assets, the skyscraper is home to **One World Observatory** (Map p244; ☎212-602-4000; www.oneworldobservatory.com; 285 Fulton St, cnr West & Vesey Sts, Lower Manhattan; adult/child $34/28; 🕒9am-9pm Sep-Apr, from 8am May-Aug; [S]E to World Trade Center, 2/3 to Park Pl, A/C, J/Z, 4/5 to Fulton St, R/W to Cortlandt St), the city's loftiest observation deck. While the observatory spans levels 100 to 102, the experience begins at the ground-floor Global Welcome Center, where an electronic world map highlights the many homelands of the building's visitors (with data relayed from ticket scans). The bitter bickering that plagued much of the project's development is all but forgotten in the adjoining *Voices* exhibition, where architects and construction workers wax lyrical about the tower's formation on 144 video screens.

After a quick rundown of the site's geology, the real thrills begin as you step inside one of five Sky Pod elevators, among the fastest in the world. As the elevators begin their 1250ft skyward journey, LED wall panels kick into action. Suddenly you're in a veritable time machine, watching Manhattan's evolution from forested island to teeming concrete jungle. Forty-seven seconds (and 500 years) later, you're on level 102, where another short presentation ends with a spectacular reveal.

Skip the overpriced eateries on level 101 and continue down to the real highlight: level 100. Waiting for you is an epic 360-degree panorama guaranteed to keep you busy searching for landmarks, from the Brooklyn and Manhattan Bridges to Lady Liberty and the Woolworth, Empire State and Chrysler Buildings. If you need a hand, interactive mobile tablets programmed in eight languages are available for hire ($15). As expected, the view is extraordinary – try to go on a clear day – taking in all five boroughs and three adjoining states. For a close-up view of the Midtown skyscrapers, however, you're better off scaling the Empire State Building or the Rockefeller Center's Top of the Rock.

Woolworth Building

What's Nearby?

Woolworth Building Notable Building

(Map p244; ☎203-966-9663; www.woolworthtours.com; 233 Broadway, at Park Pl, Lower Manhattan; 30/60/90min tours $20/30/45; [S]R/W to City Hall, 2/3 to Park Pl, 4/5/6 to Brooklyn Bridge-City Hall) The world's tallest building upon completion in 1913, Cass Gilbert's 60-story, 792ft-tall Woolworth Building is a neo-Gothic marvel, elegantly clad in masonry and terracotta. Surpassed in height by the Chrysler Building in 1930, its landmarked lobby is a breathtaking spectacle of dazzling, Byzantine-like mosaics. The lobby is only accessible on prebooked guided tours, which also offer insight into the building's more curious original features, among them a dedicated subway entrance and a secret swimming pool.

At its dedication, the building was described as a 'cathedral of commerce'; though meant as an insult, FW Woolworth, head of the five-and-dime chain-store empire headquartered there, took the comment as a compliment and began throwing the term around himself.

★ Did You Know?

One World Trade Center has green credentials, including a gray-water system that collects and uses rainwater .and building materials made substantially of post-industrial recycled content.

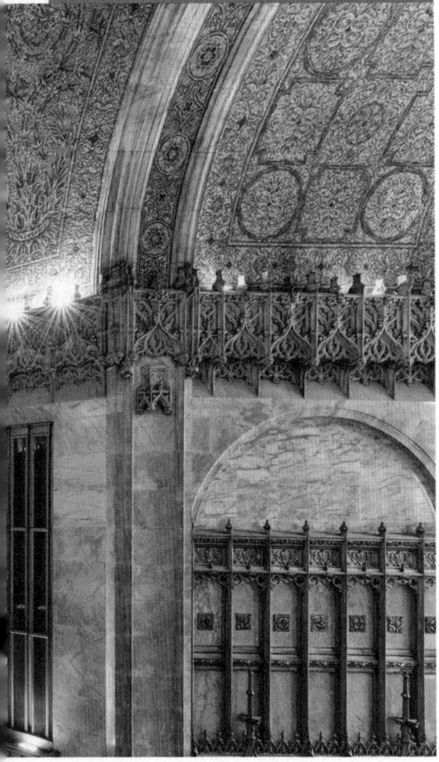

FELIX LIPOV/SHUTTERSTOCK ©

South Street Seaport District Area

(Map p244; www.seaportdistrict.nyc; Lower Manhattan; [S]2/3, 4/5, A/C, J/Z to Fulton St) The Seaport District is east of the Financial District along the river, but a whole world away. This neighborhood of cobblestone and heritage buildings proudly carries on the traditions of its nautical past, which stretches back to the early-17th-century Dutch colony of New Amsterdam. Bars and restaurants have a funky, carefree vibe, there's a farmers market on Sunday in the warmer months, and the development of Pier 17 is returning cuisine, commerce and culture to the area.

Find out more about the district's long and vibrant history at the **South Street Seaport Museum** (Map p244; ☎212-748-8600; www.southstreetseaportmuseum.org; 12 Fulton St, btwn Water & Front Sts, Lower Manhattan; exhibitions & ships $5, printing press & shop free; ⏲ships & visitor center 11am-5pm Wed-Sun, print shop 11am-7pm Tue-Sun; 👪; [S]2/3, 4/5, A/C, J/Z to Fulton St).

★ Famous Residents

The building's most famous tenant is Condé Nast Publications (publisher of *Vogue* and *The New Yorker*, among others), which made the move from 4 Times Square in 2014.

Lower East Side Tenement Museum

In a neighborhood once teeming with immigrants, this immersive museum opens a window to the past on guided tours through meticulously preserved tenements.

Great For...

ℹ️ Need to Know

Map p246; ☎877-975-3786; www.tenement. org; 103 Orchard St, btwn Broome & Delancey Sts, Lower East Side; tours adult/student & senior $25/20; ⏰visitor center 10am-6:30pm Fri-Wed, to 8:30pm Thu; 🚇; 🚇B/D to Grand St, F, J/M/Z to Delancey-Essex Sts

★ **Top Tip**

If there's a tour you're particularly interested in, buy your tickets early, because they do sell out.

Inside the Tenement

A wide range of tenement tours lead visitors into the building where hundreds of immigrants lived and worked over the years. 'Hard Times,' one of the most popular tours, visits apartments from two periods – the 1870s and the 1930s. There you'll see the squalid conditions tenants faced – in the early days there was a wretched communal outhouse and no electricity or running water – and what life was like for the families who lived there. Recorded testimony from a surviving member of the Baldizzi family, who lived here during the Depression, makes it easier to relate to what you see. Other tours focus on Irish immigrants and the harsh discrimination they faced, sweatshop workers and 'shop life' (with a tour through a recreated 1870s German beer hall).

103 Orchard St

The visitor center at 103 Orchard St (built 1888) has a museum shop and a small screening room that plays an original film about the history and influence of immigrants on the Lower East Side. Several evenings a month the museum hosts talks here, often relating to the present immigrant experience in America. The building itself was, naturally, a tenement, too – ask the staff about the interesting families of Eastern European and Italian descent that once dwelled here.

Meet Victoria

Travel back to 1916 and meet Victoria Confino, a 14-year-old girl from a Greek Sephardic family. Played by a costumed interpreter, Victoria 'lives' at 97 Orchard

St, interacting with visitors and answering questions about what her life was like in those days. It's especially recommended for kids, as visitors are free to handle household objects. This one-hour tour is held four times on Saturday and Sunday year-round, daily during the summer.

Neighborhood Tours

A great way to understand the immigrant experience is on a walking tour around the neighborhood. These tours, ranging from 90 minutes to two hours, explore a variety of topics. 'Foods of the Lower East Side' looks at the ways traditional foods have shaped American cuisine; 'Outside the Home' and 'Building on the Lower East Side' look at life beyond the apartment – where immigrants stored (and lost) their life savings, the churches and synagogues so integral to community life, and the meeting halls where poorly paid workers gathered to fight for better conditions.

☑ Don't Miss

The museum offers a prix-fixe dinner called Tasting at the Tenements every Thursday at 6:30pm.

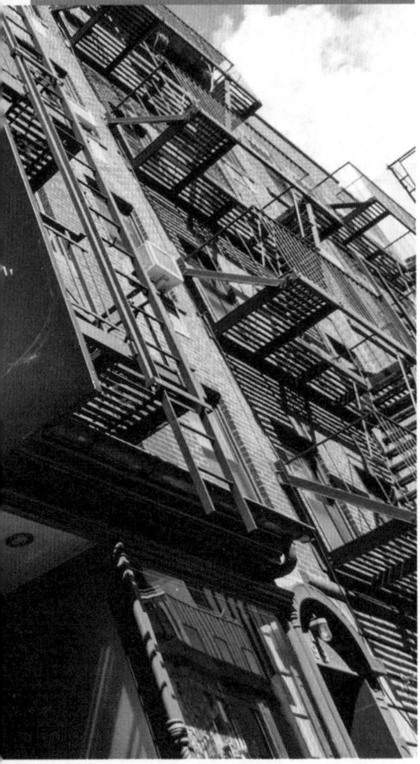

PATTI MCCONVILLE/ALAMY STOCK PHOTO ©

What's Nearby?

New Museum of Contemporary Art Museum

(Map p246; ☎212-219-1222; www.newmuseum.org; 235 Bowery, btwn Stanton & Rivington Sts, Lower East Side; adult/child $18/free, 7-9pm Thu by donation; ⏰11am-6pm Tue, Wed & Fri-Sun, to 9pm Thu; [S]F to 2nd Ave, R/W to Prince St, J/Z to Bowery, 6 to Spring St) The New Museum of Contemporary Art is a sight to behold: a seven-story stack of ethereal, off-kilter white boxes (designed by Tokyo-based architects Kazuyo Sejima and Ryue Nishizawa of SANAA and New York firm Gensler) rearing above its medium-rise neighborhood. It was a long-awaited breath of fresh air along what was a completely gritty Bowery strip when it arrived back in 2007 – since the museum's opening, many glossy new constructions have joined it, quickly transforming this once down-and-out avenue.

Founded in 1977 by Whitney curator Marcia Tucker and housed in five locations over the years, the museum's mission statement is simple: 'New art, new ideas.' True to its word, it gave gallery space to Keith Haring, Jeff Koons, Joan Jonas, Mary Kelly and Andres Serrano at the beginning of their careers, and remains Manhattan's only dedicated contemporary-art museum. It closes occasionally to install new exhibitions, so be sure to check the website before you visit.

🍴 Take a Break

Take a bite out of history at famed Jewish deli Russ & Daughters (p151), in business since 1914.

Prospect Park

Opened in 1867, Brooklyn's favorite green space is a 585-acre wonderland with a gorgeous meadow, a scenic lake, forested pathways and rambling hills cut by a tangled ravine. Its 19th-century architects, Frederick Olmsted and Calvert Vaux, considered this an improvement on their other New York project: Central Park.

Great For...

🐦 🥾 🎆

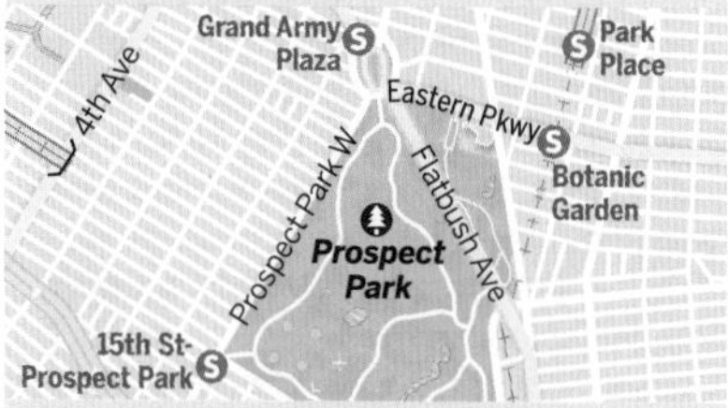

🛈 Need to Know

Map p256; ☎718-965-8951; www.prospectpark.org; Grand Army Plaza; 🕐5am-1am; [S]2/3 to Grand Army Plaza, F, G to 15th St-Prospect Park, B, Q to Prospect Park, Q to Parkside Ave)

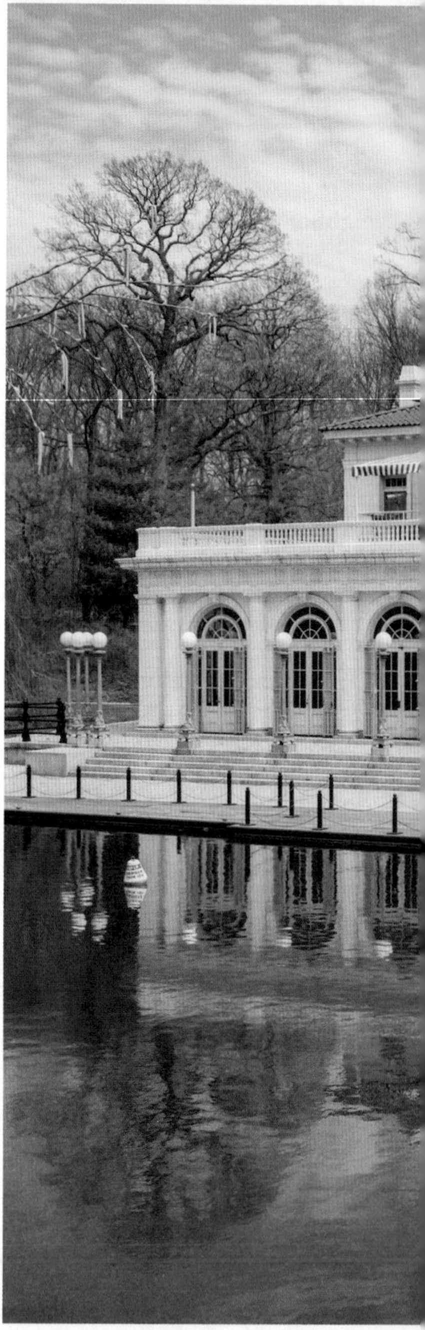

Audubon Center Boathouse (p101)

★ **Top Tip**

One of the prettiest places for a park stroll is alongside the Lullwater, near the Boathouse.

Grand Army Plaza

Inspired by the Place de la Concorde in Paris, this plaza with its dominant ceremonial arch sits at the intersection of Flatbush Ave and Prospect Park West, marking the beginning of Eastern Pkwy and the entrance to Prospect Park. The arch was built in the 1890s as a memorial to Union soldiers who fought in the Civil War; there's also a fountain with a bronze statue to Pomona, goddess of abundance. A **Greenmarket** is held here at the corner of Flatbush Ave on Saturdays from 8am to 4pm year-round.

Long Meadow

The 90-acre Long Meadow, bigger than Central Park's Great Lawn, lies to the south of the park's formal entrance at Grand Army Plaza. It's a super spot for strolling and lounging, filled with pickup ball games, frolicking dogs and families flying kites. On the south end is the **Picnic House**, with a snack stand and public bathrooms.

Children's Corner

Near Flatbush Ave, the Children's Corner contains a terrific 1912 **carousel**, originally from Coney Island, and the **Prospect Park Zoo** (Map p256; ☎718-399-7339; www.prospectparkzoo.com; 450 Flatbush Ave, Prospect Park; adult/child $10/7; 🕙10am-5pm Mon-Fri, to 5:30pm Sat & Sun Apr-Oct, to 4:30pm Nov-Mar; 👪; 🚌B41 to Flatbush Ave, [S]B, Q to Prospect Park, 2/3 to Grand Army Plaza), featuring sea lions, red pandas, wallabies and a small petting zoo. To the northeast of the carousel is the 18th-century **Lefferts Historic House** (Map p256; ☎718-789-2822; www.prospectpark.org/lefferts; near Flatbush Ave & Empire Blvd,

Grand Army Plaza

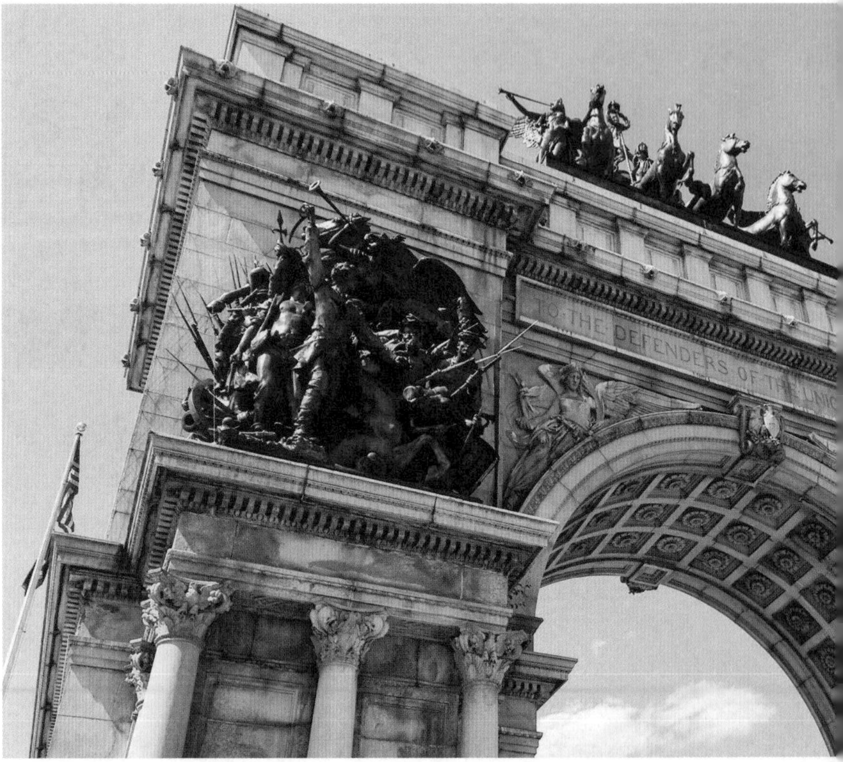

Prospect Park; adult/child $3/free; ⏰noon-5pm Thu-Sun Apr-Jun, Sep & Oct, to 6pm Jul & Aug, to 4pm Sat & Sun Nov & Dec; 👪; [S]B, Q to Prospect Park), where kids can imagine themselves on an 18th-century Brooklyn Dutch farm.

Audubon Center Boathouse

Sitting on a northern finger of Prospect Park Lake, the photogenic boathouse (aka Prospect Park Audubon Center) hosts a range of activities throughout the year: guided bird-watching sessions, free yoga classes, nature-themed art exhibitions, hands-on craft activities for kids and more. From here, there's a trailhead for 2.5 miles of woodsy **nature trails** (the route that takes you along Lullwater Creek is particularly scenic). Check the website for downloadable maps or ask at the boathouse for details.

☑ Don't Miss

Free outdoor concerts in the summer at the Prospect Park Bandshell.

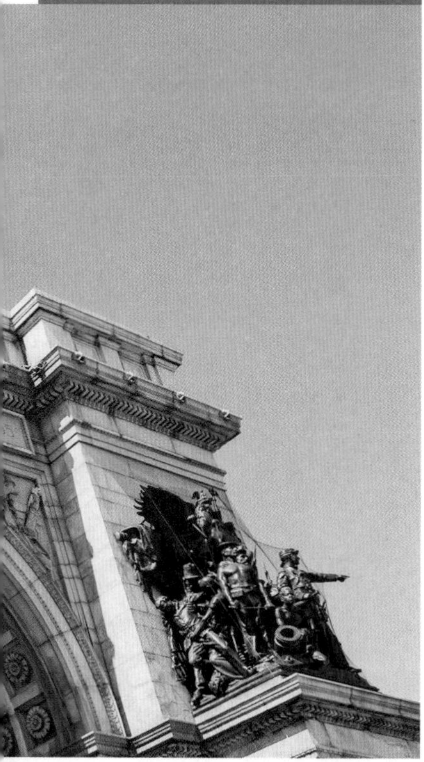

FELIX LIPOV/SHUTTERSTOCK ©

LeFrak Center at Lakeside

Prospect Park's newest attraction is this 26-acre complex (p198), which has summer and winter activities, as well as a cafe, new walking trails and a small concert space.

What's Nearby?

Brooklyn Museum Museum

(Map p256; ☎718-638-5000; www.brooklynmuseum.org; 200 Eastern Pkwy, Prospect Park; suggested admission adult/child $16/free; ⏰11am-6pm Wed & Fri-Sun, to 10pm Thu year-round, to 11pm 1st Sat of month Oct-Aug; 👪; [S]2/3 to Eastern Pkwy-Brooklyn Museum) This encyclopedic museum, imagined as the centerpiece of the 19th-century Brooklyn Institute, occupies a five-story, 560,000-sq-ft beaux-arts building stuffed with more than 1.5 million objects – ancient artifacts, 19th-century period rooms and a cornucopia of art. It's a great alternative to Manhattan's manic museums.

Brooklyn Botanic Garden Gardens

(Map p256; ☎718-623-7200; www.bbg.org; 150 Eastern Pkwy, Prospect Park; adult/student/child $15/8/free, 8am-noon Fri free, Tue-Fri Dec-Feb free; ⏰8am-6pm Tue-Fri, from 10am Sat & Sun Mar-Oct, shorter hours rest of year; 👪; [S]2/3 to Eastern Pkwy-Brooklyn Museum, B, Q to Prospect Park) Opened in 1911 and now one of Brooklyn's most picturesque sights, this 52-acre garden is home to thousands of plants and trees and a **Japanese garden** where river turtles swim alongside a Shinto shrine.

🍴 Take a Break

Every Sunday from April through October, an open-air street-food market called Smorgasburg (p140) sets up shop in the park just south of the boathouse.

Brooklyn Bridge Park

The pride and joy of Brooklyn, this 85-acre waterfront park sits in the lee of the city's most famous bridge. Skirting the East River for 1.3 miles from Dumbo to Cobble Hill, it has brilliantly revitalized a barren shore and offers grand views of Manhattan skyscrapers.

Great For...

ℹ Need to Know

Map p256; ☎718-222-9939; www.brooklyn bridgepark.org; East River Waterfront, btwn Atlantic Ave & John St, Brooklyn Heights/ Dumbo; ☉6am-1am, some sections to 11pm, playgrounds to dusk; 👭🐶; 🚌B63 to Pier 6/ Brooklyn Bridge Park, B25 to Old Fulton St/ Elizabeth Pl, 🚢East River or South Brooklyn routes to Dumbo/Pier 1, 🚇A/C to High St, 2/3 to Clark St, F to York St **FREE**

★ **Top Tip**

Be sure to check out what's on when you're in town: the website lists outdoor yoga and dance classes, theater and cinema, family activities and more.

Empire Fulton Ferry

This section of the park, between the Brooklyn and Manhattan Bridges in the northern section of Dumbo, contains a sweeping grassy lawn with stunning views of the East River. As well as the lovingly restored 1922 **Jane's Carousel** (Map p256; ☎718-222-2502; www.janescarousel.com; Old Dock St, Brooklyn Bridge Park, Dumbo; tickets $2; ⊙11am-7pm Wed-Mon mid-May–mid-Sep, to 6pm Thu-Sun mid-Sep–mid-May; 🚼), there are shrubby landscaped gardens and walking tracks to find the best vantage point for that essential Brooklyn Bridge photograph. The park is bordered on one side by the **Empire Stores & Tobacco Warehouse** (Map p256; www.empirestoresdumbo.com; 53-83 Water St, Dumbo; ⊙8am-7:30pm; 🚌B25 to Water/Main Sts), a cluster of Civil War–era warehouses that now house restaurants, shops and an acclaimed avant-garde theater.

Pier 1

Sunbathing, picnicking, playgrounds and photography are all invited by the greenery on this 9-acre pier just south of the Brooklyn Bridge. Every Thursday from July through August, free films are screened alfresco against the stunning backdrop of Manhattan; other free open-air events (dance parties, group yoga classes, Shakespeare performances, history tours) happen throughout the summer; check the park's website for the event calendar. At the north end of the pier, you can catch **NYC Ferry's** (Map p244; www.ferry.nyc; Pier 1, Brooklyn Bridge Park; adult 1 way $2.75) South Brooklyn and East River services to Manhattan.

Brooklyn Heights Promenade

Piers 2–5

Pier 2 is all about sweat, with a roller rink, an outdoor gym with free fitness equipment, courts for bocce, handball, basketball and shuffleboard, and a free summer kayaking program. Pier 3 has more lawns and granite steps for sitting and contemplating, while Pier 4 has a small beach where you can launch a paddle boat or dip your toes in the East River. Pier 5 has walkways, beach-volleyball courts, soccer fields and a 'picnic peninsula' with shade umbrellas and barbecues.

☑ Don't Miss

The views of Manhattan and the East River from Empire Fulton Ferry at sunset.

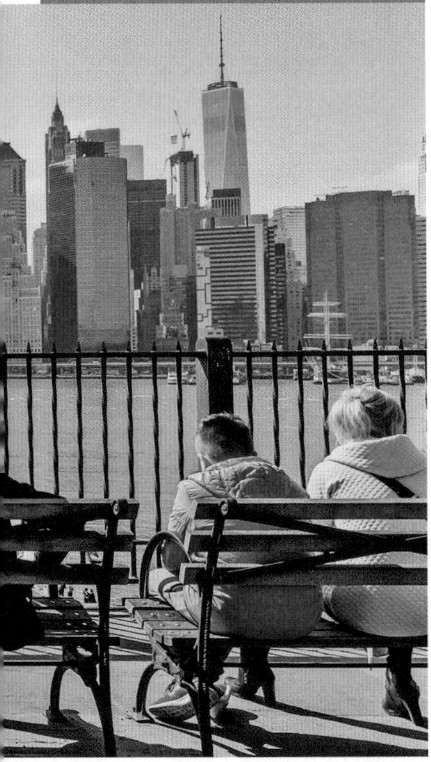

DROP OF LIGHT/SHUTTERSTOCK ©

Pier 6

At the southern end of the park, off Atlantic Ave, Pier 6 has five fantastic playgrounds and a small water-play area for tots. There's also a dog run, beach-volleyball courts and a few seasonal concessions (May to October), including wood-fired pizza, beer and Italian treats at **Fornino** (Map p256; ☎718-422-1107; www.fornino.com; Pier 6, Brooklyn Bridge Park; pizzas $15-16; 🕐10am-midnight Memorial Day–mid-Sep, weather permitting Apr, May & Oct; 🚌B63 to Brooklyn Bridge Park/Pier 6, [S]2/3, 4/5 to Borough Hall, R to Court St), which has a rooftop deck that's perfect for sundowners. A free ferry runs on weekends from Pier 6 to **Governors Island** (www.govisland.com; 🕐10am-6pm Mon-Fri, to 7pm Sat & Sun May-Oct, later hours Fri Jun-Aug; 👪; [S]4/5 to Bowling Green, 1 to South Ferry) [FREE].

What's Nearby?

Brooklyn Heights Promenade — Viewpoint

(Map p256; www.nycgovparks.org; btwn Orange & Remsen Sts, Brooklyn Heights; 🕐24hr; [S]N/R/W to Court St, 2/3 to Clark St, A/C to High St) Six of the east–west streets of well-to-do Brooklyn Heights (such as Montague and Clark Sts) lead to the area's number-one attraction: a narrow, paved walking strip with breathtaking views of Lower Manhattan and New York Harbor that is blissfully removed from the busy Brooklyn–Queens Expwy (BQE) over which it sits. This little slice of urban beauty is a great spot for a sunset walk.

An innovatively designed footbridge called the **Squibb Park Bridge**, just past the northern end of the promenade, links it with the shoreside Pier 1 in Brooklyn Bridge Park.

🍴 Take a Break

Great coffee and cookies from Dumbo's **One Girl Cookies** (Map p256; ☎212-675-4996; www.onegirlcookies.com; 33 Main St, at Water St, Dumbo; cookies $1.50-2, cupcakes $3.25, salads & sliders $5-8; 🕐8am-7pm Mon-Fri, from 9am Sat & Sun) make for perfect strolling fodder.

Walking Tour: The West Village

Of all the neighborhoods in New York City, the West Village is easily the most walkable, its cobbled corners straying from the signature gridiron that carves up the rest of Manhattan. An afternoon stroll is not to be missed; hidden landmarks and quaint cafes abound.

Start Commerce St
Distance 1.2 miles
Duration one hour

5 At Christopher Park, visit the **Stonewall National Monument** and Stonewall Inn – where 1969 riots sparked the Gay Rights Movement.

4 For another TV landmark, head to **66 Perry St**, Carrie Bradshaw's apartment in *Sex and the City*.

3 Stop at **Buvette** (p170), a dreamy Francophile wine bar perfect for people-watching with coffee or *vin*.

2 The apartment block at **90 Bedford** was the fictitious home of the cast of *Friends*.

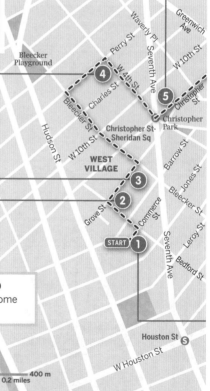

400 m
0.2 miles

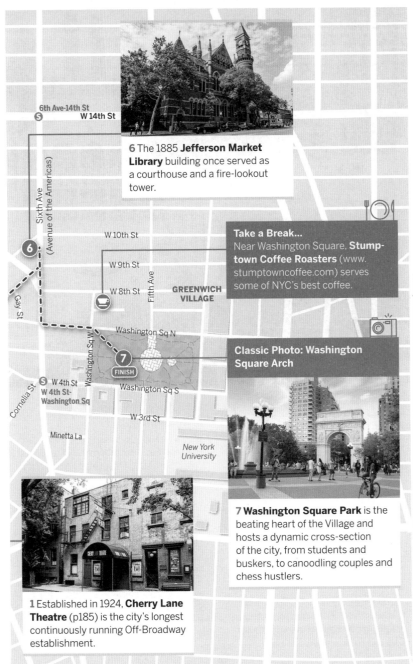

6 The 1885 **Jefferson Market Library** building once served as a courthouse and a fire-lookout tower.

6th Ave-14th St
W 14th St

W 10th St

W 9th St

W 8th St

Sixth Ave (Avenue of the Americas)

Fifth Ave

GREENWICH VILLAGE

Gay St

Take a Break...
Near Washington Square, **Stumptown Coffee Roasters** (www.stumptowncoffee.com) serves some of NYC's best coffee.

Washington Sq N

Washington Sq W

7
(FINISH)

W 4th St
W 4th St-Washington Sq

Washington Sq S

W 3rd St

Cornelia St

Minetta La

New York University

Classic Photo: Washington Square Arch

7 Washington Square Park is the beating heart of the Village and hosts a dynamic cross-section of the city, from students and buskers, to canoodling couples and chess hustlers.

1 Established in 1924, **Cherry Lane Theatre** (p185) is the city's longest continuously running Off-Broadway establishment.

1 JJFARQ/SHUTTERSTOCK © 5 GLYNNIS JONES/SHUTTERSTOCK © 6 MASSIMO SALESI/SHUTTERSTOCK © 7 LITTLENYSTOCK/SHUTTERSTOCK ©

Metropolitan Opera (p110)

EILEEN_10/SHUTTERSTOCK ©

Lincoln Center

This stark arrangement of gleaming modernist temples contains some of Manhattan's most important performance spaces, home to the finest opera, ballet and symphony orchestra in New York City.

Great For...

☑ Don't Miss

The Met Opera gift shop is full of operatic knickknacks (like binoculars), and an extensive collection of classical music CDs and DVDs – many from past Met performances.

A History of Building & Rebuilding

Built in the 1960s, this imposing arts campus replaced a neighborhood of tenements called San Juan Hill (gleefully bulldozed by urban planner Robert Moses), a predominantly African American neighborhood where the exterior shots for the movie *West Side Story* were filmed. In addition to being a controversial urban-planning move, Lincoln Center wasn't exactly well-received at an architectural level – it was relentlessly criticized for its conservative design, fortresslike aspect and poor acoustics. For the center's 50th anniversary (2009–10), Diller Scofidio + Renfro and other architects gave the complex a much-needed and critically acclaimed freshening up.

ℹ **Need to Know**

Map p254; 📞212-875-5456, tours 212-875-5350; www.lincolncenter.org; Columbus Ave, btwn W 62nd & 66th Sts; tours adult/student $25/20; ⏱tours 11:30am & 1:30pm Mon-Sat, 3pm Sun; 🚇 🅂1, 2, 3 to 66th St-Lincoln Center, A/C or B/D to 59th St-Columbus Circle FREE

✕ **Take a Break**

Across the road from Lincoln Center, the Empire Hotel's rooftop bar (p174) is one of NYC's largest and most glamorous.

★ **Top Tip**

The New York Philharmonic, New York City Ballet and Metropolitan Opera House all offer some form of cheap tickets for last-minute buyers, normally available only online. Often they're called 'rush tickets.'

Highlights

A survey of the three classic buildings surrounding the central Revson Fountain is a must. These include the **Metropolitan Opera** – its lobby walls are dressed with brightly saturated murals by painter Marc Chagall – **David Geffen Hall** and the **David H Koch Theater**, the latter designed by Philip Johnson. They're all located on the main plaza at Columbus Ave, between 62nd and 65th Sts. The **Revson Fountain** is spectacular in the evenings when it puts on Las Vegas–like light shows (from about 6pm).

Of the refurbished structures, there are a number that are worth examining, including **Alice Tully Hall**, now displaying a very contemporary translucent, angled facade, and the **David Rubenstein Atrium** (Map p254; 📞212-721-6500; http://atrium.lincolncenter.org; 61 W 62nd St, at Broadway; ⏱atrium 8am-10pm

Mon-Fri, 9am-10pm Sat & Sun, box office noon-7pm Mon-Sat, to 5pm Sun; 🅂1 to 66th St-Lincoln Center), a public space behind the Empire Hotel offering a lounge area (with free wi-fi), a cafe, and an information desk. Free events are held here on Thursday evenings, and this is also where Lincoln Center tours depart.

Performances & Screenings

On any given night, there are at least 10 performances happening throughout Lincoln Center – and even more in summer, when **Lincoln Center Out of Doors** (a series of dance and music concerts) and **Midsummer Night Swing** (ballroom dancing under the stars) lure those who love their culture alfresco. For details on seasons, tickets and programming – which runs the gamut from opera to dance, theater and ballet – check the Lincoln Center website.

Metropolitan Opera House

New York's premier **opera company** (Map p254; 🎫tickets 212-362-6000, tours 212-769-7028; www.metopera.org; Lincoln Center, Columbus Ave at W 64th St; 🚇1 to 66th St-Lincoln Center) is the place to see classics such as *La Boheme, Madame Butterfly* and *Macbeth*. It also hosts premieres and revivals of more contemporary works, such as John Adams' *The Death of Klinghoffer*. The season runs from September to April.

Tickets start at $32 and can get close to $500. Note that the box seats can be a bargain, but unless you're in boxes right over the stage, the views are dreadful: seeing the stage requires sitting with your head cocked over a handrail – a literal pain in the neck.

New York City Ballet

This prestigious **ballet company** (Map p254; 🎫212-496-0600; www.nycballet.com; Lincoln Center, Columbus Ave at W 63rd St; tickets $35 to $199; ⏲box office 10am-8:30pm Mon-Sat, 11:30am-7:30pm Sun; ♿; 🚇1 to 66th St-Lincoln Center) was first directed by renowned Russian-born choreographer George Balanchine in the 1940s. Today, it's the largest ballet organization in the US, performing 23 weeks a year at Lincoln Center's David H Koch Theater. Rush tickets for those under age 30 are $30. During the holidays the troupe is best known for its annual production of *The Nutcracker* (tickets go on sale in September: book early).

American Museum of Natural History

New York Philharmonic

The oldest professional **orchestra** (Map p254; ☎212-875-5656; www.nyphil.org; Lincoln Center, Columbus Ave at W 65th St; tickets $29-125; 👪; [S]1 to 66 St-Lincoln Center) in the US (dating to 1842) holds its season every year at David Geffen Hall; music director Jaap van Zweden took over from Alan Gilbert in 2017. The orchestra plays a mix of classics (Tchaikovsky, Mahler, Haydn) and contemporary works, as well as concerts geared toward children. If you're on a budget, check out the open rehearsals held several times a month (starting at 9:45am) on the day of the concert for only $22.

★ Behind the Scenes

Tours of Lincoln Center ($25) usually run twice a day Monday to Saturday and once on Sunday, departing from the David Rubenstein Atrium. Behind-the-scenes tours of the Metropolitan Opera House ($30) are offered weekdays at 3pm and Sundays at 10:30am and 1:30pm during the performance season.

DIEGO GRANDI/SHUTTERSTOCK ©

What's Nearby?

American Museum of Natural History

Museum

(Map p254; ☎212-769-5100; www.amnh.org; Central Park West, at W 79th St; suggested admission adult/child $23/13; 🕐10am-5:45pm; 👪; [S]C to 81st St-Museum of Natural History; 1 to 79th St) Founded in 1869, this classic museum contains a veritable wonderland of more than 30 million artifacts – including lots of menacing dinosaur skeletons – as well as the **Rose Center for Earth & Space**, which has a cutting-edge planetarium. From October through May, the museum is home to the **Butterfly Conservatory**, a glasshouse featuring 500-plus butterflies from all over the world that will flutter about and land on your outstretched arm.

The museum is perhaps best known for its light and airy **Fossil Halls** containing nearly 600 specimens, including crowd pleasers such as a mammoth, stegosaurus, triceratops and fearsome *Tyrannosaurus rex*.

There are also plentiful animal exhibits, galleries devoted to gems and minerals, and an IMAX theater. At the 77th St Lobby Gallery, there's a 63ft canoe carved by Native Americans from the Pacific Northwest in the 1870s. For the astronomical set, the Rose Center planetarium is the star of the show.

Note that while you can pay what you wish for general admission (in person only), in order to see space shows, IMAX films or ticketed exhibits you'll need to pay the posted prices for admission plus one show (adult/child $28/16.50) or admission plus all shows ($33/20).

★ Top Tip

Daily 75-minute tours are a great way to get acquainted with the complex. Get more info and buy tickets online or by phone.

Food court

Chelsea Market

In a shining example of redevelopment and preservation, the Chelsea Market has transformed a former factory into a shopping concourse that caters to foodies.

The long brick edifice occupied by Chelsea Market was built in the 1890s to house a massive bakery complex that became the headquarters of the National Biscuit Company (better known as Nabisco, makers of Saltines, Fig Newtons and Oreos). The market, which opened in the 1990s, is now a base camp for gourmet outlets and fashionistas on the lookout for something unique. Cellists and bluegrass players fill the main walkway with music, and the High Line passes right by the rear of the building.

Foodie Hub

More than two dozen food vendors ply their temptations. Try **Mokbar** for ramen with Korean accents, and **Takumi** for fusion tacos mixing Japanese and Mexican ingredients. Stop by **Very Fresh Noodles** and you'll

---

Great For...

🍴 🛍️ 💬

☑ **Don't Miss**

Fusion tacos from Takumi and a browse through the stalls at Artists and Fleas.

POLUDZIBER/SHUTTERSTOCK ©

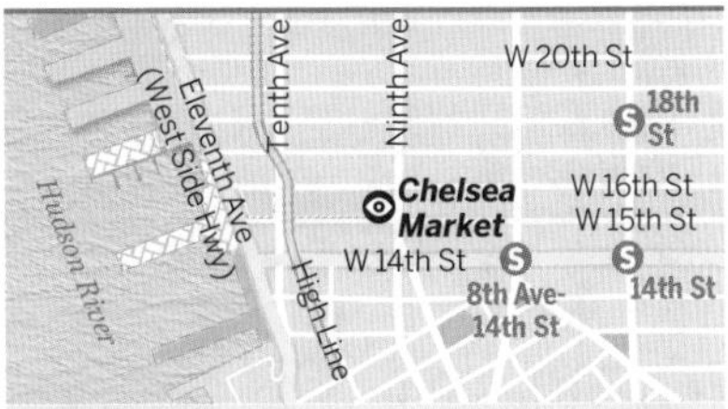

[i] Need to Know

Map p250; ☎212-652-2110; www.chelseamarket.com; 75 Ninth Ave, btwn W 15th & W 16th Sts, Chelsea; ⏲7am-2am Mon-Sat, 8am-10pm Sun; [S]A/C/E, L to 8th Ave-14th St

🍴 Take a Break

Hop up to the High Line (p52) from the entrance on 16th St and Tenth Ave to grab some fresh air.

★ Top Tip

Get your food to go – seating is limited at most of the eateries.

see hand-pulled northern Chinese noodles being stretched behind the counter. There's also **Bar Suzette** for crepes and **Num Pang** for Cambodian sandwiches. Perfect lattes can be found at **Ninth St Espresso** – grab one to go with a piping-hot mini-donut from **Doughnuttery** or brownie from **Fat Witch Bakery**. Also worth visiting is long-time tenant **The Lobster Place**, for overstuffed lobster rolls and killer sushi.

Retail Bonanza

Those looking for a bargain on high-end fashions should head to the event space near the Ninth Ave entrance. There are frequent **pop-up shops** and sample sales featuring racks of quality, discounted men and women's clothing. At the other end of the market near the Tenth Ave entrance is **Artists and Fleas** (10am to 9pm Monday to Saturday and to 8pm Sunday), a permanent market for local designers and craftspeople to sell their wares. It's the place to stop for a quirky new wallet, trendy pair of sunglasses or a piece of statement jewelry. Also check out Imports from Marrakesh, which specializes in Moroccan art and design. Browse the latest literary hits at Posman Books; or pick up a bottle at the expert-staffed Chelsea Wine Vault.

New Horizons

The market only takes up the lower part of a larger, million-sq-ft space, occupying a full city block, which housed several TV channels but in 2018 was bought by Google for $2.4 billion, with a view to becoming its new NYC headquarters.

KEEP SMILING PHOTOGRAPHY/SHUTTERSTOCK ©

Coney Island

One of New York's most popular beachside amusement areas, Coney Island draws summertime crowds for hot dogs, roller coasters, minor-league baseball games and strolls down the boardwalk.

Great For...

☑ **Don't Miss**

Ride the Cyclone, then head to the boardwalk for a cold beer.

Seaside Fun By Day

Coney Island – a name synonymous in American culture with antique seaside fun and frolicking – achieved worldwide fame as a working-class amusement park and beach-resort area at the turn of the 20th century. After decades of decline, its kitschy charms have experienced a 21st-century revival. Though it's no longer the booming, peninsula-wide attraction it once was, it still draws crowds of tourists and locals alike for legendary roller-coaster rides, hot dogs and beer on the beachside boardwalk.

Luna Park (☎718-373-5862; www.lunaparknyc.com; 1000 Surf Ave, at W 10th St, Coney Island; ⏰Apr-Oct; [S]D/F, N/Q to Coney Island-Stillwell Ave) is one of Coney Island's most popular amusement parks and contains one of its most legendary rides:

Deno's Wonder Wheel

PJ0J/SHUTTERSTOCK ©

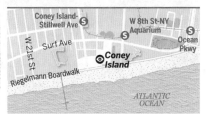

❶ Need to Know

Surf Ave & Boardwalk, btwn W 15th & W 8th Sts; ♿; Ⓢ D/F, N/Q to Coney Island-Stillwell Ave

✕ Take a Break

Totonno's (📞718-372-8606; www.totonnos coneyisland.com; 1524 Neptune Ave, at W 16th St, Coney Island; pizzas $19-22, extra toppings $2.50; ⏱noon-8pm Thu-Sun; �; Ⓢ D/F, N/Q to Coney Island-Stillwell Ave) is one of Brooklyn's oldest and most authentic pizza joints.

★ Top Tip

Go weekdays during the daytime to avoid crowds and long lines.

the Cyclone ($10), a wooden roller coaster that reaches speeds of 60mph and makes near-vertical drops. The pink-and-mint-green **Deno's Wonder Wheel** (📞718-372-2592; www.denoswonderwheel.com; 1025 Riegelmann Boardwalk, at W 12th St, Coney Island; rides $8; ⏱from noon Jul & Aug, from noon Sat & Sun Apr-Jun, Sep & Oct; ♿; Ⓢ D/F, N/Q to Coney Island-Stillwell Ave), which has been delighting New Yorkers since 1920, is the best place to survey Coney Island from up high.

The hot dog was invented in Coney Island in 1867, and there's no better place to eat one than **Nathan's Famous** (📞718-333-2202; www.nathansfamous.com; 1310 Surf Ave, at Stillwell Ave, Coney Island; hot dogs from $4; ⏱10am-11pm Mon-Thu, to midnight Fri, 9am-midnight Sat, to 11pm Sun; 🛜; Ⓢ D/F to Coney Island-Stillwell Ave), established 1916. When thirst strikes, head to **Ruby's** (📞718-

975-7829; www.rubysbar.com; 1213 Riegelmann Boardwalk, btwn Stillwell Ave & W 12th St, Coney Island; ⏱11am-10pm Sun-Thu, to 1am Fri & Sat Apr-Sep, weekends only Oct; Ⓢ D/F, N/Q to Coney Island-Stillwell Ave), a legendary dive bar right on the boardwalk.

...and By Night

Cap off your day with an evening game of minor-league baseball to cheer on the **Brooklyn Cyclones** (📞718-372-5596; www.brooklyncyclones.com; 1904 Surf Ave, at W 17th St, Coney Island; tickets $10-19, all tickets Wed $10; Ⓢ D/F, N/Q to Coney Island-Stillwell Ave) (especially if they're playing crosstown rivals the Staten Island Yankees), or else just relax with some beer on the boardwalk and watch the sun go down.

If you're there on a Friday night in July or August, stick around for the fireworks show at 9:30pm.

DINING OUT

Pizza, high-end cuisine and cheap eats

Dining Out

New York City's dining scene is infinite, all-consuming and a proud testament to its kaleidoscope of citizens. Even if you're not an obsessive foodie hitting ethnic enclaves or the newest cult-chef openings, an outstanding meal is always only a block away. Unlike California or the South, New York doesn't have one defining cuisine. Food in this multicultural town is global by definition and, just like the city itself, it's a scene that's constantly evolving. Quintessential NYC can mean anything from soul food in Harlem or American Italian in Little Italy, to lox bagels in the Upper East Side's Jewish delis, pancakes at an old-school diner or pizza in Brooklyn.

In This Section

Price Ranges & Tipping

The following price ranges refer to a main dish, exclusive of tax and tip:

$ under $15

$$ $15–25

$$$ more than $25

New Yorkers tip between 18% and 20% of the final price of the meal. For takeout, it's polite to drop a few dollars in the tip jar.

Harlem & Upper Manhattan
Comfort cuisine meets global flavors (p138)

Upper West Side & Central Park
Old-school delis and a few
neighborhood gems (p138)

Upper East Side
Ladies who lunch meet
cafe culture (p137)

Midtown
Fine dining, cocktail-literate
bistros and fast food (p135)

**West Village, Chelsea &
Meatpacking District**
See-and-be-seen brunch spots, wine
bars and New American darlings (p130)

Union Square, Flatiron District & Gramercy
Everything from Michelin-starred
meccas to parkside burgers (p133)

SoHo & Chinatown
Dirt-cheap noodles, hip cafes and
fashionable foodie hangouts (p124)

East Village & Lower East Side
Unpretentious spectrum of eats,
from Asia to the Middle East (p128)

**Financial District &
Lower Manhattan**
Celebrity-chef hot spots and a gourmet
French marketplace (p122)

Brooklyn
Neighborhood pizzerias, Michelin-star
dining and retro–New American fare (p139)

Useful Blogs & Websites

Yelp (www.yelp.com) Comprehensive
user-generated content and reviews.

Open Table (www.opentable.com)
Click-and-book reservation service for
many restaurants.

Tasting Table (www.tastingtable.com)
Sign up for handy news blasts about the
latest and greatest.

Eater (https://ny.eater.com) Food news
and restaurant roundups.

Grub Street (www.grubstreet.com)
In-the-know articles on NYC dining.

Classic NYC Dishes

Bagel A great start to the day, best
served with cream cheese and lox
(smoked salmon).

Pizza The perfect anytime snack,
served up at ubiquitous pizza parlors.

Hot Dog Served both high- and lowbrow style, best with brown mustard
and caramelized onions.

New York–Style Cheesecake Iconic
dessert with cream cheese and a cookie
crust.

The Best...

Experience New York City's finest eating establishments.

By Budget: $

Chelsea Market (p130) Foods from around the world.

Nom Wah Tea Parlor (p124) Authentic 1920s dim sum joint.

Burger Joint (p135) Scruffy bar with juicy patties in a hidden Midtown locale.

Berg'n (p140) Food market with craft brews.

Mamoun's (p128) Famous, spicy shawarma sandwiches at rock-bottom prices.

By Budget: $$$

Eleven Madison Park (p133) Arresting, cutting-edge cuisine laced with whimsy.

Blue Hill (p132) A West Village classic using ingredients sourced straight from the upstate farm.

Jeffrey's Grocery (pictured above; p130) Much-loved West Village neighborhood spot.

Agern (p136) Surprising Michelin-starred New Nordic food inside Grand Central Terminal.

By Budget: $$

Upstate (p129) A seafood feast awaits in the East Village.

Ivan Ramen (p128) Sublime steaming bowls from a Long Islander by way of Tokyo.

Roberta's (pictured above; p141) Hip Williamsburg pizza place with garden bar.

Butcher's Daughter (p126) Beloved vegan cafe and bar with a West Coast vibe and plenty of meat-eating fans.

COOKSHOP

Brunch

Cookshop (pictured above; p130) Great indoor-outdoor dining spot in west Chelsea.

Big Daddy's (p133) Satisfying American diner food near Union Sq with breakfast burritos and, of course, fluffy pancakes.

Dutch (p127) Wholesome, New Yorker–sized plates with global influences and standout lox and scrambled-egg bagels.

Italian

Il Buco Alimentari & Vineria (p127) Taste the old country in this Nolita standout.

Rosemary's (pictured above; p133) A West Village spot with memorable cooking.

Barbuto (p132) Serves creative modern Italian fare in a buzzing space in the Meatpacking District.

Vegetarian & Vegan

Nix (p132) Michelin-starred veg dishes.

Butcher's Daughter (pictured above; p126) Inventive vegetarian menu in Nolita.

Hangawi (p136) Meat-free Korean fare.

Modern Love (p141) Fab vegan plates.

Two Boots Pizza (p134) Get your pizza fix with vegan and gluten-free options.

Old-School NYC

Barney Greengrass (p138) Perfect plates of smoked salmon and sturgeon for over 100 years in the Upper West Side.

Russ & Daughters (p151) A celebrated Jewish deli in the Lower East Side.

Di Fara Pizza (p134) First-rate pies served in a well-loved joint that's been around since the 1960s.

JG Melon (p137) Classic New Yorkers' pub with burgers at the counter.

★ Lonely Planet's Top Choices

Modern (p136) Mouthwatering Michelin-starred morsels beside MoMA's sculpture garden.

Smorgasburg (p140; pictured above) Gourmet food market with more than 100 vendors and no fixed abode.

Uncle Boons (p125) Michelin-starred Thai with good-time vibes and Asian-inspired cocktails.

RedFarm (p132) Savvy Sino-fusion dishes boast bold flavors, but it doesn't take itself too seriously.

Foragers Table (p130) A triumph of farm-to-table cooking with flavorful sustainable recipes in Chelsea.

🍴 Financial District & Lower Manhattan

Arcade Bakery Bakery $

(Map p246; ☎212-227-7895; www.arcadebakery.com; 220 Church St, btwn Worth & Thomas Sts, Tribeca; pastries from $3, sandwiches $9, pizzas $10; ⏰8am-3pm Mon-Fri; [S]1 to Franklin St) It's easy to miss this little treasure in the vaulted lobby of a 1920s office building, with a counter trading in beautiful, just-baked goods. Edibles include artful sandwiches and (between noon and 3pm, or whenever the dough runs out) a small selection of puff-crust pizzas with combos like mushroom, caramelized onion and goat's cheese. Arcade also makes sensational almond croissants.

Bluestone Lane Coffee

(Map p244; ☎718-374-6858; www.bluestonelaneny.com; 30 Broad St, Financial District; ⏰7am-5:30pm Mon-Fri, 8am-5pm Sat & Sun; [S]J/Z to Broad St, 2/3, 4/5 to Wall St) The second installment in Bluestone Lane's booming US empire of Aussie-style coffee shops, this tiny outpost in the corner of an art-deco office block is littered with Melbourne memorabilia. Alongside Wall St suits you'll find homesick antipodeans craving a decent, velvety flat white and a small selection of edibles, including the Australian cafe standard smashed avocado on toast ($9).

Kaffe 1668 South Coffee

(Map p244; ☎212-693-3750; www.kaffe1668.com; 275 Greenwich St, btwn Warren & Murray Sts, Lower Manhattan; ⏰6:30am-9pm Mon-Thu, to 8:30pm Fri, 7am-8pm Sat & Sun; 📶; [S]A/C, 1/2/3 to Chambers St) A coffee-geek mecca, Kaffe 1668 has dual Synesso machines pumping out single-origin magic from across Africa and the Americas. There's a large communal table speckled with suits and laptop-tapping creatives, and more seating downstairs. You can snack on eggs, breakfast bowls, avocado toast, soups and more (mains $8 to $10). Other locations at 530 5th Ave and 401 Greenwich St.

Coffee bar, Le District

Brookfield Place Food Hall $$

(Map p244; ☎212-978-1673; www.brookfieldplaceny.com; 230 Vesey St, at West St, Lower Manhattan; 📶; [S]E to World Trade Center, 2/3 to Park Pl, R/W to Cortlandt St, 4/5 to Fulton St, A/C to Chambers St) This polished, high-end office and retail complex offers two fabulous food halls.

Francophile foodies should hit **Le District** (Map p244; ☎212-981-8588; www.ledistrict.com; Brookfield Place, 225 Liberty St, at West St, Lower Manhattan; market mains $12-30, Beaubourg dinner mains $31-36; 🕐Beaubourg 8am-10pm Mon, to 11pm Tue-Fri, 10am-11pm Sat, to 10pm Sun, other hours vary; 📶), a charming and mouthwatering marketplace with several stand-alone restaurants and counters selling everything from stinky cheese to steak-*frites*.

One floor above is **Hudson Eats** (Map p244; ☎212-978-1698; https://bfplny.com/directory/food; Brookfield Place, 225 Liberty St, at West St, Lower Manhattan; dishes from $7; 🕐8am-9pm Mon-Sat, to 7pm Sun; 📶), a fashionable enclave of upmarket fast bites, from sushi and tacos to salads and burgers.

Locanda Verde Italian $$$

(Map p246; ☎212-925-3797; www.locandaverdenyc.com; 377 Greenwich St, at N Moore St, Tribeca; mains lunch $25-32, dinner $38-54; 🕐7am-11pm Mon-Thu, to 11:30pm Fri, 8am-11:30pm Sat, to 11pm Sun; [S]1 to Franklin St, A/C/E to Canal St) Curbside at the Greenwich Hotel you'll find this Italian fine diner by Andrew Carmellini, where velvet curtains part onto a scene of loosened button-downs, black dresses and slick bar staff. It's a place to see and be seen, but the food – perhaps Sicilian cod with chickpeas, *orecchiette* with duck sausage and kale, or truffle ravioli – is the main event.

Tiny's & the Bar Upstairs American $$$

(Map p246; ☎212-374-1135; www.tinysnyc.com; 135 W Broadway, btwn Thomas & Duane Sts, Tribeca; mains $29-32; 🕐8am-11pm Mon-Thu, to midnight Fri, 9am-midnight Sat, 9am-10pm

🍴 Reach for the Stars

There are only four cities in the world with more Michelin-starred restaurants than New York. While most are likely to make your wallet weep, the positive in NYC is that many only open their reservation books one to two months in advance, which means organized visitors can get a table at one of NYC's 75+ Michelin-starred restaurants.

Options include Midtown's triple-Michelin-starred **Le Bernardin** (www.le-bernardin.com) for exquisite seafood from French celebrity chef Éric Ripert, and art-worthy morsels at two-starred Modern (p136) overlooking MoMA's sculpture garden. Three-starred Eleven Madison Park (p133), named the world's best restaurant in 2017, is now more accessible than ever thanks to the addition of dining tables in the bar, offering an abbreviated tasting menu (five rather than 10 courses) for $175.

There are several cheaper one-starred options, too. In Tribeca there's French–Italian **Bâtard** (www.batardtribeca.com), which has BYOB Mondays with no corkage fees. New Nordic Agern (p136) has bargain lunch deals, and **Finch** (www.thefinchnyc.com) serves modern American in a Brooklyn brownstone. For Asian cuisine try atmospheric Uncle Boons (p125) in SoHo, or JeJu Noodle Bar (p130) in the West Village. Vegetarians should make a beeline for Nix (p132).

Desserts at Le Bernardin

★ Best Bakeries

Four & Twenty Blackbirds (p140)

Supermoon Bakehouse (p128)

Little Cupcake Bakeshop

Arcade Bakery (p122)

From left: Little Cupcake Bakeshop; Nom Wah Tea Parlor; Canal St Market

Sun; S 1 to Franklin St, A, C to Chambers St) The rustic interior of this 1810 Tribeca town house – replete with antique wallpaper, salvaged wood paneling, original tin ceilings, pressed copper and marble bar tops, and handmade tiles – alone makes it worth a visit, but you won't regret staying for a meal or a cocktail. Food is modern American with French accents: perhaps seared duck with turnip and shallots or hand-dived scallops.

Marc Forgione   American $$$

(Map p246; ✆212-941-9401; www.marcforgione. com; 134 Reade St, btwn Hudson & Greenwich Sts, Tribeca; mains $41-43; ◷5-10pm Sun-Thu, to 11pm Fri & Sat; S 1/2/3 to Chambers St) Marc Forgione's gorgeous modern American food finds an apt setting in this convivial, wide-open, brick-lined dining room. Utmost attention is given to seasonality, freshness and the proper treatment of each ingredient in dishes such as Aegean branzino with wild mushrooms, chestnuts, wild rice and Douglas fir needles, or Icelandic cod with butternut-squash clam chowder with house-made bacon.

✖ SoHo & Chinatown

Nom Wah Tea Parlor   Chinese $

(Map p246; ✆212-962-6047; www.nomwah. com; 13 Doyers St, Chinatown; dim sum from $3.75; ◷10:30am-10pm Sun-Wed, to 11pm Fri & Sat; S J/Z to Chambers St; 4/5/6 to Brooklyn Bridge-City Hall) Hidden down a narrow lane, 1920s Nom Wah Tea Parlor is NYC's original dim-sum place. Grab a table or seat at one of the red banquettes or counter stools and simply tick off what you want on the paper menu provided. Roast pork buns, Shanghainese soup dumplings, shrimp siu mai... it's all finger-licking good.

Little Cupcake Bakeshop   Desserts $

(Map p246; ✆212-941-9100; www.littlecupcake bakeshop.com; 30 Prince St, at Mott St, Nolita; cakes from $4; ◷7:30am-11pm Mon-Fri, to midnight Fri, 8am-midnight Sat, 8am-11pm Sun; S 6 to Spring St, R/W to Prince St) ✐ Famed for its version of the Brooklyn blackout cake, regularly called out as the best chocolate cake in the USA, this prim little bakeshop has plenty of other tricks up its sleeve. The four Italian brothers from Brooklyn

RICHARD LEVINE/ALAMY STOCK PHOTO ©

who own the shop also ruin waistlines with homemade ice-cream flavors such as peanut butter and jelly, key lime pies and moist mini cupcakes.

Canal St Market Food Hall $

(Map p246; www.canalstreet.market; 265 Canal St, btwn Broadway & Lafayette St; 🕐food 10am-8pm, retail 11am-7pm Mon-Sat, noon-6pm Sun; [S]6, N/Q/R/W to Canal St) In the borderlands where Chinatown morphs into SoHo, this new food and retail market is unavoidably turning heads. The warehouse-like dining area is a world tour of food trends – Japanese shaved ice, ceviche, seasonal farm food, etc. The shopping floor is the place to hunt for unusual indie gems such as vintage skateboards, K-pop clothing and locally made jewelry.

Xi'an Famous Foods Chinese $

(Map p246; www.xianfoods.com; 45 Bayard St, btwn Elizabeth St & Bowery, Chinatown; dishes $4.70-12; 🕐11:30am-9pm Sun-Thu, to 9:30pm Fri & Sat; [S]N/Q/R/W, J/Z, 6 to Canal St, B/D to Grand St) Food bloggers hyperventilate at the mere mention of this small chain's hand-pulled noodles. The burgers are also menu stars: tender lamb sautéed with ground cumin and toasted chili seeds, or melt-in-the-mouth stewed pork. There are 11 other locations throughout the city.

Mamacha Cafe

(Map p246; www.mamacha.nyc; 312 Bowery, NoHo; 🕐10am-8pm; 📶; [S]B/D/F/M to Broadway-Lafayette St) Although it's essentially a matcha-with-art bar, this gallery-like cafe has made its name selling drinks infused with CBD – a non-psychoactive (completely legal) compound found in the hemp plant used to make cannabis. Take a shot of it in a turmeric ginger latte or zingy pomegranate and peppermint fizz, and wait to see if it has the calming effect it's supposed to.

Uncle Boons Thai $$

(Map p246; ☎646-370-6650; www.uncleboons.com; 7 Spring St, btwn Elizabeth St & Bowery, Nolita; small plates $13-16, large plates $22-32; 🕐5:30-11pm Sun-Thu, to midnight Fri & Sat; 📶; [S]J/Z to Bowery; 6 to Spring St) Michelin-star Thai is served up in a fun, tongue-in-cheek combo of retro wood-paneled dining room with Thai film posters and old family snaps. Spanning the old and the new, dishes are tangy, rich and creative. Standouts include the *kob woonsen* (garlic and soy marinated frogs legs), *koong* (grilled baby octopus) and *kaduuk* (roasted bone marrow satay).

Gelso & Grand   Italian $$
(Map p246; ☎212-226-1600; www.gelsoand grand.com; 186 Grand St, at Mulberry St, SoHo; mains $17-31; ☺11am-1am Sun-Thu, to 2am Fri & Sat; Ⓢ6 to Canal St/Spring St, J/Z to Bowery) 'Gelso' means mulberry in Italian – a nod to this refined Italian restaurant's location at a historic intersection in Little Italy. Except here the red checkered tablecloths have been banished, the bricks exposed, and the menu updated with nods to modern American food. The menu sings with homemade pasta dishes and pizzas, but it's the fresh perspective on Italian cuisine that makes Gelso & Grand stand out.

ATLA   Mexican $$
(Map p246; www.atlanyc.com; 372 Lafayette St, at Great Jones St, NoHo; dishes $12-26; ☺11am-11pm Sun-Wed, to midnight Thu-Sat; Ⓢ6 to Bleecker St, B/D/F/M to Broadway-Lafayette St) The Mexican dishes on ATLA's menu – enchiladas, quesadillas, tacos, *chilaquiles* – might sound like standard fare, but here they've been elevated to fine-dining level. Settle into the striking black-and-white dining hall with a mezcal negroni, and order a banquet of sharing dishes such as arctic char and farmer's cheese tostada, striped bass black *aguachile* or duck wings and scallions.

Butcher's Daughter   Vegetarian $$
(Map p246; ☎212-219-3434; www.thebutchers daughter.com; 19 Kenmare St, at Elizabeth St, Nolita; salads & sandwiches $13-16, dinner mains $15-18; ☺8am-10pm; 🍴; Ⓢ J to Bowery; 6 to Spring St) The butcher's daughter certainly has rebelled, peddling nothing but fresh herbivorous fare in her whitewashed cafe. While healthy it is, boring it's not: everything from the soaked organic muesli to the spicy kale Caesar salad with almond Parmesan or the dinnertime Butcher's burger (vegetable and black-bean patty with cashew cheddar cheese) is devilishly delicious.

Gelso & Grand

ED ROONEY/ALAMY STOCK PHOTO ©

Chefs Club
Fusion $$$

(Map p246; 212-941-1100; www.chefsclub.com; 275 Mulberry St, Nolita; mains $20-40; 5:30-10:30pm Mon-Sat; S R/W to Prince St, B/D/F/M to Broadway-Lafayette St) In a building used in part for the show *Will & Grace*, Chefs Club sounds more like a discount warehouse than the spectacular dining spot it really is: visiting chefs prepare a menu for anywhere from three weeks to three months, offering their finest selections in menus that span the flavors of the globe.

Dutch
American $$$

(Map p246; 212-677-6200; www.thedutchnyc. com; 131 Sullivan St, at Prince St, SoHo; mains lunch $18-38, dinner $27-68; 11:30am-3pm & 5:30-10:30pm Mon-Thu, to 11:30pm Fri, 10am-3pm & 5:30-11:30pm Sat, to 10:30pm Sun; S C/E to Spring St; R/W to Prince St; 1 to Houston St) Whether perched at the bar or dining snugly in the back room, you can always expect smart, farm-to-table comfort grub at this see-and-be-seen stalwart. Flavors traverse the globe, from wagyu steak tartare with béarnaise aioli ($22) to grilled lamb chops with jerk sauce and roti pancake ($46). Reservations are recommended, especially for dinner and all day on weekends.

Il Buco Alimentari & Vineria
Italian $$$

(Map p246; 212-837-2622; www.ilbucovineria. com; 53 Great Jones St, btwn Bowery & Lafayette St, NoHo; mains lunch $14-34, dinner $34-70; 8am-11pm Mon-Thu, to midnight Fri, 9am-midnight Sat, to 11pm Sun; ; S 6 to Bleecker St; B/D/F/M to Broadway-Lafayette St) Whether it's espresso at the front bar, cheese from the deli or long-and-lazy Italian feasting in the sunken dining room, Il Buco's trendier spin-off delivers the goods. Brickwork and giant industrial lamps set a hip and rustic tone, echoed in the menu. The lunchtime paninis are huge, decadent and divine: try the porchetta with fried eggs, salsa verde and arugula ($18).

Estela
American $$$

(Map p246; 212-219-7693; www.estelanyc. com; 47 E Houston St, btwn Mulberry & Mott Sts, Nolita; mains $18-39; 5:30-11pm Mon-Thu,

Markets & Food Halls

Don't let the concrete streets and buildings fool you – NYC has a thriving greens scene and many neighborhoods in NYC have their own greenmarket. One of the biggest is the **Union Square Greenmarket** (Map p250; 212-788-7476; www.grownyc.org/unionsquaregreen market; E 17th St, btwn Broadway & Park Ave S, Union Sq; 8am-6pm Mon, Wed, Fri & Sat; S 4/5/6, N/Q/R/W, L to 14th St-Union Sq) , open four days a week year-round. Check Grow NYC (www.grownyc.org/ greenmarket) for a list of the other 50-plus markets around the city.

The number of food halls and markets in NYC has exploded in recent years. These often-trendy affairs are fun for grazing and usually excellent environments in which to try fledgling, independent foodie businesses that don't have the big bucks to open their own restaurants. Top of the list – and one of the originals – is Chelsea Market (p130), which is packed with gourmet goodies of all kinds. Some of the best are in Brooklyn, such as Smorgasburg (p140) and Berg'n (p140), which bring together scores of small gourmet businesses. There's also Gansevoort Market (p130) in the Meatpacking District, the new Canal St Market (p125) in Chinatown and a trio of food halls at Brookfield Place (p122), in Lower Manhattan.

Union Square Greenmarket

11:30am-3pm & 5:30-11:30pm Fri & Sat, to 11pm Sun; S B/D/F/M to Broadway-Lafayette St; 6 to

 Where's the Real Little Italy?

Italian immigration to NYC peaked around the 1880s to 1920s, and the area between SoHo and Chinatown became a hive of micro-communities: Sicilians lived on Elizabeth St, Neapolitans on Mulberry St, and Cantabrians on Mott St. This was the 'hood that spawned the New York mafia and Martin Scorsese – the latter grew up on Elizabeth St and was an altar boy at Mulberry St's Old St Patrick's Cathedral, where he later filmed a scene in *Mean Streets*.

Yet in the past 50 years, this once-strong Italian neighborhood has turned into a micro pastiche of its former self. There's still an endearingly kitsch strip of gingham-tableclothed restaurants around Mulberry St, including Lombardi's – the first pizzeria in America, which opened in 1905 – but they're mainly the preserve of tourists rather than a home for exceptional Italian food. If a real-deal American–Italian meal is on your hit list, or you want to hunt out the best cannelloni bakeries, see artisan pasta being kneaded in shop windows and stringy mozzarella stretched and heaped into panini, head to what is now considered NYC's 'real Little Italy': Arthur Ave in the Bronx. The easiest way to reach it is by taking the Metro North from Grand Central Terminal to Fordham, or the B/D subway to Fordham Rd.

Old St Patrick's Cathedral
ED ROONEY/ALAMY STOCK PHOTO ©

Bleecker St) Estela is on many of NYC's top spots to eat lists, but it may be resting on its laurels just a bit. The food is tasty, no question, with quirky flavor combos that will keep you guessing, but tables are so tightly packed it's tough to have a conversation without meeting those sitting next to you, and portions are tiny.

✖ East Village & Lower East Side

Supermoon Bakehouse   Bakery $
(Map p246; www.supermoonbakehouse.com; 120 Rivington St, at Essex St, Lower East Side; pastries $6-8; ⊗8am-10pm Mon-Thu, to 11am Fri, 9am-11pm Sat, to 10pm Sun; Ⓢ F to Delancey St) This super-friendly Aussie-owned bakery, where the bakers can be seen doing their thing behind glass, produces perhaps Manhattan's most imaginative and remarkable doughnuts. Everything is luridly colorful and elaborately baked and decorated: perhaps a Green & Red croissant filled with a white-chocolate and peppermint ganache and raspberry jam; a Ferrero Rocher croissant; or a tumeric-golden doughnut filled with salted caramel.

Mamoun's   Middle Eastern $
(Map p246; ☎646-870-5785; www.mamouns.com; 30 St Marks Pl, btwn Second & Third Aves, East Village; sandwiches $4-7, plates $9-13; ⊗11am-1am Mon-Wed, to 3am Thu, to 5am Fri & Sat, to 1am Sun; ⊘; Ⓢ 6 to Astor Pl, L to 3rd Ave) This former grab-and-go outpost of the beloved NYC falafel chain has expanded its St Marks storefront with more seating inside and out. Late on weekends a line of inebriated bar-hoppers ends the night with a juicy shawarma covered in Mamoun's famous hot sauce. If you don't do lamb, perhaps a falafel wrap or a sustaining bowl of *fool mudammas* (stewed beans)?

Ivan Ramen   Ramen $$
(Map p246; ☎646-678-3859; www.ivanramen.com; 25 Clinton St, btwn Stanton & E Houston Sts, East Village; mains $16-19; ⊗12:30-10pm Sun-Thu, to 11pm Fri & Sat; Ⓢ F, J/M/Z to Delancey-Essex Sts, F to 2nd Ave) After creating two thriving ramen spots in Tokyo, Long

MAURITIUS IMAGES GMBH/ALAMY STOCK PHOTO ©

Momofuku Noodle Bar

Islander Ivan Orkin brought his talents back home. Few can agree about NYC's best ramen, but this intimate shop, where solo ramen fans sit at the bar watching their bowls take shape, is on every short list. The *tsukumen* (dipping-style) ramen with pickled collard greens and shoyu-glazed pork belly is unbeatable.

Momofuku Noodle Bar Noodles $$

(Map p246; ☎212-777-7773; https://momofukunoodlebar.com; 171 First Ave, btwn E 10th & E 11th Sts, East Village; mains $17-23; 🕐noon-4pm & 5:30-11pm Sun-Thu, noon-4pm & 5:30pm-1am Fri & Sat; ✍; [S]L to 1st Ave, 6 to Astor Pl) With just a handful of tables and a no-reservations policy, this bustling phenomenon may require you to wait. But you won't regret it: spicy short-rib ramen; ginger noodles with pickled shiitake; cold noodles with Sichuan sausage and Thai basil – it's all amazing. The ever-changing menu includes buns (perhaps brisket and horseradish), snacks (smoked chicken wings) and desserts.

Russ & Daughters Cafe Jewish $$

(Map p246; ☎212-475-4880; www.russanddaughterscafe.com; 127 Orchard St, btwn Delancey & Rivington Sts, Lower East Side; mains $18-21; 🕐9am-10pm Mon-Fri, from 8am Sat & Sun; [S]F, J/M/Z to Delancey-Essex Sts) Sit down and feast on shiny boiled bagels and perhaps the best lox in the city in all the comfort of an old-school diner, in this extension of the storied Jewish delicatessen Russ & Daughters, just up Orchard St. Aside from thick, smoky fish, there are potato latkes, borscht, eggs plenty of ways, and even chopped liver, if you must.

Upstate Seafood $$

(Map p246; ☎646-791-5400; www.upstatenyc.com; 95 First Ave, at E 6th St, East Village; mains $15-18; 🕐5-10pm Mon-Wed, to 11pm Fri & Sat, to 10pm Sun; [S]F to 2nd Ave) Upstate keeps it simple: serving outstanding seafood dishes and craft beers. The small, always changing menu features the likes of beer-steamed mussels, seafood stew, scallops over mushroom risotto, *uni* (urchin roe) and wondrous oyster selections. There's no freezer – seafood comes from the market daily, so you know you'll be getting only the freshest. Lines can be long, so go early.

🍴 West Village, Chelsea & Meatpacking District

Chelsea Market Market $

(Map p250; www.chelseamarket.com; 75 Ninth Ave, btwn W 15th & W 16 Sts, Chelsea; mains $10-15; 🕐7am-2am Mon-Sat, 8am-10pm Sun; [S]A/C/E, L to 8th Ave-14th St) In a shining example of redevelopment and renaissance, Chelsea Market has taken a 19th-century Nabisco cookie factory and turned it into an 800ft-long food court of mouthwatering diversity. On the site where the beloved Oreo was first conceived, now more than 35 vendors sell everything from tongue-tingling hand-pulled dan dan noodles to Jamaican jerk, fine cheese and whole lobsters.

Gansevoort Market Market $

(Map p246; ☎646-449-8400; www.gansmarket.com; 353 W 14th St, btwn Eighth & Ninth Aves, Meatpacking District; mains $10-15; 🕐7am-9pm; 📶; [S]A/C/E, L to 8th Ave-14th St) Inside a brick building in the heart of the Meatpacking District, this buzzing place is the latest and greatest food emporium to land in NYC. A raw, industrial space lit by skylights, it features a bar and over a dozen gourmet vendors slinging Korean bibimbap, 'Irish' fish and chips, ceviche, pizza, Thai noodles, ramen, Belgian waffles and more.

JeJu Noodle Bar Noodles $$

(Map p246; ☎646-666-0947; http://jejunoodlebar.com; 679 Greenwich St, at Christopher St, West Village; noodles $18-19; 🕐5-10pm Sun-Wed, to 11pm Thu-Sat; 🚌M8 to Greenwich St-Christopher St, [S]1 to Christopher St-Sheridan Sq) With classic ramen continuing to rampage across the world's tables, perhaps it's time to explore its variations – such as the Korean *ramyun* served at this welcoming restaurant on Christopher St's quieter western stretch. Start with *toro ssam bap* (fatty tuna, toasted seaweed, *tobiko* rice and scrambled egg) before slurping down a *so ramyun* – brisket and noodles in veal broth.

Cookshop American $$

(Map p250; ☎212-924-4440; www.cookshopny.com; 156 Tenth Ave, at W 20th St, Chelsea; mains brunch $16-18, lunch $18-24, dinner $24-30; 🕐8am-11:30pm Mon-Fri, from 10am Sat, 10am-10pm Sun; ✎; [S]1, C/E to 23rd St) A brilliant brunching pit stop before (or after) tackling the verdant High Line (p52) across the street, Cookshop is a lively place that knows its niche and nails it. Excellent service, eye-opening cocktails (good morning, Blushing Monk!), a perfectly baked bread basket, outdoor seating for warm days and inventive egg dishes make this a Chelsea favorite.

Foragers Table American $$$

(Map p250; ☎212-243-8888; www.foragersmarket.com/restaurant; 300 W 22nd St, at Eighth Ave, Chelsea; mains $28-32; 🕐dinner 5:30-10pm Mon-Sat, to 9pm Sun, brunch 9am-3pm Sat & Sun; ✎; [S]1, C/E to 23rd St) The owners of this outstanding restaurant run a 28-acre Hudson Valley farm, from which much of the seasonal menu is sourced. It changes frequently, but recent temptations included fettuccine with a medley of exotic mushrooms cooked in sherry and butter, fish with young chard, puffed rice and yuzu-pickled apple, and Berkshire pork on red polenta with daikon kimchi.

Jeffrey's Grocery American $$$

(Map p246; ☎646-398-7630; www.jeffreysgrocery.com; 172 Waverly Pl, at Christopher St, West Village; mains $26-29; 🕐8am-11pm Mon-Wed, to 1am Thu-Fri, 9:30am-1am Sat, to 11pm Sun; [S]1 to Christopher St-Sheridan Sq) This West Village classic is a lively eating and drinking spot that hits all the right notes. Seafood is the focus: there's an oyster bar and beautifully executed mains such as mussels with madras curry, coconut milk and herbs, fresh tuna Nicoise, and lobster bisque. Meat dishes include hanger steak with yukon potatoes in a *romesco* (nut and red-pepper) sauce.

★ Best Bagels

Russ & Daughters Cafe (p129)
Barney Greengrass (p138)
Eli's Essentials (p137)

Clockwise from top: Chelsea Market; Barney Greengrass (p138); Jeffrey's Grocery

BRUCE YUANYUE BI/ALAMY STOCK PHOTO ©

Eataly

RedFarm Fusion $$$

(Map p246; ☎212-792-9700; www.redfarmnyc.com; 529 Hudson St, btwn W 10th & Charles Sts, West Village; mains $28-52, dumplings $15-17; ⏰dinner 5-11:45pm Mon-Sat, to 11pm Sun, brunch 11am-2:30pm Sat & Sun; [S]1 to Christopher St-Sheridan Sq, A/C/E, B/D/F/M to W 4th St-Washington Sq) Experience Chinese cooking as unique, delectable artistry in this small, buzzing space. Diced tuna and eggplant bruschetta, juicy rib steak (marinated in papaya, ginger and soy) and pastrami egg rolls are among the many stunning, genre-defying dishes. Other hits include lobster sautéed with egg and chopped pork, cheeseburger spring rolls, and black-truffle chicken-soup dumplings.

Barbuto Italian $$$

(Map p246; ☎212-924-9700; www.barbutonyc.com; 775 Washington St, at W 12th St, West Village; mains $31-32; ⏰lunch noon-3:30pm, dinner 5:30-11pm Mon-Thu, to midnight Fri & Sat, to 10pm Sun; [S]A/C/E, L to 8th Ave-14th St, 1 to Christopher St-Sheridan Sq) Occupying a stripped-yet-stylish former garage space with roller doors that allow alfresco dining during the warmer months, Barbuto produces a delightful assortment of nouveau-Italian dishes, such as swordfish with honeynut squash, smoked cabbage and brown butter, or ricotta cavatelli with wild mushrooms and Parmesan.

Blue Hill American $$$

(Map p246; ☎212-539-1776; www.bluehillfarm.com; 75 Washington Pl, btwn Sixth Ave & Washington Sq W, West Village; prix-fixe menu $95-108; ⏰5-11pm Mon-Sat, to 10pm Sun; [S]A/C/E, B/D/F/M to W 4th St-Washington Sq) A place for Slow Food junkies with deep pockets, Blue Hill was an early crusader in the farm-to-table movement. Gifted chef-patron Dan Barber, who hails from a farm family in the Berkshires, MA, uses regional harvests to create his widely praised fare.

Nix Vegetarian $$$

(Map p246; ☎212-498-9393; www.nixny.com; 72 University Pl, btwn E 10th & E 11th Sts, West Village; mains $26-28; ⏰11:30am-2:30pm & 5:30-11pm Mon-Thu, 11:30am-2:30pm & 5-11pm Fri, 10:30am-2:30pm & 5-11pm Sat, 10:30am-2:30pm & 5-10:30pm Sun; 🌿; [S]4/5/6, N/Q/R/W, L to 14th St-Union Sq) At this modest yet

Michelin-starred restaurant, chefs John Fraser and Garrett Eagleton transform vegetables into beautifully executed dishes that delight the senses. Start with tandoor bread with dips such as red pepper and walnut, then move to more complex plates such as burrata with winter-truffle pesto, figs and walnuts or cauliflower tempura with steamed buns and pickles.

Chumley's   American $$$

(Map p246; 212-675-2081; http://chumleys newyork.com; 86 Bedford St, btwn Grove & Barrow Sts, West Village; mains $29-36; 5:30-10:15pm Mon-Thu, to 10:30pm Fri & Sat, 11:30am-3:30pm Sun; S1 to Christopher St-Sheridan Sq, A/C/E, B/D/F/M to W 4th St-Washington Sq) Occupying the site of a legendary 1922 West Village speakeasy, Chumley's maintains its historic air while upgrading everything else. The ambitious seasonal menu includes arctic char cooked in parchment and a burger with two 4oz patties, bone marrow and shallots. Walls are lined with the portraits and book jackets of Prohibition-era writers.

Rosemary's   Italian $$$

(Map p246; 212-647-1818; www.rosemarysnyc. com; 18 Greenwich Ave, at W 10th St, West Village; mains $24-28, lunch/dinner prix fixe $24/34; 8am-4pm & 5-11pm Mon-Thu, 8am-4pm & 5pm-midnight Fri, 10am-4pm & 5pm-midnight Sat, 10am-4pm & 5-11pm Sun; S1 to Christopher St-Sheridan Sq) One of the West Village's hottest restaurants, Rosemary's serves fantastic high-end Italian fare. In a vaguely farmhouse-like setting, diners tuck into generous portions of house-made pastas, rich salads, and cheese and *salumi* (cured meat) boards. Everything, from the bitter greens with hazelnuts to the 'Meiller Farm' pork with orange mustard fruits, is incredible.

❷ Union Square, Flatiron District & Gramercy

Eataly   Food Hall $$

(Map p250; 212-229-2560; www.eataly.com; 200 Fifth Ave, at W 23rd St, Flatiron District; 7am-11pm; ; SR/W, F/M, 6 to 23rd St)

Mario Batali's sleek, sprawling temple to Italian gastronomy is a veritable wonderland. Feast on everything from vibrant *crudo* (raw fish) and *fritto misto* (tempura-style vegetables) to steamy pasta and pizza at the emporium's string of sit-down eateries. Alternatively, guzzle espresso at the bar and scour the countless counters and shelves for a DIY picnic hamper *nonna* would approve of.

Big Daddy's   Diner $

(Map p250; 212-477-1500; www.bigdaddysnyc. com; 239 Park Ave S, btwn E 19th & E 20th Sts, Gramercy; mains $10-16; 8am-midnight Mon-Thu, to 5am Fri & Sat, to 11pm Sun; ; S6 to 23rd St; 4/5/6, L, N/Q/R/W to 14th St-Union Sq) Giant, fluffy omelets, hearty burgers and heaps of tater tots (regular or sweet potato) have made Big Daddy's a top choice for both breakfast and late-night treats. The interior is all Americana kitsch, but unlike some theme restaurants the food doesn't break the bank and actually satisfies.

Maialino   Italian $$$

(Map p250; 212-777-2410; www.maialinonyc. com; Gramercy Park Hotel, 2 Lexington Ave, at 21st St, Gramercy; mains lunch $24-36, dinner $34-58; 7:30-10am, noon-2pm & 5:30-10pm Mon-Wed, to 10:30pm Thu & Fri, 10am-2:30pm & 5:30-10:30pm Sat, to 10pm Sun; S6, R/W to 23rd St) Fans reserve tables up to four weeks in advance at this Danny Meyer classic, but the best seats in the house are at the walk-in bar, with sociable, knowledgeable staffers. Wherever you're plonked, take your taste buds on a Roman holiday. Maialino's lip-smacking, rustic Italian fare is created using produce from the nearby Union Square Greenmarket (p127).

Eleven Madison Park   American $$$

(Map p250; 212-889-0905; www.eleven madisonpark.com; 11 Madison Ave, btwn 24th & 25th Sts, Flatiron District; tasting menu $315; 5:30-10pm Mon-Wed, to 10:30pm Thu, noon-1pm & 5:30-10:30pm Fri-Sun; SR/W, 6 to 23rd St) Eleven Madison Park consistently bags a spot on top restaurant lists. Frankly, we're not surprised: this revamped poster child

New York City on a Plate

The dough base is hand-tossed and baked into a thin crust.

Typical toppings include pepperoni, green peppers, onions and mushrooms. (Never pineapple!)

The tomato sauce must perfectly balance acidity and sweetness.

Grated mozzarella cheese is used (ricotta is added for a 'white pie').

The proper way to hold a NY slice is folded lengthwise.

ADIDAS4747/SHUTTERSTOCK ©

The Best Pizza Slice

A Slice of Heaven

Whether grabbed on the go as a slice or eaten whole at a sit-down restaurant, pizza is one of New York's most ubiquitous and beloved foods. The light, springy crunch of the thin NY-style crust combines with the slightly sweet tomato sauce and thick, melted mozzarella cheese to create a symphony in your mouth. Add on some meat or vegetable toppings for a classic New York meal.

Juliana's (p141)
ROBERT CICCHETTI/SHUTTERSTOCK ©

★ Top Five Places for Pizza

Juliana's (p141)

Roberta's (pictured below; p141)

Two Boots Pizza (Map p246; ☎ 212-633-9096; http://twoboots.com; 201 W 11th St, at Greenwich Ave, West Village; ⏱11am-midnight Sun-Wed, to 1am Thu, to 2am Fri & Sat; Ⓢ A/C/E, L to 8th Ave-14th St)

Totonno's (p115)

Di Fara Pizza (☎ 718-258-1367; www.difarany.com; 1424 Ave J, cnr E 15th St, Midwood; pizza slices $5-6; ⏱noon-8pm Tue-Sat, from 1pm Sun; Ⓢ Q to Ave J)

SIVAN ASKAYO/LONELY PLANET ©

of modern, sustainable American cooking is also one of only five NYC restaurants sporting three Michelin stars. Insane attention to detail, intense creativity and whimsy are all trademarks of chef Daniel Humm's approach.

Craft American $$$

(Map p250; ☎212-780-0880; www.craftrestaurant.com; 43 E 19th St, btwn Broadway & Park Ave S, Union Sq; lunch $17-23, dinner mains $35-55; 🕑noon-2:30pm & 5:30-10pm Mon-Thu, to 11pm Fri, 5:30-11pm Sat, to 9pm Sun; 📶; [S]4/5/6, N/Q/R/W, L to 14th St-Union Sq) 🍃 Humming, high-end Craft flies the flag for small, family-owned farms and food producers, their bounty transformed into pure, polished dishes. Whether nibbling on flawlessly charred braised octopus, juicy roasted quail or pumpkin mezzaluna pasta with sage, brown butter and Parmesan, expect every ingredient to sing with flavor. Book ahead Wednesday to Saturday or head in by 6pm or after 9:30pm.

Gramercy Tavern American $$$

(Map p250; ☎212-477-0777; www.gramercytavern.com; 42 E 20th St, btwn Broadway & Park Ave S, Flatiron District; tavern mains $32-36, dining room 3-course menu $134, tasting menus $164-184; 🕑tavern 11:30am-11pm Sun-Thu, to midnight Fri & Sat, dining room 11:30am-2pm & 5-9:45pm Sun-Thu, to 10:30pm Fri & Sat; 📶🖉; [S]R/W, 6 to 23rd St) 🍃 Seasonal, local ingredients drive this perennial favorite, a vibrant, country-chic institution aglow with copper sconces, murals and dramatic floral arrangements. Choose from two spaces: the walk-in-only tavern and its à la carte menu, or the swankier dining room and its fancier prix-fixe and degustation feasts. Regardless of where you sit, you'll find service is excellent. New Yorkers LOVE this place: book ahead.

🍴 Midtown

Totto Ramen Japanese $

(Map p252; ☎212-582-0052; www.tottoramen.com; 366 W 52nd St, btwn Eighth & Ninth Aves; ramen $12-18; 🕑noon-4:30pm & 5:30pm-midnight Mon-Sat, 4-11pm Sun; [S]C/E to 50th St) There might be another two branches in Midtown, but purists know that neither beats the tiny 20-seat original. Write your name and number of guests on the clipboard and wait your turn. Your reward: extraordinary ramen. Go for the butter-soft *char siu* (pork), which sings in dishes like miso ramen (with fermented soybean paste, egg, scallion, bean sprouts, onion and home-made chili paste).

Burger Joint Burgers $

(Map p252; ☎212-708-7414; www.burgerjointny.com; Le Parker Meridien, 119 W 56th St, btwn Sixth & Seventh Aves; burgers $9-17; 🕑11am-11:30pm Sun-Thu, to midnight Fri & Sat; [S]F to 57th St) With only a small neon burger as your clue, this speakeasy-style burger hut lurks behind the lobby curtain in the Parker New York hotel. Though it might not be as secret as it once was (you'll see the queues), it still delivers the same winning formula of graffiti-strewn walls, retro booths and attitude-loaded staff slapping up beef 'n' patty brilliance.

Stumptown Coffee Roasters Coffee

(Map p250; ☎855-711-3385; www.stumptowncoffee.com; 18 W 29th St, btwn Broadway & Fifth Ave; 🕑6am-8pm Mon-Fri, from 7am Sat & Sun; [S]R/W to 28th St) Hipster baristas in fedora hats brewing killer coffee? No, you're not in Williamsburg, you're at the Manhattan outpost of Portland's cult-status coffee roaster. The queue is a small price to pay for proper espresso, so count your blessings. It's standing-room only, though weary punters might find a seat in the adjacent **Ace Hotel** (☎212-679-2222; www.acehotel.com/newyork; 20 W 29th St, btwn Broadway & Fifth Ave, Midtown West; r from $399; ❄📶; [S]R/W to 28th St) lobby.

Turnstyle Underground Market Street Food $

(Map p254; www.turn-style.com; Eighth Ave, btwn W 58th & 57th Sts; 🕑hours vary; [S]A/C, 1, B/D to 59th St-Columbus Circle) Genius idea: take a neglected subway passage and turn it into an underground food hall and shopping avenue where commuters can grab a morning coffee or pause to scarf up tacos, chicken and waffles, Russian dumplings or sushi for lunch or dinner. Anything goes in this buzzing strip of food joints, which are complemented by small independent shops.

Fournos Theophilos Greek $

(Map p252; ☎212-278-0015; www.fournos.com; 45 W 45th St, btwn Fifth & Sixth Aves; lunch $11.90; ⏰7am-10pm Mon-Sat, from 8am Sun; [S]B/D/F/M to 47th-50th Sts-Rockefeller Center) Named in honor of a poor Greek painter who was paid for his art in food, Fournos Theophilos is a scrumptious archive of Greek food heritage in an area of Midtown that can feel like a culinary wasteland. Greek pies, pastries and even baklava milkshakes can be grabbed upfront in the bakery; head to the back for flavor-packed hot lunch boxes.

Sons of Thunder Seafood $

(Map p250; ☎646-863-2212; www.sonsofthunder.com; 204 E 38th St, btwn 3rd Ave & Tunnel Exit St; poke bowls $9-14; ⏰11am-9pm Mon-Fri, noon-8pm Sat; [S]6 to 33rd St) New York has clearly embraced the poke trend, but some places do it better than others. Sons of Thunder's version of the Hawaiian dish can be tailored to your taste (choose from octopus, salmon, tuna, tofu or beets served atop rice, greens or cauliflower rice). If you don't appreciate raw fish, specials like Baja fish tacos and chili bowls will hit the spot.

Hangawi Korean $$

(Map p250; ☎212-213-0077; www.hangawirestaurant.com; 12 E 32nd St, btwn Fifth & Madison Aves; mains lunch $13-14, dinner $18-30; ⏰noon-2:30pm & 5:30-10:15pm Mon-Thu, to 10:30pm Fri, 1-10:30pm Sat, 5-9:30pm Sun; 🌿; [S]B/D/F/M, N/Q/R/W to 34th St-Herald Sq) Meat-free Korean is the draw at high-achieving Hangawi. Leave your shoes at the entrance and slip into a soothing, Zen-like space of meditative music, soft low seating and clean, complex dishes. Dishes include pumpkin noodles, spicy kimchi pancakes and a seductively smooth tofu claypot in ginger sauce. At lunchtime there's a four-course prix-fixe deal for $25.

Modern French $$$

(Map p252; ☎212-333-1220; www.themodernnyc.com; 9 W 53rd St, btwn Fifth & Sixth Aves; 3-/6-course lunch $138/178, 6-course dinner $228; ⏰restaurant noon-2pm & 5-10pm Mon-Wed, noon-2pm & 5-10:30pm Thu-Sat, bar 11:30am-10pm Mon-Wed, to 10:30pm Thu-Sat, to 9:30pm Sun; 📶; [S]E, M to 5th Ave-53rd St) Shining two (Michelin) stars bright, the Modern delivers rich, confident creations like foie gras tart and 'ants on a log' peanut butter cake. Service is friendly and meals are presented in a light-filled space reminiscent of MoMA's galleries, with giant windows overlooking the sculpture garden. Fans of *Sex and the City* may know that it was here that Carrie announced her impending marriage to Mr Big.

O-ya Sushi $$$

(Map p250; ☎212-204-0200; https://o-ya.restaurant/o-ya-nyc; 120 E 28th St; nigiri $6-25; ⏰5:30-10pm Mon-Sat; [S]4/6 to 28th St) With the cheapest nigiri pairs at close to $15, this is not a spot you'll come to every day. But if you're looking for a special night out and sushi's in the game plan, come here for exquisite flavors, fish so tender it melts like butter on the tongue, and preparations so artful you almost apologize for eating them.

Agern New Nordic $$$

(Map p252; ☎646-568-4018; www.agernrestaurant.com; 89 E 42nd St, Grand Central Terminal; dinner mains $28-44, 2-/3-course prix fixe lunch $40/48; ⏰11:30am-2:30pm & 5:30-10pm Mon-Fri, 5:30-10pm Sat; 📶🌿; [S]S, 4/5/6, 7 to Grand Central-42nd St, 🚆Metro North to Grand Central-42nd St) Showing off the sleek design principles and seasonal, creative flair you'd expect from an architect of Denmark's New Nordic food revolution, Claus Meyer's restaurant in Grand Central Station features deceptively simple dishes, such as endive with preserved blackberries and pork shoulder with sorrel. Agern is also refreshingly affordable – especially the $40 lunch menu.

Grand Central Oyster Bar & Restaurant Seafood $$$

(Map p252; ☑212-490-6650; www.oyster barny.com; lower level, Grand Central Terminal, 42nd St, at Park Ave; mains $15-39; ⊗11:30am-9:30pm Mon-Sat; ⑤S, 4/5/6, 7 to Grand Central-42nd St) This buzzing bar and restaurant within Grand Central is hugely atmospheric, with a vaulted tiled ceiling by Catalan-born engineer Rafael Guastavino. Ignore the formal dining area on your left as you enter: the prize seats are at the sleek communal tables on your right, where diners happily slurp oysters as quick as staff can shuck them.

⊗ Upper East Side

JG Melon Pub Food $

(Map p254; ☑212-744-0585; 1291 Third Ave, at E 74th St; mains $10-30; ⊗11:30am-4am; ⑤Q to 72nd St-2nd Ave) JG's is a loud, old-school neighborhood pub that has been serving reasonably priced drinks and juicy burgers ($12) on tea plates since 1972. It's a local favorite for both eating and drinking (the Bloody Marys are excellent) and it gets crowded in the after-work hours. Cash only.

Papaya King Hot Dogs $

(Map p254; ☑212-369-0648; www.papayaking. com; 179 E 86th St, at Third Ave; hot dogs $2.75-4.50; ⊗8am-midnight Sun-Thu, to 1am Fri & Sat; ⑤4/5/6, Q to 86th St) The *original* hot-dog-and-papaya-juice shop, from 1932, over 40 years before crosstown rival **Gray's Papaya** (Map p254; ☑212-799-0243; 2090 Broadway, at 72nd St, entrance on Amsterdam Ave; hot dogs $2.50; ⊗24hr; ⑤1/2/3, B, C to 72nd St) opened, Papaya King has lured many a New Yorker to its neon-lit corner for a cheap and tasty snack of hot dogs and fresh-squeezed papaya juice. (Why papaya? The informative wall signs will explain all.) Try the Homerun, with sauerkraut and New York onion relish.

� Urban Farm to Table

Whether it's upstate triple-cream Kunik at **Bedford Cheese Shop** (Map p250; ☑718-599-7588; www.bedfordcheeseshop. com; 67 Irving Pl, btwn E 18th & 19th Sts, Gramercy; ⊗8am-8pm Sun-Thu, to 9pm Fri-Sat; ⑤4/5/6, N/Q/R/W, L to 14th St-Union Sq) or Montauk Pearl oysters at fine-dining Craft (p135), New York City's passion for all things local and artisanal continues unabated. The city itself has become an unlikely food bowl, with an ever-growing number of rooftops, backyards and community gardens finding new purpose as urban farms. The current queen of the crop is **Brooklyn Grange** (www.brooklyngrangefarm. com), a 2.5-acre organic farm covering two rooftops in Long Island City and the Brooklyn Navy Yards. The project is the brainchild of young farmer Ben Flanner; obsessed with farm-to-table eating he kick-started NYC's rooftop revolution in 2009 with the opening of its first rooftop soil farm – **Eagle Street Rooftop Farm** – in nearby Greenpoint. Flanner's collaborators include some of the city's top restaurants, among them Roberta's (p141) in Brooklyn, and Gramercy Tavern (p135) in Manhattan.

Eagle Street Rooftop Farm

Eli's Essentials American $

(Map p254; ☑646-755-3999; www.elizabar.com/ ElisEssentials_91_Madison.aspx; 1270 Madison Ave, at E 91st St; buffet per lb $16.95, sandwiches from $7; ⊗7am-11pm; 🛜🍴; ⑤6 to 96th St) The youngest son of the founders of Zabar's (p157) delicatessen is building a mini empire on the Upper East Side, and this update on New York's traditional Jewish deli is perfect for a pit stop near Fifth Ave's Museum Mile. As well as lox bagels and Eli's signature egg brioche roll, there's a buffet with fried chicken, mac 'n' cheese and salads.

Tanoshi Sushi **$$$**

(Map p254; ☎917-265-8254; www.tanoshisushinyc.com; 1372 York Ave, btwn E 73rd & 74th Sts; chef's sushi selection $95-100; 🕒seatings 6pm, 7:30pm & 9pm Tue-Sat; [S]Q to 72nd St) It's not easy to snag one of the 20 stools at Tanoshi, a wildly popular, pocket-sized sushi spot. The setting may be humble, but the flavors are simply magnificent. Only sushi is on offer and only *omakase* (chef's selection) – which might include Hokkaido scallops, kelp-cured flake or mouthwatering *uni* (sea urchin). BYO beer, sake or whatnot. Reserve well in advance.

Café Boulud French **$$$**

(Map p254; ☎212-772-2600; www.cafeboulud.com/nyc; 20 E 76th St, btwn Fifth & Madison Aves; mains around $45; 🕒7-10:30am, noon-2:30pm & 5:30-10:30pm Mon-Fri, 8-10:30am, 11:30am-2:30pm & 5:30-10:30pm Sat, 8-10:30am, 11:30am-3pm & 5-10pm Sun; 🌿; [S]6 to 77th St) This long-standing Michelin-starred bistro by Daniel Boulud attracts a rather staid crowd with its globe-trotting French cuisine. Seasonal menus include classics like bass '*en paupiette*', as well as fare such as duck with apple gnocchi. The inventive farmers market section will appeal to vegetarians.

🍴 Upper West Side & Central Park

Peacefood Cafe Vegan **$**

(Map p254; ☎212-362-2266; www.peacefoodcafe.com; 460 Amsterdam Ave, at 82nd St; mains $11-18; 🕒10am-10pm; 🌿; [S]1 to 79th St) This bright and airy vegan haven dishes up a popular fried seitan panini (served on homemade focaccia and topped with cashew cheese, arugula, tomatoes and pesto), as well as pizzas, roasted-vegetable plates and an excellent quinoa salad. There are daily raw specials, energy-fueling juices and rich desserts, plus a more substantial dinner menu served 5pm to 10pm.

Barney Greengrass Deli **$$**

(Map p254; ☎212-724-4707; www.barneygreengrass.com; 541 Amsterdam Ave, at 86th St; mains $12-23.50; 🕒deli 8:30am-6pm Tue-Sun, cafe from 8:30am; [S]1 to 86th St) The self-proclaimed 'King of Sturgeon,' Barney Greengrass serves up the same heaping dishes of eggs and salty lox, luxuriant caviar and melt-in-your-mouth chocolate babkas that first made it famous when it opened over a century ago. Fuel up in the morning at casual tables amid the crowded produce counters, or take lunch at the serviced cafe in an adjoining room.

Boulud Sud Mediterranean **$$$**

(Map p254; ☎212-595-1313; www.bouludsud.com; 20 W 64th St, btwn Broadway & Central Park W; 3-course prix fixe 5-7pm Mon-Sat $65, mains lunch $18-35, dinner $35-63; 🕒11:30am-2:30pm & 5-11pm Mon-Fri, 11am-3pm & 5-11pm Sat, to 10pm Sun; [S]) Pear-wood paneling and a yellow-grey palette lend a 1960s *Mad Men* feel to Daniel Boulud's restaurant championing cuisines from the Mediterranean and North Africa. Dishes such as Valencian paella, Tunisian *brik* with confit tuna and Sardinian lemon saffron linguini emphasize seafood, vegetables and regional spices. Look out for specials, like the express lunch ($25), pre-theater menu ($65) and happy pasta hour (50% off).

🍴 Harlem & Upper Manhattan

Vinatería European **$$**

(☎212-662-8462; www.vinaterianyc.com; 2211 Frederick Douglass Blvd, btwn 119th & 120th Sts; mains $19-29; 🕒5-10pm Mon, to 11pm Tue-Thu, to midnight Fri, 10:30am-midnight Sat, to 10pm Sun; [S]A/C, B to 116th St) This classy Michelin-recommended neighborhood restaurant shows a new side to Harlem, taking inspiration from Italy and Spain with

RICHARD LEVINE/ALAMY STOCK PHOTO ©

Sylvia's

flavor-packed dishes such as spicy veal meatballs bedded in parmigiano polenta and grilled octopus with roasted poblano peppers and fennel pollen. Pasta is made in-house, and the black seafood spaghetti is a signature dish.

Sylvia's Southern US $$
(☎212-996-0660; www.sylviasrestaurant.com; 328 Malcolm X Blvd, btwn 126th & 127th Sts, Harlem; mains $14-27; 🕒8am-10:30pm Mon-Sat, 11am-8pm Sun; [S]2/3 to 125th St) Founded by Sylvia Woods back in 1962, this Harlem icon has been dazzling Harlemites and visitors (including a few presidents) with its lip-smackingly good down-home Southern cooking – succulent fried chicken, baked mac 'n' cheese and cornmeal-dusted catfish, plus requisite sides like collard greens. Come on Sundays for the gospel brunch, and book ahead to avoid the overwhelming scrum for a table.

Red Rooster American $$$
(☎212-792-9001; www.redroosterharlem.com; 310 Malcolm X Blvd, btwn W 125th & 126th Sts, Harlem; mains lunch $20-25, dinner $25-40; 🕒11:30am-3pm & 4:30-10:30pm Mon-Thu, to 11:30pm Fri, 10am-3pm & 4:30-11:30pm Sat, to 10pm Sun; [S]2/3 to 125th St) Transatlantic superchef Marcus Samuelsson laces upscale comfort food with a world of flavors at his effortlessly cool brasserie. Mac 'n' cheese joins forces with lobster, blackened catfish pairs with pickled mango, and Swedish meatballs salute Samuelsson's home country. The DJ-led bar atmosphere is as good as, if not better, than the food: roll in after midnight on weekends and you'll find it's still buzzing.

🍴 Brooklyn

Ample Hills Creamery Ice Cream $
(Map p256; ☎347-725-4061; www.amplehills.com; 305 Nevins St, at Union St, Gowanus; cones $4.35-7.35; 🕒noon-11pm Sun-Thu, to midnight Fri & Sat; [S]R to Union St, F, G to Carroll St) Ice-cream lovers: we found the mother ship. All of Ample Hills' magnificently creative flavors – snap mallow pop (a deconstructed Rice Krispies treat), Mexican hot chocolate,

salted crack caramel, 'ooey gooey' butter cake – are whipped up right here in the creamery's Gowanus factory. Grab a cone and watch the goods being made through the kitchen's picture window.

Four & Twenty Blackbirds — Bakery $

(Map p256; ☎718-499-2917; www.birdsblack.com; 439 Third Ave, cnr 8th St, Gowanus; pie slices $6; 🕐8am-8pm Mon-Fri, from 9am Sat, 10am-7pm Sun; 📶; [S]R to 9th St) Inspired by their grandma, sisters Emily and Melissa Elsen use local fruit and foraged foods in season to create NYC's best pies, hands down. Any time is just right to drop in for a slice – perhaps salted-caramel apple, or brown-butter pumpkin – and a cup of Stumptown coffee. Ardent bakers can also pick up a copy of their *Pie Book*.

Berg'n — Food Hall $

(Map p256; www.bergn.com; 899 Bergen St, btwn Classon & Franklin Aves, Crown Heights; mains $13-16; 🕐food 9am-10pm Tue-Thu, 10am-11pm Fri & Sat, to 10pm Sun, bar 11am-late Tue-Sun; 📶🥕👪; [S]C, 2/3, 4/5 to Franklin Ave) From the team behind Smorgasburg and Brooklyn Flea (p159), Berg'n is a large brick food hall with long wooden tables where you can feast on smoky brisket (Mighty Quinn's), gourmet grilled cheese and burgers (LandHaus), Shanghai-inspired street food (Jianbing) and blistered, hand-stretched pizzas (Pizza by Charlie). There's also a coffee stand and a bar serving local and regional microbrews.

Smorgasburg — Market $

(www.smorgasburg.com; mains $12-16; 🕐Williamsburg 11am-6pm Sat, Prospect Park 11am-4pm Sun Apr-Oct, Atlantic Center 11am-8pm Sat, to 5pm Sun Nov-Feb; 👪) The largest foodie event in Brooklyn (perhaps the US) brings together more than 100 vendors selling an incredible array of goodness: Italian street snacks, duck confit, Indian flatbread tacos, roasted-mushroom burgers, vegan Ethiopian food, sea-salt-caramel ice cream, passion-fruit doughnuts, craft beer and much more. Locations tend to change from season to season, so check the website for the latest.

Smorgasburg

LITTLENYSTOCK/SHUTTERSTOCK ©

Fette Sau Barbecue $

(Map p257; ☎718-963-3404; www.fettesaubbq.com; 354 Metropolitan Ave, btwn Havemeyer & Roebling Sts, Williamsburg; meats per half-pound $12-13; 🕐5-11pm Mon, from noon Tue-Sun; [S]L to Bedford Ave) The atmosphere is unfussy, but the reverence for smoky meat is indubitable at the 'Fat Pig,' Brooklyn's best house of barbecue. The cement floor and inside-outside feel echo the garage that once operated from this space, while shared trestles and an 'order by the pound' system put lovers of brisket, pulled pork and ancho-chili-spiced sausage further at ease.

Juliana's Pizza $$

(Map p256; ☎718-596-6700; www.julianaspizza.com; 19 Old Fulton St, btwn Water & Front Sts, Brooklyn Heights; pizzas $26-29; 🕐11:30am-10pm, closed 3:15-4pm; ✎; [S]A/C to High St) Legendary pizza maestro Patsy Grimaldi has returned to Brooklyn, offering delicious, thin-crust perfection in both classic and creative combos – like the No 1, with mozzarella, *scamorza affumicata* (an Italian smoked cow's cheese), pancetta, scallions and white truffles in olive oil. Note that Juliana's closes for 45 minutes every afternoon to stoke the coal-fired pizza oven.

Olmsted American $$

(Map p256; ☎718-552-2610; www.olmstednyc.com; 659 Vanderbilt Ave, btwn Prospect Pl & Park Pl, Prospect Heights; small plates $15-16, large plates $23-24; 🕐dinner 5:30-10pm Mon-Thu, 5-10:30pm Fri & Sat, 5-9:30pm Sun, brunch 11:30am-2:30pm Fri, 11am-3pm Sat & Sun; [S]B, Q to 7th Ave) 🌿 Chef-owner Greg Baxtrom, alumnus of a string of hot kitchens, cooks such great, seasonally inspired food that even Manhattanites will cross the river to eat here. Olmsted is so 'locavore' that much of the menu comes from the restaurant's backyard garden – which doubles as a lovely spot for cocktails or dessert. Reservations are recommended, but Mondays are for walk-ins only.

Modern Love Vegan $$

(Map p257; ☎929-298-0626; www.modernlovebrooklyn.com; 317 Union Ave, at S 1st St, East Williamsburg; mains brunch $16-18, dinner $20-23; 🕐5:30-10pm Tue-Thu, to 11pm Fri, 5-11pm Sat, 10am-3pm & 5-10pm Sun; ✎; [S]G to Metropolitan Ave, L to Lorimer St) Celebrated chef Isa Chandra Moskowitz's 'swanky vegan comfort food' has been received with open, watering mouths in Williamsburg. Delicious vegan renditions of classics include 'mac 'n' shews' (with creamy cashew cheese and pecan-cornmeal-crusted tofu), Manhattan 'glam chowder', seitan Philly cheesesteak and truffled poutine. It's always buzzing, so bookings are a good idea (though not mandatory).

Roberta's Pizza $$

(Map p257; ☎718-417-1118; www.robertaspizza.com; 261 Moore St, near Bogart St, East Williamsburg; pizzas $19-20; 🕐11am-midnight Mon-Fri, from 10am Sat & Sun; ✎; [S]L to Morgan Ave) This hiply renovated warehouse restaurant in one of Brooklyn's booming food enclaves makes some of the best pizza in NYC. Service is relaxed, but the brick-oven pies are serious: chewy, fresh and topped with knowing combinations of outstanding ingredients. The classic margherita is sublime; more adventurous palates can opt for seasonal fancies like 'Beastmaster' (Gorgonzola, pork sausage and jalapeño).

Zenkichi Japanese $$$

(Map p257; ☎718-388-8985; www.zenkichi.com; 77 N 6th St, at Wythe Ave, Williamsburg; tasting menus vegetarian/regular $65/75; 🕐6pm-midnight Mon-Sat, 5:30-11:30pm Sun; ✎; [S]L to Bedford Ave) Created by a homesick Tokyo chef, this hushed restaurant promises peace and pleasure in equal proportions. Sink into one of the secluded booths, order the *omakase* (tasting menu) and abandon yourself to a precise succession of seasonal delights: in winter, these might include monkfish *(anou)* with tempura celery, Washugyu beef in sweet soy, and rice with truffles and *shimeji* mushrooms.

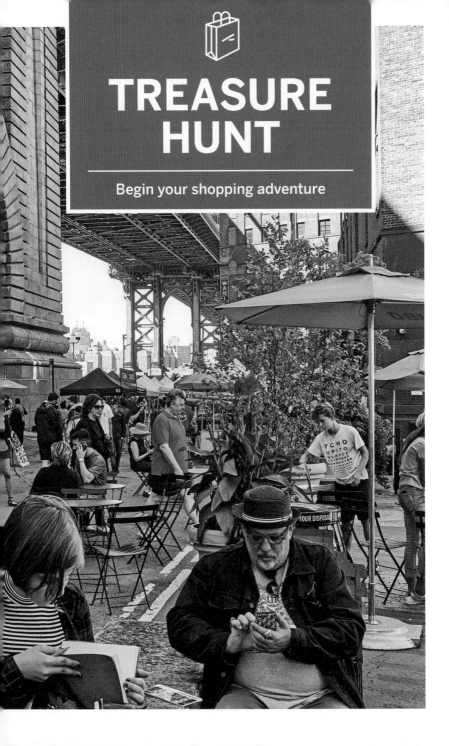

TREASURE HUNT

Begin your shopping adventure

Treasure Hunt

Not surprisingly for a capital of commercialism, creativity and fashion, New York City is quite simply one of the best shopping destinations on the planet. World-class designers, crafters and entrepreneurs gravitate towards the bright lights of NYC, lining its streets and markets with unique wares and retail flagship stores of dizzying proportions and flair. Between the independent boutiques and landmark department stores, it's quite easy to blow your budget here. Christmas is an especially popular time, when people jet in from all over the world for retail blow-outs.

In This Section

Useful Websites

Time Out (www.timeout.com/newyork/shopping) The latest info on store openings, sales and pop-up shops.

New York Magazine (www.nymag.com) Trustworthy opinions on the Big Apple's best places to swipe your plastic.

The Stylish City (www.thestylishcity.com) Comprehensive listings of NYC sample sales.

Previous page: Brooklyn Flea (p159)
NIELSKLIIM/SHUTTERSTOCK ©

Harlem & Upper Manhattan
Tend to be locally minded, with shops
catering to a neighborhood crowd (p158)

Upper West Side & Central Park
Home to some great bookstores (new and used),
along with some little boutiques (p157)

Upper East Side
The country's most expensive boutiques
are found along Madison Ave (p157)

Midtown
Epic department stores, global chains
and the odd in-the-know treasure –
window shoppers unite! (p155)

West Village, Chelsea &
Meatpacking District
Bleecker St, running off Abingdon Sq, is lined with
boutiques, with a handful on nearby W 4th St (p153)

Union Square, Flatiron District & Gramercy
This big block of neighborhoods harbors a
sprinkling of NYC's most interesting stores (p154)

SoHo & Chinatown
West Broadway is chain heaven,
but it's SoHo and Nolita's boutiques that
make the area world-class for retail fans (p149)

East Village & Lower East Side
Hipster treasure trove of vintage wares
and design goods (p151)

Financial District & Lower Manhattan
While not a shopping hot spot per se, Lower
Manhattan serves up a trickle of gems (p148)

Brooklyn
A healthy mix of independent
boutiques and thrift stores (p158)

Opening Hours

In general, most businesses are open
from 10am to around 7pm on weekdays
and 11am to around 8pm Saturdays.
Sundays can be variable – some stores
stay closed while others keep weekday
hours. Stores tend to stay open later in
the neighborhoods downtown. Small
boutiques often have variable hours –
many open at noon.

Sales Seasons

Clothing sales usually happen at the end
of each season. Other big retail sales are
timed with long weekends such as Memorial Day and Labor Day. Black Friday
has become one of the biggest sales
of the year, occurring the Friday after
Thanksgiving; prepare for big crowds
on Fifth Ave. Typical discounts can be as
much as 30% to 50%.

The Best...

Shop till you drop in New York City's best stores.

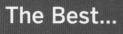

For Women

Shishi (p157) Get a new wardrobe without breaking the bank at this Upper West Side gem.

Galeria Melissa (p149) Stylish Brazilian-designed plastic footwear.

Resurrection (p150) Valhalla for lovers of designer vintage, and friendly staff to help you.

Barneys (pictured below; p156) Serious fashionistas shop at Barneys, well-known for its spot-on collections of in-the-know labels.

For Children

FAO Schwarz (pictured above; p156) New York institution with a new lease of life: nirvana for kids big and small.

Dinosaur Hill (p153) In the East Village, you'll find fun, creative toys, books and music to inspire young minds.

Yoya (p154) Small, pretty clothing store in the West Village.

For Men

By Robert James (p151) Rugged menswear by a celebrated local designer.

Nepenthes New York (p156) Japanese collective selling covetable labels.

New York Shaving Company (p149) Classic SoHo-inspired colognes and traditional shaving kit in a barbershop beloved by celebs.

Opening Ceremony (p150) Showstopping streetwear threads and a customization bar.

Homewares & Design

Shinola (p149) Unusual accessories.

Fishs Eddy (p154) Playful New York designs.

Guggenheim Store (p32) Homewares and objet d'arts inspired by artists.

Museum of Art & Design Store (p65) Striking bowls, vases and kitchen paraphernalia alongside affordable designer jewelry.

Bookshops

Strand Book Store (pictured above; p153) Hands-down NYC's best used bookstore.

Housing Works Bookstore (p150) Used books and a cafe in an atmospheric setting in Nolita.

192 Books (p153) The perfect neighborhood bookshop in Chelsea.

NYC Souvenirs

Lower East Side Tenement Museum (p94) Books, bags, scarves and more from the museum shop.

Strand Book Store (p153) An entire aisle dedicated to Americana and books about New York.

Artists & Fleas (pictured above; p158) Locally made jewelry, homewares and threads in a market environment.

Vintage Stores

Housing Works Thrift Shop (p153) Always a fun place to browse, with locations around the city.

Screaming Mimis (p154) Lots of appealing clothes from decades past.

Resurrection (pictured above; p150) Mint-condition pieces from couture labels.

★ Lonely Planet's Top Choices

Bergdorf Goodman (p155) The most magical of NYC's legendary department stores, with stellar store displays.

Brooklyn Flea (p159) Brooklyn's flea market offers plenty of vintage furnishings, retro clothing and bric-a-brac.

ABC Carpet & Home (p154) Spread over six floors like a museum, ABC is packed with treasures large and small.

MoMA Design & Book Store (p155) The perfect one-stop shop for coffee-table tomes, art prints and 'Where-did-you-get-that?' homewares.

FAO Schwarz (p156) New York's greatest toy shop has been reborn in the Rockefeller Center.

📍 Financial District & Lower Manhattan

Philip Williams Posters — Vintage
(Map p244; ☎212-513-0313; www.poster
museum.com; 122 Chambers St, btwn Church St
& W Broadway, Lower Manhattan; ⏰10am-7pm
Mon-Sat; 🚇A/C, 1/2/3 to Chambers St) You'll
find more than 100,000 posters dating
back to 1870 in this cavernous treasure
trove, from oversized French advertise-
ments for perfume and cognac to Eastern
European film posters and decorative Chinese *Nianhua* posters. Prices range from
$15 for small reproductions to thousands
of dollars for rare, showpiece originals
like an AM Cassandre. There's a second
entrance at 52 Warren St.

Century 21 — Fashion & Accessories
(Map p244; ☎212-227-9092; www.c21stores.
com; 22 Cortlandt St, btwn Church St & Broadway,
Financial District; ⏰7:45am-9pm Mon-Wed, to
9:30pm Thu & Fri, 10am-9pm Sat, 11am-8pm
Sun; 🚇A/C, J/Z, 2/3, 4/5 to Fulton St, R/W to
Cortlandt St) For frugal fashionistas, this
giant cut-price department store is danger-
ously addictive. It's physically dangerous
as well, considering the elbows you might
have to throw to ward off the competition
beelining for the same rack. Not everything
is a knockout or a bargain, but persistence
pays off. You'll also find bespoke tailoring,
accessories, shoes, cosmetics, homewares
and toys.

Pearl River Mart — Department Store
(Map p246; ☎212-431-4770; www.pearlriver.com;
395 Broadway, at Walker St, Tribeca; ⏰10am-
7:20pm; 🚇N/Q/R/W, J/M/Z, 6 to Canal St)
Pearl River has been a downtown shopping
staple since 1971, peddling a dizzying array
of Asian gifts, housewares, clothing and
accessories: silk men's pajamas, cheong-
sam dresses, blue-and-white Japanese
ceramic tableware, clever kitchen gadgets,
paper lanterns, origami and calligraphy kits,
bamboo plants and an abundance of lucky-
cat figurines. A great place for gifts.

Century 21

TUPUNGATO/SHUTTERSTOCK ©

Shinola Fashion & Accessories
(Map p246; ☏917-728-3000; www.shinola.
com; 177 Franklin St, btwn Greenwich & Hudson
Sts, Tribeca; ⏱11am-7pm Wed-Sat, to 6pm Sun,
10am-5pm Mon; Ⓢ1 to Franklin St) Well known
for its coveted wristwatches, Detroit-based
Shinola branches out with a super-cool
selection of made-in-USA life props. Bag
anything from leather tablet cases and
journal covers to jewelry, limited-edition
bicycles with customized bags and even
high-end turntables. Bonuses include
complimentary monogramming of leather
goods and stationery, and an in-house
artisan watchmaker.

🔒 SoHo & Chinatown

Galeria Melissa Shoes
(Map p246; ☏212-775-1950; www.melissa.com.
br/us/galerias/ny; 500 Broadway, btwn Broome
& Spring Sts, SoHo; ⏱10am-7pm Mon-Fri, to 8pm
Sat, 11am-7pm Sun; 🚻; Ⓢ6 to Spring St, R/W to
Prince St) This Brazilian designer specializes in downpour-friendly plastic footwear.
Recyclable, sustainable, stylish – women's
and kids' shoes run the gamut from mod
sandals to brogues, runners and, of course,
boots.

Saturdays Fashion & Accessories
(Map p246; ☏212-966-7875; www.saturdays
nyc.com; 31 Crosby St, btwn Broome & Grand Sts,
SoHo; ⏱store 10am-7pm, coffee bar 8am-6pm
Mon-Sat, 10am-6pm Sun; 🛜; Ⓢ N/Q/R/W, J/Z
to Canal St; 6 to Spring St) SoHo's version of a
surf shop sees boards and wax paired up
with designer grooming products, graphic
art and surf tomes, and Saturdays' own line
of high-quality, fashion-literate threads for
dudes. There's a second branch in the **West
Village** (Map p246; ☏347-246-5830; www.
saturdaysnyc.com; 17 Perry St, at Waverly St,
West Village; ⏱10am-7pm; ⓈA/C/E, L to 8th Ave-
14th St; 1/2/3 to 14th St).

**New York
Shaving Company** Health & Wellness
(Map p246; ☏212-334-9495; www.nyshaving
company.com; 202b Elizabeth St, btwn Prince &

💳 Sampling NYC's Sales

While clothing sales happen year-round,
sample sales are held frequently, mostly
in the huge warehouses in the Fashion
District of Midtown or in SoHo, and
often inside **Chelsea Market**. While
the original sample sale was a way for
designers to get rid of one-of-a-kind
prototypes that weren't quite up to
snuff, most sample sales these days are
for high-end labels to dispose of over-
stock at wonderfully deep discounts. For
the latest sample sales, check out *The
Stylish City* (www.thestylishcity.com).
Consignment stores are another fine
place to look for top (gently used) fashions at reduced prices; label hunters
find the Upper East Side prime territory,
with standouts like Michael's (p157).

Chelsea Market
YMGERMAN/SHUTTERSTOCK ©

Spring Sts, Nolita; ⏱11am-8pm Mon-Fri, from
10am Sat, 11am-7pm Sun; Ⓢ6 to Spring St, J/Z to
Bowery) This lovely male grooming shop was
founded by John Scala, a Brooklyn-born
Sicilian. Wooden cabinets display gorgeous
traditional grooming products, like beard
creams, shaving gels and razor kits, as well
as a series of colognes – the classic Elizabeth St fragrance is said to be a favorite of
Justin Timberlake.

Rag & Bone Fashion & Accessories
(Map p246; ☏212-219-2204; www.rag-bone.
com; 117-119 Mercer St, btwn Prince & Spring Sts,
SoHo; ⏱11am-8pm Mon-Sat, to 7pm Sun; ⓈR/W
to Prince St) Downtown label Rag & Bone
is a hit with many of New York's coolest,

Flea Markets & Vintage Adventures

As much as New Yorkers gravitate toward all that's shiny and new, it can be infinitely fun to riffle through closets of unwanted wares and threads. The most popular flea market is the Brooklyn Flea (p159), housed in all sorts of spaces throughout the year. Another gem is Artists & Fleas (p158), with scores of vendors, and there's also the weekly **Hell's Kitchen Flea Market** (Map p250; ☎212-220-0239; www.annexmarkets.com/hells-kitchen-foundation; W 39th St, btwn Ninth & Tenth Aves; 🕒9am-5pm Sat & Sun; [S]A/C/E to 42nd St-Port Authority Bus Terminal), slap-bang in the middle of Midtown. The East Village is the city's de facto neighborhood for secondhand and vintage stores – the uniform of the unwavering legion of hipsters.

Hell's Kitchen Flea Market
LIUZZI.PHOTOGRAPHY/SHUTTERSTOCK ©

sharpest dressers – both men and women. Detail-oriented pieces range from clean-cut shirts and blazers and graphic tees to monochromatic sweaters, feather-light strappy dresses, leather goods and Rag & Bone's highly prized jeans (from $200). Accessories include shoes, hats, bags and wallets.

Resurrection Vintage
(Map p246; ☎212-625-1374; www.resurrectionvintage.com; 45 Great Jones St, btwn Lafayette & Bowery Sts, NoHo; 🕒10am-6pm Mon-Fri, 11am-7pm Sat; [S]6 to Spring St; N/R to Prince St) Resurrection gives new life to cutting-edge designs from past decades. Striking, mint-condition pieces cover the eras of mod, glam-rock and new-wave design, and design deities such as Marc Jacobs have dropped by for inspiration. Top picks include Halston dresses, Courrèges coats and Jack Boyd jewelry.

MiN New York Cosmetics
(Map p246; ☎212-206-6366; www.min.com; 117 Crosby St, btwn Jersey & Prince Sts, SoHo; 🕒11am-7pm Tue-Sat, noon-6pm Sun & Mon; [S]B/D/F/M to Broadway-Lafayette St; N/R to Prince St) This chic, library-like fragrance apothecary has exclusive perfumes, bath and grooming products, and scented candles. Look out for artisanal fragrance 'stories' from MiN's own line. Prices span affordable to astronomical (from $70), and the scents are divine. Unlike many places, here there's no pressure to buy.

Opening Ceremony Fashion & Accessories
(Map p246; ☎212-219-2688; www.openingceremony.com; 35 Howard St, btwn Broadway & Lafayette St, SoHo; 🕒11am-8pm Mon-Sat, noon-7pm Sun; [S]N/Q/R/W, J/Z, 6 to Canal St) Opening Ceremony is famed for its never-boring edit of A-list indie and streetwear labels. It showcases a changing roster of names from across the globe, both established and emerging, catering for men, women and unisex; complementing them are Opening Ceremony's own avant-garde creations. No matter who's hanging on the racks, you can always expect showstopping, 'where-did-you-get-that?!' threads that are bold and refreshingly unexpected.

Housing Works Bookstore Books
(Map p246; ☎212-334-3324; www.housingworks.org/locations/bookstore-cafe; 126 Crosby St, btwn E Houston & Prince Sts, SoHo; 🕒10am-9pm Mon-Thu, to 6pm Fri-Sun; 📶; [S]B/D/F/M to Broadway-Lafayette St; N/R to Prince St) Relaxed, earthy and featuring a great selection of secondhand books, vinyl, CDs and comics you can buy for a good cause (proceeds go to the city's HIV-positive and AIDS-infected homeless population), this creaky hideaway is a very local place to while away a few quiet afternoon hours

Tictail Market

browsing, sitting in the on-site cafe, or rummaging in its adjoining thrift store.

🅐 East Village & Lower East Side

Russ & Daughters   Food
(Map p246; ☑212-475-4800; www.russand
daughters.com; 179 E Houston St, btwn Orchard &
Allen Sts, Lower East Side; ☺8am-6pm Fri-Wed,
to 7pm Thu; ⓈF to 2nd Ave) Since 1914 this
much-loved deli has served up Eastern
European Jewish delicacies, such as
caviar, herring, sturgeon and, of course, lox.
Perhaps the high-water mark of New York's
Jewish delis, it's a great place to load up for
a picnic or stock your fridge with breakfast
goodies. Foodies, history buffs and interior
designers will love it.

Tictail Market   Fashion & Accessories
(Map p246; ☑917-388-1556; www.tictail.com; 90
Orchard St, at Broome St, Lower East Side; ☺noon-
9pm Mon-Sat, to 6pm Sun; ⓈB/D to Grand St,
F, J/M/Z to Delancey-Essex Sts) Tictail Market
specializes in clothing, accessories, trinkets

and art from a global 'community' of artisans. All products are sourced directly from
the designers and artists, so you can be sure
you're supporting a small business with
each purchase. The collection is eclectic but
leans toward a cool, minimalist aesthetic.

Obscura Antiques   Antiques
(Map p246; ☑212-505-9251; www.obscura
antiques.com; 207 Ave A, btwn E 12th & E 13th
Sts, East Village; ☺noon-8pm Mon-Sat, to 7pm
Sun; ⓈL to 1st Ave) This trove of the eclectic
pleases both curio-lovers and inveterate
antique hunters. Here you'll find taxidermied animal heads, tiny rodent skulls and
skeletons, butterfly displays in glass boxes,
Victorian-era postmortem photography,
disturbing little (dental?) instruments, German land-mine flags, old poison bottles and
glass eyes. A six-series TV show, *Oddities,*
focuses on the shop, bizarre things, and
those who seek them.

By Robert James   Fashion & Accessories
(Map p246; ☑212-253-2121; www.byrobert
james.com; 74 Orchard St, btwn Broome & Grand

Top Five NYC Souvenirs

Guggenheim Mug

The Guggenheim's modernist ziggurat form has been stylishly applied to mugs, teapots and salt-and-pepper shakers in the museum shop (p78).

Distinctive Scents

Head to the New York Shaving Company (p149) for old-school colognes inspired by the streets of Little Italy.

Local Wears

Add something NYC-made to your wardrobe, like a Brooklyn hoodie from Artists & Fleas (p158).

Strand Books Totes & Tees

Stop by NYC's largest independent bookstore (p153) to get its iconic logo on a canvas tote bag or T-shirt.

NYC Skyline Christmas Decoration

If visiting in November or December, pick up a bauble from the Empire State (p66) shop.

Sts, Lower East Side; ⏰noon-8pm Mon-Sat, to 6pm Sun; [S]F, J/M/Z to Delancey-Essex Sts) Rugged, beautifully tailored menswear is the signature of Robert James, who sources and manufactures right in NYC (the design studio is just upstairs). The racks are lined with slim-fitting denim, handsome button-downs and classic-looking sports coats. Lola, James' black lab, sometimes roams the store.

Dinosaur Hill Toys

(Map p246; ☎212-473-5850; www.dinosaurhill.com; 306 E 9th St, btwn First & Second Aves, East Village; ⏰11am-7pm; 👪; [S]6 to Astor Pl) Through high windows glow the myriad colors of the handmade, unusual and stimulating items this small, old-fashioned and wholly wonderful toy store stocks. Czech marionettes, shadow puppets, micro building blocks, calligraphy sets, toy pianos, art and science kits, kids' music from around the globe, and wooden blocks in various languages, plus natural-fiber clothing for infants: there's so much to want.

🛍 West Village, Chelsea & Meatpacking District

Strand Book Store Books

(Map p246; ☎212-473-1452; www.strandbooks.com; 828 Broadway, at E 12th St, West Village; ⏰9:30am-10:30pm Mon-Sat, from 11am Sun; [S]L, N/Q/R/W, 4/5/6 to 14th St-Union Sq) Beloved and legendary, the iconic Strand embodies downtown NYC's intellectual bona fides – a bibliophile's Oz, where generations of book lovers carrying the store's trademark tote bags happily lose themselves for hours. In operation since 1927, the Strand sells new, used and rare titles, spreading an incredible 18 miles of books (over 2.5 million of them) among three labyrinthine floors.

Murray's Cheese Food & Drinks

(Map p246; ☎212-243-3289; www.murrayscheese.com; 254 Bleecker St, btwn Morton & Leroy Sts, West Village; sandwiches $7-8; ⏰8am-9pm Mon-Sat, 9am-8pm Sun; [S]A/C/E, B/D/F/M to W 4th St-Washington Sq, 1 to Christopher St-Sheridan Sq) Founded in 1940 by Spanish Civil War veteran Murray Greenberg, this is one of New York's best cheese shops. Former owner (now 'adviser') Rob Kaufelt is known for his talent for sniffing out the best curds from around the world: you'll find (and be able to taste) all manner of *fromage*, all aged in cheese caves on site and in Queens.

Meadow Chocolate

(Map p246; ☎212-645-4633; https://themeadow.com; 523 Hudson St, btwn W 10th & Charles Sts, West Village; ⏰11am-9pm Mon-Thu, to 10pm Fri & Sat, to 8pm Sun; [S]1 to Christopher St-Sheridan Sq) An import from Portland, this peaceful, pretty little shop is the place to go for single-origin chocolate, fine salt, honey and other pantry essentials. The owner selects exquisite chocolate from around the world (and has also written a 300-page book on salt). You may be offered hot, sticky chocolate (blended in-store), or popcorn generously sprinkled with truffle salt.

Housing Works Thrift Shop Vintage

(Map p250; ☎718-838-5050; www.housingworks.org; 143 W 17th St, btwn Sixth & Seventh Aves, Chelsea; ⏰10am-7pm Mon-Sat, noon-6pm Sun; [S]1 to 18th St) The flagship for 13 other branches around town, this shop with its swank window displays looks more boutique than thrift, but its selections of clothes, accessories, furniture, books and records are great value. It's the place to go to find discarded designer clothes for a bargain, and all proceeds benefit the charity serving the city's HIV-positive and AIDS-affected homeless communities.

192 Books Books

(Map p250; ☎212-255-4022; www.192books.com; 192 Tenth Ave, btwn W 21st & W 22nd Sts, Chelsea; ⏰11am-7pm; [S]1, C/E to 23rd St) This small indie bookstore in the thick of the gallery district has great selections of fiction, history, travel, art and criticism. Rotating art exhibits, during which the owners organize special displays of books related to the featured show or artist, are a special

New York Legends

A few stores have cemented their status as NYC legends. This city just wouldn't quite be the same without them. For label hunters, Century 21 (p148) is a Big Apple institution, with wears by D&G, Prada, Marc Jacobs and many others at low prices. Book lovers of the world unite at the Strand (p153), the city's biggest and best bookseller. Run by Hassidic Jews and employing mech-anized whimsy, B&H Photo Video is a mecca for digital and audio geeks. For secondhand clothing, home furnishings and books, good-hearted **Housing Works** (Map p252; ☏646-963-2665; http://shop.housingworks.org; 730-732 Ninth Ave, btwn 49th & 50th Sts, Midtown West; ☺noon-8pm Mon-Sat, to 6pm Sun; ⓈC/E to 50th St), with many locations around town, is a perennial favorite. Remember the legendary toy store where Tom Hanks danced on a floor piano in the movie *Big*? It was based on NYC's FAO Schwarz (p156), which was mourned when it closed in 2015 but in 2018 was resurrected in a magical new space in the Rockefeller Center.

Housing Works
NEW YORK CITY/ALAMY STOCK PHOTO ©

treat. Weekly readings feature acclaimed authors and intellectuals.

Screaming Mimis
Vintage

(Map p246; ☏212-677-6464; www.screaming mimis.com; 240 W 14th St, btwn Seventh & Eighth Aves, Chelsea; ☺noon-8pm Mon-Sat, 1-7pm Sun; ⓈA/C/E, L to 8th Ave-14th St) If you dig vintage, designer and rare threads, or flamboyant costumes, you may just scream, too. This funtastic shop carries an excellent selection of yesteryear pieces, organized by decade, from the '40s to the '90s. From prim beaded wool cardigans to suede minidresses, fluoro furs, white leather go-go boots, accessories and jewelry, the stock is in great condition.

Yoya
Children's Clothing

(Map p246; ☏646-336-6844; www.yoyanyc.com; 605 Hudson St, btwn Bethune & W 12th Sts, West Village; ☺11am-7pm Mon-Sat, noon-5pm Sun, shorter hours winter; ⓈA/C/E, L to 8th Ave-14th St) For well-made and stylishly curated kids' clothes and accessories, visit Yoya, which stocks such high-end brands as Bobo Choses, Bangbang Copenhagen and 1+ In The Family.

ⓕ Union Square, Flatiron District & Gramercy

Fishs Eddy
Homewares

(Map p250; ☏212-420-9020; www.fishseddy. com; 889 Broadway, at E 19th St, Union Sq; ☺10am-9pm Mon-Fri, to 8pm Sat-Sun; ⓈR/W, 6 to 23rd St) High-quality and irreverent design has made Fishs Eddy a staple in the homes of hip New Yorkers for years. Its store is a veritable landslide of cups, saucers, butter dishes, carafes and anything else that belongs in a cupboard. Styles range from tasteful color blocking to delightfully outrageous patterns.

ABC Carpet & Home
Homewares

(Map p250; ☏212-473-3000; www.abchome. com; 888 Broadway, at E 19th St; ☺10am-7pm Mon-Wed, Fri & Sat, to 8pm Thu, 11am-6pm Sun; Ⓢ4/5/6, N/Q/R/W, L to 14th St-Union Sq) A mecca for home designers and decorators brainstorming ideas, this beautifully curat-ed, seven-level temple to good taste heaves with all sorts of furnishings, small and large. Shop for easy-to-pack knickknacks, boho textiles and jewelry, as well as statement furniture, designer lighting, ceramics and antique carpets. Come Christmas the shop is a joy to behold and it's a great place to buy decorations.

ⓐ Midtown

MoMA Design
& Book Store   Gifts & Souvenirs

(Map p252; ☏212-708-9700; www.momas tore.org; 11 W 53rd St, btwn Fifth & Sixth Aves; ◷9:30am-6:30pm Sat-Thu, to 8pm Fri; Ⓢ E, M to 5th Ave-53rd St) The flagship store at the Museum of Modern Art (p32) is a fab spot for souvenir shopping. Besides gorgeous books (from art and architecture tomes to pop-culture readers and kids' picture books), you'll find art prints and posters and one-of-a-kind knickknacks. For furniture, lighting, homewares, jewelry, bags and arty gifts, head to the **MoMA Design Store** across the street.

Bergdorf
Goodman   Department Store

(Map p254; ☏212-753-7300; www.bergdorf goodman.com; 754 Fifth Ave, btwn W 57th & 58th Sts; ◷10am-9pm Mon-Fri, to 8pm Sat, 11am-8pm Sun; Ⓢ N/R/W to 5th Ave-59th St, F to 57th St) Not merely loved for its Christmas windows (the city's best), plush BG, at this location since 1928, leads the fashion race, led by its industry-leading fashion director Linda Fargo. A mainstay of ladies who lunch, its draws include exclusive collections and a coveted women's shoe department. The men's store is across the street.

Saks Fifth Ave   Department Store

(Map p252; ☏212-753-4000; www.saksfifth avenue.com; 611 Fifth Ave, at E 50th St; ◷10am-8:30pm Mon-Sat, 11am-7pm Sun; Ⓢ B/D/F/M to 47th-50th Sts-Rockefeller Center, E, M to 5th Ave-53rd St) Graced with vintage escalators, Saks' 10-floor flagship store is home to the 'Shoe Salon,' NYC's biggest women's shoe department (complete with express elevator and zip code). Other fortes include the revamped beauty floor and men's departments, the latter home to destination grooming salon John Allan's and a sharply edited offering of fashion-forward labels. The store's January sale is legendary.

Saks Fifth Ave

Bloomingdale's

Bloomingdale's Department Store

(Map p254; ☑212-705-2000; www.bloom
ingdales.com; 1000 Third Ave, at E 59th St;
⏰10am-8:30pm Mon-Sat, 11am-7pm Sun; 🛜;
Ⓢ4/5/6 to 59th St; N/R/W to Lexington Ave-59th
St) Blockbuster Bloomie's is something
like the Metropolitan Museum of Art of
the shopping world – historic, sprawling,
overwhelming and packed with bodies, but
you'd be sorry to miss it. Raid the racks
for clothes and shoes from a who's who of
US and global designers, including many
'new-blood' collections. Refueling pit stops
include a branch of cupcake heaven Mag-
nolia Bakery.

FAO Schwarz Toys

(Map p252; ☑800-326-8638; www.faoschwarz.
com; 30 Rockefeller Plaza; ⏰9am-10pm Mon-Sat,
from 11am Sun; ⓈB/D/F/M 47-50 Sts-Rockefeller
Center) New Yorkers mourned the loss of
this landmark toy store (c 1862) when it
closed its famed flagship on Fifth Ave in
2015 (this was where Tom Hanks played
a huge floor keyboard in the film *Big*). It was
resurrected in this new Rockefeller location
in 2018, looking jazzier than ever. Even the

giant floor piano for kids to dance over has
made a comeback.

Nepenthes
New York Fashion & Accessories

(Map p250; ☑212-643-9540; www.nepenthesny.
com; 307 W 38th St, btwn Eighth & Ninth Aves;
⏰noon-7pm Mon-Sat, to 5pm Sun; ⓈA/C/E to
42nd St-Port Authority Bus Terminal) Occupying
an old sewing machine shop in the Garment District, this cult Japanese collective
stocks edgy menswear from the likes of
Engineered Garments and Needles, known
for their quirky detailing and artisanal
production value, with a vintage-inspired
Americana workwear feel. Accessories
include bags and satchels, gloves, eyewear
and footwear.

Barneys Department Store

(Map p254; ☑212-826-8900; www.barneys.
com; 660 Madison Ave, at E 61st St; ⏰10am-8pm
Mon-Wed & Sat, to 9pm Thu & Fri, 11am-7pm Sun;
🛜; ⓈN/R/W to 5th Ave) Serious fashionistas
swipe their plastic at Barneys, respected
for its collections of top-tier labels like
Isabel Marant Étoile, Mr & Mrs Italy and

Lanvin – all spaced out adequately enough to show just how precious each collection is. If you're not armed with the big bucks, expect to find it a little intimidating.

⊕ Upper East Side

Michael's
Clothing

(Map p254; ☑212-737-7273; www.michaels consignment.com; 1125 Madison Ave, btwn E 84th & 85th Sts; ☺10am-6:30pm Mon-Sat, to 8pm Thu, noon-6pm Sun, closed Sun Jul & Aug; Ⓢ6 to 77th St) In operation since the 1950s and as of 2018 in a new street-facing location, this vaunted Upper East Side resale store features high-end labels, including Chanel, Gucci, Prada and Jimmy Choo. Almost everything on display is less than two years old. It's pricey but cheaper than shopping the flagship boutiques on Madison Ave.

⊕ Upper West Side & Central Park

Shishi
Fashion & Accessories

(Map p254; ☑646-692-4510; www.shishi boutique.com; 2488 Broadway, btwn 92nd & 93rd Sts; ☺11am-8pm Mon-Sat, to 7pm Sun; Ⓢ1/2/3 to 96th St) Shishi is a delightful Israeli-owned boutique stocking an ever-changing selection of stylish, affordable apparel: elegant sweaters, sleeveless shift dresses and eye-catching jewelry from Brazilian designers, among others. (All its clothes are wash-and-dry friendly too.) It's fun for browsing, and with the enthusiastic staff kitting you out in the glamorous changing area, you'll feel like you have your own personal stylist.

Zabar's
Food

(Map p254; ☑212-787-2000; www.zabars.com; 2245 Broadway, at W 80th St; ☺8am-7:30pm Mon-Fri, to 8pm Sat, 9am-6pm Sun; Ⓢ1 to 79th St) A bastion of gourmet kosher foodie-ism, this sprawling local market has been a neighborhood fixture since the 1930s. And what a fixture it is! It features a heavenly array of cheeses, meats, olives, caviar,

 New York's Landmark Department Stores

A tour of New York's legendary Midtown department stores is a quintessential pastime for shopping fans vacationing in the Big Apple, but don't be surprised if you quickly get retail fatigue in these giant emporiums. Most of them carry very similar selections of fashion, shoes, handbags and beauty products, at prices you would expect from the world's top designer labels. **Macy's** (Map p250; ☑212-695-4400; www.macys.com; 151 W 34th St, at Broadway; ☺10am-10pm Mon-Sat, 11am-9pm Sun; ⓈB/D/F/M, N/Q/R/W to 34th St-Herald Sq; A/C/E to Penn Station) is geared the most towards midrange shopping (tourists also get 10% off if you show ID at the in-house tourist office), while Bloomingdale's (p156) and Saks Fifth Ave (p155) have gorgeous heritage appeal. Barneys (p156) and Bergdorf Goodman (p155) are where the trendsetters and fashionistas come to browse eye-wateringly-priced show-stoppers. Visit these department stores because they are icons in their own rights, not because they truly represent New Yorkers' style or local designers.

Brooklyn (p159) and the area around SoHo are both hot spots for boutiques and markets, while New York's art and design museums all have wonderfully creative in-house shops selling everything from clocks to handmade jewelry, dinnerware and wall art.

Macy's

smoked fish, pickles, dried fruits, nuts and baked goods, including pillowy, fresh-out-of-the-oven *knishes* (Eastern European–style potato dumplings wrapped in dough).

🅗 Harlem & Upper Manhattan

Harlem Haberdashery   Fashion & Accessories

(📞646-707-0070; www.harlemhaberdashery.com; 245 Malcolm X Blvd, btwn 122nd & 123rd Sts, Harlem; ⊗noon-8pm Mon-Sat; Ⓢ2/3 to 125th St) Keep your wardrobe fresh at this uberhip uptown boutique, which has covetable apparel in all shapes and sizes. Lovely T-shirts, high-end sneakers, dapper woven hats are among the ever-changing collections.

🅑 Brooklyn

Artists & Fleas   Market

(Map p257; 📞917-488-4203; www.artistsandfleas.com; 70 N 7th St, btwn Wythe & Kent Aves, Williamsburg; ⊗10am-7pm Sat & Sun; Ⓢ L to

Bedford Ave) This exuberant flea market provides stripped-back vending space for more than 75 purveyors of vintage and craft wares. Clothing, records, paintings, photographs, hats, handmade jewelry, unique T-shirts and canvas bags, plus an in-store cafe and DJ – it's all here. Two locations in Manhattan are smaller but open daily, one in SoHo, the other inside the Chelsea Market (p113).

Dellapietras   Food

(Map p256; 📞718-618-9575; 193 Atlantic Ave, btwn Court & Clinton Sts, Downtown Brooklyn; sandwiches $12; ⊗10am-7pm Mon-Sat, to 5pm Sun; Ⓢ4/5 to Borough Hall) Meet the meat – dry-aged prominently in the front window of this outstanding deli-butcher. Great cuts of meat and sausages are augmented by charcuterie and a huge range of lovingly prepared food. Fried chicken, salads, stews and amazing carvery sandwiches make this an ideal lunch stop. The porchetta, broccoli rabe and pecorino sandwich is a thing of immense pleasure.

Brooklyn Flea

Brooklyn Flea Market

(Map p256; www.brooklynflea.com; 80 Pearl St, Manhattan Bridge Archway, Anchorage Pl, at Water St, Dumbo; ⏰10am-6pm Sun Apr-Oct; 👪; 🚌B67 to York/Jay Sts, [S]F to York St) Every Sunday from spring through early fall, numerous vendors sell their wares inside a giant archway under the Manhattan Bridge. There's everything from antiques to records, vintage clothes, homemade foods, quirky handicrafts, housewares and furniture. Locations can change, so check the website before you head out.

Rough Trade Music

(Map p257; ☎718-388-4111; www.roughtradenyc.com; 64 N 9th St, btwn Kent & Wythe Aves, Williamsburg; ⏰11am-11pm Mon-Sat, to 9pm Sun; 📶; [S]L to Bedford Ave) This 10,000-sq-ft record store – a London import – stocks deep racks of vinyl and CDs, music books and magazines, and clothing. It also has in-store DJs, listening stations, exhibitions, and coffee and doughnuts from the on-site Brompton Bike Cafe. A small stage hosts acts as diverse as Gang of Four and the Get Up Kids (tickets range from $10 to $42).

Desert Island Comics Comics

(Map p257; ☎718-388-5087; http://desertislandcomics.tumblr.com; 540 Metropolitan Ave, btwn Union Ave & Lorimer St, Williamsburg; ⏰2-7pm Mon, noon-8pm Tue-Fri & Sun, to 9pm Sat; 👪; [S]L to Lorimer St, G to Metropolitan Ave) Desert Island is a charming, well-curated indie comic-book shop located inside a former bakery. Inside, you'll find hundreds of comics, graphic novels, local zines, prints and handmade artists' books. Also on sale are original prints and lithographs by artists such as Adrian Tomine and Peter Bagge, while good tunes spin on the turntable in back.

Twisted Lily Perfume

(Map p256; ☎347-529-4681; www.twistedlily.com; 360 Atlantic Ave, btwn Bond & Hoyt Sts, Boerum Hill; ⏰12:30-7:30pm Wed-Sun; [S]F, G to Hoyt-Schermerhorn) Come out smelling like a rose (or, if you'd prefer, bergamot, clary sage or honeysuckle) from this 'fragrance boutique and apothecary' specializing in unusual scents from around the world. The attentive staff will help you shop by fragrance for personalized perfumes, scented candles, and skincare and grooming products.

Shopping in Brooklyn

Whatever your preferred flavor of retail therapy, Brooklyn's got it. Williamsburg and Greenpoint are full of home-design shops, vintage furniture and clothing stores, and indie boutiques, bookstores and record shops. In southern Brooklyn, you'll find some satisfying browsing (and good consignment) in the vicinity of Boerum and Cobble Hills. Atlantic Ave, running east to west near Brooklyn Heights, is sprinkled with antique stores, while Park Slope features a good selection of laid-back clothing shops.

Park Slope

SOLEPSIZM/SHUTTERSTOCK ©

Industry City Design

(☎718-736-2516; www.industrycity.com; 220 36th St, btwn Second & Third Aves, Sunset Park; ⏰9am-9pm; 📶; [S]D, N, R to 36th St) These six towering warehouses by the Brooklyn waterfront have been repurposed as a bustling hub of art, commerce and consumerism. Home to nonprofits, design studios, tech start-ups and many other kinds of enterprise, the 35-acre site also houses galleries, furniture and clothing stores, and plenty of fantastic food. The courtyards stage an ever-changing program of festivals, classes and performances.

BAR OPEN

Thirst-quenching venues, craft-beer culture and beyond

Bar Open

You'll find all species of thirst-quenching venues here, from historic dive bars to specialty taprooms and glamorous rooftop bars that feel suspended between the skyscrapers. Here in the land where the term 'cocktail' was born, mixed drinks are stirred with the utmost gravitas – NYC remains one of the hottest destinations for talented mixologists. Prohibition-style cocktail lounges and hidden speakeasies are all the rage. Then there's the legendary club scene, spanning everything from celebrity staples to gritty, indie hangouts. Head downtown or to Brooklyn for the parts of the city that, as they say, truly never sleep.

In This Section

Opening Hours

Opening times vary. While some dive bars open as early as 8am, most drinking establishments get rolling around 5pm. Numerous bars stay open until 4am, while others close around 1am early in the week and 2am from Thursday to Saturday. Clubs generally operate from 10pm to 4am or 5pm.

Harlem & Upper Manhattan
A burgeoning mix of fabulous live
music spots, speakeasy-style bars
and old-school dives (p174)

Upper West Side & Central Park
Not party central, but there are some beer halls
and wine bars worth checking out (p174)

Upper East Side
Traditionally the home of pricey,
luxe lounge bars, but downtown-cool
gastropubs are arriving (p173)

Midtown
Rooftop bars with skyline views, historic
cocktail salons and rough-and-ready
dive bars: welcome to Midtown (p172)

**West Village, Chelsea &
Meatpacking District**
Jet-setters flock here, with wine bars,
backdoor lounges and gay hangouts (p169)

Union Square, Flatiron District & Gramercy
Vintage drinking dens, swinging cocktail bars and
fun student hangouts – this trio spans all tastes (p171)

SoHo & Chinatown
Stylish cocktail lounges, a sprinkling of dives
and a few speakeasy-style bars (p167)

East Village & Lower East Side
Proud home of the original-flavor dive bar,
the East Village is brimming with options (p168)

**Financial District &
Lower Manhattan**
FiDi office slaves loosen their ties in
everything from specialist beer and brandy
bars to revered cocktail hot spots (p166)

Brooklyn
Offers everything on the nightlife
spectrum, with Williamsburg as its heart (p175)

Costs & Tipping

New York is an expensive place to drink,
so try to take advantage of happy hours
(usually from around 4pm to 6pm).
Beers start at around $8, a glass of wine
starts from $10 and specialty cocktails
usually cost $17 to $20.

Tip $1 per drink at the bar; $2 to $3 for
fancier cocktails. Sit-down bars with
waitstaff may expect a restaurant-style
18% to 20% tip.

Useful Websites

New York Magazine (www.nymag.
com/nightlife) Brilliantly curated
nightlife options by the people who
know best.

Thrillist (www.thrillist.com) A roundup
of what's hot or coming soon on the
NYC bar scene, including interviews
with industry peeps.

Urbandaddy (www.urbandaddy.com)
More up-to-the-minute info and a handy
'hot right now' list.

partyearth (www.partyearth.com/
new-york) Detailed club reviews from
some of the city's savviest party kids.

The Best...

Drinking and nightlife spots to sip the night away.

Cocktails

Bar Goto (p169) Lower East Side icon under the helm of Kenta Goto, New York's most famous mixologist.

Dead Rabbit (p166) Meticulously researched cocktails, punches and pop-inns – lightly hopped ales spiked with different flavors – in a snug FiDi den.

Employees Only (p169) Award-winning barkeeps and arresting libations.

Raines Law Room (p171) Well-composed cocktails from serious mixologists in a Prohibition-style den near Union Sq.

Dance Clubs & House DJs

Le Bain (pictured above; p171) Well-dressed crowds still pack this favorite.

Berlin (p169) Yesteryear's free-spirited dance days live on at this concealed East Village bolt-hole.

Bossa Nova Civic Club (p177) A hip little Bushwick haunt for those craving off-the-radar thrills.

Beer

Spuyten Duyvil (p177) A much-loved Williamsburg spot serving unique, high-quality crafts.

Harlem Hops (p175) Pair craft brews with spicy meat pies at Harlem's only 100% African American–owned beer bar.

Dead Rabbit (pictured above; p166) A world-class gem in the Financial District, with one floor dedicated to specialty beers.

Dive Bars

Cowgirl SeaHorse (p167) Always a good time at this nautically themed drinkery in Lower Manhattan.

Ear Inn (pictured above; p167) Expect friendly and diverse patrons at one of the oldest drinking establishments in NYC.

Montero Bar & Grill (p175) Ramshackle Brooklyn charm with cheap beer and karaoke.

Solo Travelers

Brandy Library (p166) Civilized Tribeca spot in which to take your time over top-shelf cognac, whiskey and brandy.

Spuyten Duyvil (pictured above; p177) Brooklyn beer bar with sociable locals.

Caledonia (p174) A long, comfortable bar staffed by folk who love to chat about whiskey, on the Upper East Side.

La Compagnie des Vins Surnaturels (p168) Frenchified Nolita wine cavern with bar-counter seating and a top-class list of wines by the glass.

Wine

La Compagnie des Vins Surnaturels (p168) A love letter to Gallic wines steps away from Little Italy.

Buvette (p170) A buzzing, candlelit wine bar on a tree-lined West Village street.

Immigrant (p169) Wonderful wines and service in a skinny East Village setting.

Classic Date Bars

Manhattan Cricket Club (p174) Intimate, handsomely designed cocktail spot in the Upper West Side.

Pegu Club (p167) Made-from-scratch concoctions in a Burma-inspired SoHo hideaway.

Maison Premiere (p175) Risqué New Orleans–style cocktail bar with oysters.

★ Lonely Planet's Top Choices

House of Yes (pictured above; p175) Unrivaled destination for a wild night out at this Bushwick warehouse space.

Apothéke (p167) An atmospheric lounge and former opium den with great cocktails hidden away in Chinatown.

Rue B (p169) An appealing little East Village venue with live jazz and a fun crowd.

Ear Inn (p167) Creaking old-school SoHo pub with jazz on Sundays and wooden tables.

Maison Premiere (p175) Absinthe, juleps and oysters shine bright at this Big Easy tribute in Williamsburg.

Financial District & Lower Manhattan

Dead Rabbit — Bar

(Map p244; ☎646-422-7906; www.deadrabbitnyc.com; 30 Water St, btwn Broad St & Coenties Slip, Financial District; ⏰Taproom 11am-4am, Parlor 11am-2:30pm & 5pm-2am Mon-Sat, 5pm-midnight Sun; [S]R/W to Whitehall St, 1 to South Ferry) Named for a feared 19th-century Irish American gang, this three-story drinking den is regularly voted one of the world's best bars. Hit the sawdust-sprinkled Taproom for specialty beers, historic punches and pop-inns (lightly soured ale spiked with different flavors). On the next floor there's the cozy Parlor, serving meticulously researched cocktails, and above that the reservation-only Occasional Room, 'for whiskey explorers.'

Pier A Harbor House — Bar

(Map p244; ☎212-785-0153; www.piera.com; 22 Battery Pl, Battery Park, Financial District; ⏰Harbor House 11am-midnight Sun-Wed, to 2am Thu-Sat, BlackTail 5pm-2am; 📶; [S]4/5 to Bowling Green, R/W to Whitehall St, 1 to South Ferry) Built in 1886 as the New York City Board of Dock Commissioners' Headquarters, Pier A is a super-spacious casual eating and drinking house right on New York Harbor. Go for a seat on the waterside deck in warm weather – picnic benches, sun umbrellas and the New York skyline create a brilliant spot for sipping craft beers or on-tap house cocktails.

Brandy Library — Cocktail Bar

(Map p246; ☎212-226-5545; www.brandylibrary.com; 25 N Moore St, btwn Varick & Hudson Sts, Tribeca; ⏰5pm-1am Sun-Wed, 4pm-2am Thu, 4pm-4am Fri & Sat; [S]1 to Franklin St) This brandy-hued bastion of brown spirits is the place to go for top-shelf cognac, whiskey and brandy. Settle into handsome club chairs facing floor-to-ceiling, bottle-lined shelves and sip your tipple of choice, paired with nibbles such as Gruyère-cheese puffs, hand-cut steak tartare and foie gras. Saturday nights are generally quieter than weeknights, making it a civilized spot for a weekend tête-à-tête.

Pier A Harbor House

ARTYOORAN/SHUTTERSTOCK ©

Smith & Mills Cocktail Bar

(Map p246; ☎212-226-2515; www.smithandmills.com; 71 N Moore St, btwn Hudson & Greenwich Sts, Tribeca; 🕒11am-2am Mon & Wed-Sun, to 3am Thu-Sat; [S]1 to Franklin St) Petite Smith & Mills ticks all the cool boxes: unmarked exterior, design-conscious industrial interior, and expertly crafted cocktails with a penchant for the classics. Space is limited, so head in early if you fancy kicking back on a plush banquette. A seasonal menu spans light snacks to a particularly notable burger adorned with caramelized onions.

Cowgirl SeaHorse Bar

(Map p244; ☎212-608-7873; www.cowgirlseahorse.com; 259 Front St, at Dover St, Lower Manhattan; 🕒11am-11pm Mon-Thu, to late Fri, 10am-late Sat, to 11pm Sun; [S]A/C, J/Z, 2/3, 4/5 to Fulton St) In an ocean of more serious bars and restaurants, Cowgirl SeaHorse is a party ship. Its ranch-meets-sea theme (wagon wheels and seahorses on the walls) and southern home cooking (blackened fish, oyster po'boy sliders, shrimp and grits etc) make it irresistibly fun. Live music on Monday, happy hour every day except Saturday and great frozen margaritas don't hurt, either.

SoHo & Chinatown

Ear Inn Pub

(Map p246; ☎212-226-9060; www.earinn.com; 326 Spring St, btwn Washington & Greenwich Sts, SoHo; 🕒bar 11:30am-4am, kitchen to 2am; 📶; [S]C/E to Spring St) Want to see what SoHo was like before the trendsetters and fashionistas? Come to the creaking old Ear Inn, proudly billed as one of the oldest drinking establishments in NYC. The house it occupies was built in the late 18th century for James Brown, an African aide to George Washington. Drinks are cheap and the crowd's eclectic.

Apothéke Cocktail Bar

(Map p246; ☎212-406-0400; www.apothekenyc.com; 9 Doyers St, Chinatown; 🕒6:30pm-2am Mon-Sat, from 8pm Sun; [S]J/Z to Chambers St; 4/5/6 to Brooklyn Bridge-City Hall) It takes a little effort to track down this former opium-den-turned-apothecary bar on Doyers St (look for the illustration of a beaker hanging above the doorway). Inside, skilled barkeeps work like careful chemists, using local, seasonal produce from Greenmarkets to produce intense, flavorful 'prescriptions.' The pineapple-cilantro spiced Sitting Buddha is one of the best drinks on the menu.

Clubbing in NYC

New Yorkers are always looking for the next big thing, so the city's club scene changes faster than a New York minute. Promoters entice revelers out all over the city for weekly events held at the finest addresses, and when there's nothing on, it's time to hit the dance floor stalwarts. When clubbing it never hurts to plan ahead; having your name on a guest list can relieve unnecessary frustration and disappointment. If you're an uninitiated partier, dress the part. If you're fed the 'private party' line, try to bluff – chances are high that you've been bounced. Also, don't forget a wad of cash as many nightspots (even the swankiest ones) often refuse credit cards, and in-house ATMs scam a fortune in fees.

ANGELINA PILARINOS/SHUTTERSTOCK ©

Pegu Club Cocktail Bar

(Map p246; ☎212-473-7348; www.peguclub.com; 2nd fl, 77 W Houston St, btwn W Broadway & Wooster St, SoHo; 🕒5pm-2am Sun-Wed, to 4am Thu-Sat; [S]B/D/F/M to Broadway-Lafayette St; C/E to Spring St, 1 to Houston St) Dark, elegant

Another Side of Gay New York

If Chelsea is a muscly, overachieving jock, then the Lower East Side is his wayward, punk younger brother. Amid the frat dives and cocktail lounges you'll find many gay bars catering to guys who prefer flannels and scruff to tank tops and six-pack abs. **Nowhere** (Map p246; ☎212-477-4744; www.nowherebarnyc.com; 322 E 14th St, btwn First & Second Aves, East Village; 🕒3pm-4am; [S]L to 1st Ave) and **Phoenix** (Map p246; ☎212-477-9979; www.phoenixbarnyc.com; 447 E 13th St, btwn First Ave & Ave A, East Village; 🕒3pm-4am; [S]L to 1st Ave) are great places to meet some new friendly faces, while the **Cock** (Map p246; 93 Second Ave, btwn E 5th & E 6th Sts, East Village; 🕒9pm-4am Mon & Tue, from 6pm Wed-Sun; [S]F/M to 2nd Ave) caters to a friskier crowd. The drinks are also typically much cheaper.

NICK BAYLIS/ALAMY STOCK PHOTO ©

Pegu Club (named after a gentleman's club in colonial-era Rangoon) is an obligatory stop for cocktail connoisseurs. Sink into a lounge chair and savor seamless libations such as the silky-smooth Earl Grey MarTEAni (tea-infused gin, lemon juice and raw egg white). Grazing options include chicken satay and crispy squid.

La Compagnie des Vins Surnaturels — Wine Bar

(Map p246; ☎212-343-3660; www.compagnienyc.com; 249 Centre St, btwn Broome & Grand Sts, Nolita; 🕒5pm-1am Mon-Wed, to 2am Thu & Fri, 3pm-2am Sat, to 1am Sun; [S]6 to Spring St; R/W to Prince St) A snug melange of Gallic-themed decor, svelte armchairs and tea lights, La Compagnie des Vins Surnaturels is an offshoot of a Paris bar by the same name. Head sommelier Theo Lieberman steers an impressive, French-heavy wine list, with some 600 drops and no shortage of arresting labels by the glass. A short, sophisticated menu includes housemade charcuterie and chicken rillettes.

Spring Lounge — Bar

(Map p246; ☎212-965-1774; www.thespringlounge.com; 48 Spring St, at Mulberry St, Nolita; 🕒8am-4am Mon-Sat, from noon Sun; [S]6 to Spring St; R/W to Prince St) This neon-red rebel has never let anything get in the way of a good time. In Prohibition days, it peddled buckets of beer. In the '60s its basement was a gambling den. These days, it's best known for its kooky stuffed sharks, early-start regulars and come-one, come-all late-night revelry. Perfect last stop on a bar-hopping tour of the neighborhood.

Ghost Donkey — Bar

(Map p246; ☎212-254-0350; www.ghostdonkey.com; 4 Bleecker St, NoHo; 🕒5pm-2am; [S]6 to Bleecker St; B/D/F/M to Broadway-Lafayette St) Rowdy meets trippy meets craft at this mezcal and tequila house, which gives vibes of Mexico, the Middle East and the Wild West. If the moon had a saloon, this place would fit right in. Yet it's more than just a gimme-a-shot-and-lime stop. The extensive mezcal and tequila menu is organized by region, and mezcal pours come with seasonal fruits and salts.

East Village & Lower East Side

Flower Shop — Bar

(Map p246; ☎212-257-4072; https://theflowershopnyc.com; 107 Eldridge St, btwn Grand & Broome Sts, Lower East Side; 🕒5pm-midnight Sun-Wed, to 2am Thu-Sat; [S]B/D to Grand St, J/Z to Bowery) Take the stairs under the humming restaurant of the same name to discover an eclectically furnished basement bar of such meticulously retro sensibility that you'll feel you've stumbled into a mash-up of your dad's pool room and your grandparents' 'best' room. The randomly assembled photos and posters often raise a smile, while flowery banquettes and good cocktails encourage lingering.

Sel Rrose Cocktail Bar

(Map p246; ☎212-226-2510; www.selrrose.com; 1 Delancey St, btwn Bowery & Chrystie St; 🕒cafe 9am-3pm Mon-Fri, bar & restaurant 4pm-late; [S]B/D to Grand St, F to Delancey St) You're likely to see quite a few people on dates at this downtown spot, which serves up clever cocktails and a wide selection of oysters and manages to exude quiet style despite its prominent corner location. It also happens to be right across the street from the **Bowery Ballroom** (Map p246; ☎800-745-3000, 212-533-2111; www.boweryballroom.com; 6 Delancey St, at Bowery, Lower East Side; [S]J/Z to Bowery, B/D to Grand St), making it perfect for a pre- or post-concert tipple.

Bar Goto Cocktail Bar

(Map p246; ☎212-475-4411; www.bargoto.com; 245 Eldridge St, btwn E Houston & Stanton Sts, Lower East Side; 🕒5pm-midnight Tue-Thu & Sun, to 2am Fri & Sat; [S]F to 2nd Ave) Maverick mixologist Kenta Goto has cocktail connoisseurs spellbound at his eponymous, intimate hot spot. Expect meticulous, elegant drinks that draw on Koto's Japanese heritage (the Umami Mary, with vodka, shiitake, dashi, miso, lemon, tomato and Clamato, is inspired), paired with authentic Japanese comfort bites, such as *okonomiyaki* (savory cabbage pancakes).

Rue B Bar

(Map p246; ☎212-358-1700; https://rueb-nyc.com; 188 Ave B, btwn E 11th & E 12th Sts, East Village; 🕒5pm-4am; [S]L to 1st Ave) There's live jazz (and the odd rockabilly group) every night from 9pm to midnight at this tiny, amber-lit drinking den on a bar-dappled stretch of Ave B. A musical, celebratory crowd packs the small space – so mind the tight corners, lest the trombonist end up in your lap. Photos and posters of jazz greats and NYC icons enhance the ambience.

Berlin Club

(Map p246; ☎reservations 347-586-7247; www.berlinundera.com; 25 Ave A, btwn E 1st & E 2nd Sts, East Village; occasional cover $5; 🕒8pm-4am; [S]F to 2nd Ave) This brick-vaulted cavern beneath Ave A does its best to hide – access is through an unmarked door behind a cafe that seems to occupy its (Berlin's) address, then steep stairs lead down into a dim, riotous indie lair. Once you're in, enjoy a night of rock, funk, disco, house and other party tunes in close proximity with your fellow revelers.

Immigrant Bar

(Map p246; ☎646-308-1724; www.theimmigrantnyc.com; 341 E 9th St, btwn First & Second Aves, East Village; 🕒5pm-2am; [S]L to 1st Ave, 6 to Astor Pl) Combining wine bar and taproom within the intimate geometry of a 19th-century tenement building, this timber-floored little charmer has all the makings of a classic neighborhood local. The staff are knowledgeable and kind, mingling with faithful regulars while dishing out tangy olives and topping up glasses with imported snifters.

🍷 West Village, Chelsea & Meatpacking District

Employees Only Bar

(Map p246; ☎212-242-3021; www.employeesonlynyc.com; 510 Hudson St, btwn W 10th & Christopher Sts, West Village; 🕒6pm-4am; [S]1 to Christopher St-Sheridan Sq) This divine cocktail bar, tucked behind a discreet green awning on Hudson St, is a world-beater. Ace mixologists shake up crazy, addictive libations like the Ginger Smash, and the wood-rich art-deco space makes everyone feel glamorous. Open until 3:30am, the kitchen plays its part, too, producing delights such as bone-marrow poppers and spicy shrimp on polenta (mains $27 to $31).

PATTI MCCONVILLE/ALAMY STOCK PHOTO ©

Birreria

Buvette Wine Bar

(Map p246; ☎212-255-3590; www.ilovebuvette.com; 42 Grove St, btwn Bedford & Bleecker Sts, West Village; small plates $12-18; ⏰7am-2am; [S]1 to Christopher St-Sheridan Sq, A/C/E, B/D/F/M to W 4th St-Washington Sq) Buzzing with the animated conversation of locals, courting couples and theater types, this devotedly Francophile wine bar and restaurant makes a great rest stop amid a West Village back-street wander. Enjoy a cocktail or a glass of wine, or settle in for a meal. Brunch dishes such as croque monsieurs are replaced by tartines and small plates at dinner.

Pier 66 Maritime Bar

(Map p250; ☎212-989-6363; www.pier66maritime.com; Pier 66, at W 26th St, Chelsea; ⏰noon-midnight May-Sep & warm days Apr & Oct; [S]1, C/E to 23rd St) Salvaged from the bottom of the sea (or at least the Chesapeake Bay), the lightship *Frying Pan* and the two-tiered dockside bar where it's moored are fine go-to spots for a sundowner. On warm days the rustic open-air space brings in the crowds, who laze on deck chairs and drink ice-cold beers ($7/25 for a microbrew/pitcher).

Cubbyhole LGBT

(Map p246; ☎212-243-9041; www.cubbyholebar.com; 281 W 12th St, at W 4th St, West Village; ⏰4pm-4am Mon-Fri, from 2pm Sat & Sun; [S]A/C/E, L to 8th Ave-14th St) This West Village dive bills itself as 'lesbian, gay and straight friendly since 1994.' While the crowd is mostly ladies, it welcomes anyone looking for a drink in good company beneath a ceiling festooned with lanterns, toys and other ephemera. It's got a great jukebox, friendly bartenders and plenty of regulars who prefer to hang and chat rather than hook up and leave.

Eagle NYC Gay

(Map p250; ☎646-473-1866; www.eagle-ny.com; 554 W 28th St, btwn Tenth & Eleventh Aves, Chelsea; ⏰10pm-4am Mon-Wed, from 7pm Thu-Sat, from 5pm Sun; [S]1, C/E to 23rd St) A relocation of the original leather bar of the same name, the Eagle is the choice for out-and-proud fetishists. Its two levels, roof deck and 'dark and sleazy' vibe are perfect for dancing, drinking and cruising, all done with abandon. There are frequent theme nights, so check the website lest you arrive without the appropriate attire (which may be nothing).

Marie's Crisis   Bar

(Map p246; ☎212-243-9323; www.mariescrisis.us; 59 Grove St, btwn Seventh Ave & Bleecker St, West Village; ◎4pm-3am Sun-Thu, to 4am Fri & Sat; Ⓢ1 to Christopher St-Sheridan Sq, A/C/E, B/D/F/M to W 4th St-Washington Sq) Ageing Broadway queens, wide-eyed out-of-town youngsters, giggly tourists and various other fans of musical theater assemble around the piano here and take turns belting out campy show tunes, often joined by the entire crowd – and the occasional celebrity. It's old-school fun, no matter how jaded you might be when you go in. Non-flash photography is allowed, but video is not.

Le Bain   Club

(Map p246; ☎212-645-7600; www.standard hotels.com; Standard, 848 Washington St, at 13th St, Meatpacking District; ◎10pm-midnight Mon, 4pm-4am Tue-Thu, 2pm-4am Fri & Sat, 2pm-3am Sun; Ⓢ A/C/E, L to 8th Ave-14th St) This sweeping rooftop venue at the painfully hip Standard hotel sees a garish parade of party promoters who do their thing on any day of the week. Brace yourself for skyline views, a giant Jacuzzi on the dance floor, legendary DJs such as Tony Humphries and Danny Krivit and an eclectic crowd getting wasted on pricey snifters.

❼ Union Square, Flatiron District & Gramercy

Raines Law Room   Cocktail Bar

(Map p250; www.raineslawroom.com; 48 W 17th St, btwn Fifth & Sixth Aves, Flatiron District; ◎5pm-2am Mon-Thu, to 3am Fri & Sat, to 1am Sun; Ⓢ F/M to 14th St, L to 6th Ave, 1 to 18th St) A sea of velvet drapes and overstuffed leather lounge chairs, the perfect amount of exposed brick, expertly crafted cocktails using hard-to-find spirits – these folks are as serious as a mortgage payment when it comes to amplified atmosphere. There's no sign from the

street; look for the '48' above the door and ring the bell to gain entry.

Birreria   Rooftop Bar

(Map p250; ☎212-937-8910; www.eataly.com; 200 Fifth Ave, at W 23rd St, Flatiron District; ◎11:30am-11pm; Ⓢ F/M, R/W, 6 to 23rd St) The crown jewel of Italian food emporium Eataly (p133) is this covered rooftop garden tucked between the Flatiron's corporate towers. The theme is refreshed each season, meaning you might find a Mediterranean beach escape one month and an alpine country retreat the next, but the setting is unfailingly impressive and food and drink always matches up to the gourmet goodies below.

Lillie's Victorian Establishment   Bar

(Map p250; ☎212-337-1970; www.lilliesnyc.com; 13 E 17th St, btwn Broadway & Fifth Ave, Union Sq; ◎11am-4am; Ⓢ 4/5/6, L, N/Q/R/W to 14th St-Union Sq) Step in and be taken to the era of petticoats and watch fobs with high, stamped-tin ceilings, red-velvet love seats and walls covered in vintage photographs in extravagant gilded frames – Lillie's feels every bit the traditional British watering hole without falling into parody. Pub grub such as shepherds pie helps fulfill the fantasy.

Old Town Bar & Restaurant   Bar

(Map p250; ☎212-529-6732; www.oldtownbar .com; 45 E 18th St, btwn Broadway & Park Ave S, Union Sq; ◎11:30am-11:30pm Mon-Fri, noon-11:30pm Sat, to 10pm Sun; ☎; Ⓢ 4/5/6, N/Q/R/W, L to 14th St-Union Sq) It still looks like 1892 in here, with the mahogany bar, original tile floors and tin ceilings – the Old Town is an old-world drinking-man's classic (and -woman's: Madonna lit up at the bar

★ Top Five Rooftop Bars

Cantor Roof Garden Bar (p173)

Empire Rooftop (p174)

Bar SixtyFive (p172)

Top of the Strand (p172)

Birreria (p171)

here – when lighting up in bars was still legal – in her 'Bad Girl' video). Most people come for beers and a burger (from $12.50).

Midtown

The Campbell Cocktail Bar

(Map p252; ☎212-297-1781; www.thecampbellnyc.com; D Hall, Grand Central Terminal; 🕑noon-2am; [S]S, 4/5/6, 7 to Grand Central-42nd St) In 1923 this hidden-away hall was the office of American financier John W Campbell. It later became a signalman's office, a jail and a gun storage before falling into obscurity. In 2017 it was restored to its original grandeur, complete with the stunning hand-painted ceiling and Campbell's original safe in the fireplace. Come for cocktails and you'll feel like you're waiting for Rockefeller or Carnegie to join you.

Bar SixtyFive Cocktail Bar

(Map p252; ☎212-632-5000; www.rainbowroom.com/bar-sixty-five; 30 Rockefeller Plaza, entrance on W 49th St; 🕑5pm-midnight Mon-Fri, 4-9pm Sun, closed Sat; [S]B/D/F/M to 47th-50th Sts-Rockefeller Center) Sophisticated SixtyFive sits on level 65 of the GE Building at Rockefeller Center (p225), making it the highest vantage point in Midtown that doesn't require a ticket. Views are undeniably breathtaking, but at peak times it can feel like a cattle market: walk-ins are herded into a central standing area. If you want to sit down by a window, you'll need to reserve a table.

Top of the Strand Cocktail Bar

(Map p250; ☎646-368-6426; www.topofthestrand.com; Marriott Vacation Club Pulse, 33 W 37th St, btwn Fifth & Sixth Aves, Midtown East; 🕑5pm-to 1am Tue-Sat, to midnight Sun & Mon; 📶; [S]B/D/F/M, N/Q/R to 34th St) For that 'oh my God, I'm in New York' feeling, head to the Marriott Vacation Club Pulse (formerly the Strand) hotel's rooftop bar, order a martini (extra dirty) and drop your jaw (discreetly). Sporting comfy cabana-style seating, a refreshingly mixed-age crowd and a retractable glass roof, its view of the Empire State Building is simply unforgettable.

The Campbell

HEMIS/ALAMY STOCK PHOTO ©

❸ Upper East Side

Cantor Roof Garden Bar   Rooftop Bar

(Map p254; ☑212-570-3711; www.metmuseum.
org/visit/dining; Metropolitan Museum, 1000
Fifth Ave, 5th fl, at E 82nd St; ⏲11am-4:30pm
Sun-Thu, to 8:15pm Fri & Sat mid-Apr–Oct; 🚇;
Ⓢ4/5/6 to 86th St) The sort of setting you
can't get enough of (even if you are a jaded
local). Located atop the Met, this rooftop
bar sits right above Central Park's tree
canopy, allowing for splendid views of the
park and the city skyline all around. Sunset
is when you'll find fools in love...then again,
it could all be those martinis.

UES NYC   Cocktail Bar

(Map p254; ☑646-559-5889; www.theuesnyc.
com; 1707 Second Ave, btwn E 88th & 89th Sts;
⏲5pm-late Mon-Sat; ⓈQ to 86th St) Scooping
delicious ice cream by day, this candy-
colored parlor lets rip as a speakeasy by
night. Cocktails are named after Upper
East Side landmarks, such as 'Meet me at
the Met' and '2nd Avenue Subway.' Beware:
there's a dress code, so no sneakers, flip-
flops, ripped jeans or T-shirts.

Entrance to the dimly lit 'Storage Room'
is through the wall of ice-cream tubs at the
back of the shop. On Sundays it becomes a
cinema from 6pm.

Bemelmans Bar   Lounge

(Map p254; ☑212-744-1600; www.thecarlyle.
com; Carlyle Hotel, 35 E 76th St, at Madison Ave;
⏲noon-1:30am; Ⓢ6 to 77th St) Sink into a
chocolate-leather banquette and take in
the glorious, old-school elegance at this
atmospheric bar – the sort of place where
the waiters wear white jackets and serve
martinis, a pianist tinkles on a baby grand
and the ceiling is 24-carat gold leaf. The
walls are covered in charming murals by
the bar's namesake Ludwig Bemelmans,
famed creator of the *Madeline* books.

Flora Bar   Bar

(Map p254; ☑646-558-5383; www.florabarnyc.
com; Met Breur, 945 Madison Ave, lower fl, at E
75th St; ⏲bar 11:30am-10pm Tue-Sat, to 9pm
Sun, cafe 10am-5:30pm Tue-Sun; 🚇; Ⓢ6 to 77th

Brooklyn Brews

Beer brewing was once a thriving industry in the city – by the 1870s, Brooklyn
boasted a belly-swelling 48 breweries. By
the eve of Prohibition in 1919, the borough
was one of the country's leading beer
peddlers, but by the end of Prohibition in
1933, most breweries had shut shop.

Though the industry rose from the
ashes in WWII, local flavor gave in to
big-gun Midwestern brands. Today, New
York's craft beer scene is still lagging behind that of the West Coast, but Brooklyn
is becoming a catchword for good beer
as a handful of craft breweries put
integrity back on tap. Head of the pack is
Williamsburg's **Brooklyn Brewery** (www.
brooklynbrewery.com), whose seasonal
offerings include a nutmeg-spiked Post
Road Pumpkin Ale (available August
to November) and a luscious Black
Chocolate Stout (a take on Imperial
Stout, available October to March). The
brewery's comrades-in-craft include **Six
Point Craft Ales** (www.sixpoint.com),
which hopes to open a taproom and offer
tours of its brewing facility in the near future, and **Threes Brewing** (www.threes
brewing.com), which operates two bars
(in Gowanus and Greenpoint). There's
also **Other Half Brewing Co** (www.
otherhalfbrewing.com), which is famed
for its Imperial IPA Green Diamonds.

Brooklyn Brewery

St; Q to 72nd St) Forget the fact that this is essentially a museum bar in the **Met Breuer**
(Map p254; ☑212-731-1675; www.metmuseum.

org/visit/met-breuer; 3-day pass adult/senior/child $25/$17/free; pay-as-you-wish for NY State residents; ⏰10am-5:30pm Tue-Thu & Sun, to 9pm Fri & Sat); Flora is a sophisticated drinking lounge that shows off the building's architectural extravagance. Park yourself at the marble bar or curl into a deep modernist armchair to marvel at the double-story concrete cathedral and gigantic glass wall that leads to a sunken garden: an oasis beneath Madison Ave.

Caledonia Bar

(Map p254; ☎212-734-4300; www.caledoniabar.com; 1609 Second Ave, btwn E 83rd & 84th Sts; ⏰5pm-4am Mon-Thu, 4pm-4am Fri-Sun, happy hour to 7pm Mon-Fri; [S]Q, 4/5/6 to 86th St) The name of this unpretentious, dimly lit bar is a dead giveaway: it's devoted to Scotch whisky, with over a hundred single malts to choose from (be they Highlands, Islands, Islay, Lowlands or Speyside), as well as some blends and even a few from the US, Ireland and Japan. The bartenders know their stuff and will be happy to make recommendations.

Upper West Side & Central Park

Manhattan Cricket Club Lounge

(Map p254; ☎646-823-9252; www.mccnewyork.com; 226 W 79th St, btwn Amsterdam Ave & Broadway; ⏰6pm-late Mon-Sat; [S]1 to 79th St) Above Australian bistro **Burke & Wills** (Map p254; ☎646-823-9251; www.burkeandwillsny.com; mains $19-32; ⏰dinner 5:30-11pm, brunch 11am-3pm Sat & Sun) (ask its host for access), this elegant drinking lounge is modeled on the classy Anglo-Aussie cricket clubs of the early 1900s. Sepia-toned photos of batsmen adorn the gold-brocaded walls, while mahogany bookshelves and Chesterfield sofas create a fine setting for quaffing well-made and inventive cocktails.

Empire Rooftop Rooftop Bar

(Map p254; ☎212-265-2600; www.empirehotelnyc.com; 44 W 63 St, at Broadway; ⏰3pm-1am Mon-Wed, to 2am Thu & Fri, 11am-2am Sat, to 1am Sun; [S]1 to 66th St-Lincoln Center) Sprawled across the top of the Empire Hotel, this stylish rooftop bar is one of New York's most expansive drinking spaces in the sky at 8000 sq ft. A bright, glass-roofed wing strewn with palms and sofas is perfect for winter and has a retractable roof for summer, and there's a handful of outdoor terraces.

Harlem & Upper Manhattan

Shrine Bar

(www.shrinenyc.com; 2271 Adam Clayton Powell Jr Blvd, btwn 133rd & 134th Sts, Harlem; ⏰4pm-4am; [S]2/3 to 135th St) Don't fret that it looks like a dive from outside: friendly, unpretentious Shrine is one of the best places in Harlem (if not New York) to hear live bands without a cover charge. Musicians take to its small stage every day of the week with blues, reggae, Afro-beat, funk, and indie rock. Beer is cheap and the crowd is as eclectic as the music.

Silvana Bar

(www.silvana-nyc.com; 300 W 116th St, Harlem; ⏰upstairs 7am-4am, downstairs from 4pm; [S]2/3 to 116th St) This appealing Middle Eastern cafe and shop whips up tasty hummus and falafel plates; the real draw, though, is the hidden downstairs club, which draws a friendly, easygoing local crowd with good cocktails and live bands (kicking off around 6pm) followed by DJs. The lineup is anything-goes, with jazz, Cuban *son*, reggae and Balkan gypsy punk all in the rotation.

Ginny's Supper Club Cocktail Bar

(☎212-421-3821; www.ginnyssupperclub.com; 310 Malcolm X Blvd, btwn W 125th & 126th Sts, Harlem; cover charge $25; ⏰6pm-midnight Thu, to 3am Fri & Sat, brunch 10:30am-12:30pm Sun; [S]2/3 to 125th St) Looking straight out of the TV series *Boardwalk Empire*, this roaring basement supper club is rarely short of styled-up regulars sipping cocktails, nibbling on soul and global bites – from the Red Rooster (p139) kitchen upstairs – and grooving to live jazz from 7:30pm Thursday

House of Yes

GUILLAUME GAUDET/LONELY PLANET ©

to Saturday and DJ-spun beats from 11pm Friday and Saturday. Don't miss the weekly Sunday gospel brunch (reservations recommended).

Harlem Hops Craft Beer

(☎646-998-3444; www.harlemhops.com; 2268 Adam Clayton Powell Jr Blvd, btwn 133th & 134th Sts, Harlem; 🕐4pm-midnight Sun-Thu, to 2am Fri & Sat; 📶; [S]2/3 to 135th St) Harlem's only 100% African American–owned beer bar has its home 'hood emblazoned on the ceiling in neon lights, and bratwurst and meat pies on the menu. Order a $15 beer paddle of four 5oz pours, pair with a habanero beef pie with African spices, and settle in.

🍸 Brooklyn

House of Yes Club

(www.houseofyes.org; 2 Wyckoff Ave, at Jefferson St, Bushwick; tickets free-$55; 🕐usually 7pm-4am Wed-Sat; [S]L to Jefferson St) Anything goes at this hedonistic warehouse venue, with two stages, three bars and a covered outdoor area that offers some of the most creative themed performance and dance nights in Brooklyn. You might see aerial-silk acrobats, punk bands, burlesque shows, drag queens or performance artists, or DJs as revered as Jellybean Benitez spinning disco, soul, house and other delights.

Montero Bar & Grill Bar

(Map p256; ☎646-729-4129; 73 Atlantic Ave, at Hicks St, Brooklyn Heights; 🕐noon-4am; [S]4/5 to Borough Hall) Montero's is the real deal: an anachronistic, neon-fronted, Pabst-peddling longshoreman's bar that's weathered every change thrown at this corner of Brooklyn since WWII. Its eclectic decor recalls the maritime types who once drank here.

Maison Premiere Cocktail Bar

(Map p257; ☎347-335-0446; www.maisonpremiere.com; 298 Bedford Ave, btwn S 1st & Grand Sts, Williamsburg; 🕐2pm-2am Mon-Wed, to 4am Thu & Fri, 11am-4am Sat, to 2am Sun; [S]L to Bedford Ave) The interior of this New Orleans–style oyster and cocktail bar must be appreciated: antique photos, elegant glassware, bentwood chairs and stripped surfaces all add to a sense of occasion.

New York City in a Glass

One part gin

One part Campari

One part
sweet vermouth

At NYC's trendy cocktail
lounges, it'll come with
a solitary brick of ice

Garnish with an
orange slice or twist

Always served short

Best NYC Negroni

SERHIY SHULLY/SHUTTERSTOCK ©

Revival of a Classic

Take the worldwide gin craze and
shake it up with a splash of NYC Italian
heritage, and it's obvious why New York
mixologists have fallen back in love with
the negroni. Served short and strong,
this grown-up cocktail is entirely savory.
It is classically made with gin, but
New York's creative barkeeps are also
serving versions mixed with mezcal for a
uniquely North American taste.

JACOB LUND/SHUTTERSTOCK ©

★ Top Places for a Negroni

Amor y Amargo (Map p246; ☏ 212-614-
6818; www.amoryamargony.com; 443 E
6th St, btwn Ave A & First Ave, East Village;
⊘ 5pm-1am Mon-Thu, to 3am Fri, 3pm-3am
Sat, 3pm-1am Sun; 𝕊 F to 2nd Ave; L to 1st
Ave; 6 to Astor Pl) A tiny 'bitters tasting
room' that faithfully sticks to the classic.

Bathtub Gin (Map p250; ☏ 646-559-1671;
www.bathtubginnyc.com; 132 Ninth Ave, btwn
W 18th & W 19th Sts, Chelsea; ⊘ 5pm-2am
Sun-Wed, to 3am Thu, to 4am Fri, 4pm-4am
Sat, noon-4pm Sun; 𝕊 A/C/E, L to 8th Ave-
14th St, 1, C/E to 23rd St, 1 to 18th St) Seasonal negronis in a hidden speakeasy
gin bar.

Ghost Donkey (p168) This SoHo mezcal bar mixes its negronis with mezcal
and mole spices.

Oysters and clams from around the country are flown in especially to be eaten fresh by the dressed-up crowd, who order cocktails with confidence from the natty, suspender-wearing bar staff.

Bossa Nova Civic Club Club

(☎718-443-1271; 1271 Myrtle Ave, at Hart St, Bushwick; occasional cover $10; 🕐7pm-4am; [S]M to Central Ave) Yet another reason you never need to leave Brooklyn, this smallish hole-in-the-wall club is a great place to get your groove on, with DJs spinning house and techno in a (somewhat) tropical-themed interior. There's a great sound system, fairly priced drinks and a celebratory crowd that's there to dance. A $10 cover applies after midnight on Friday and Saturday.

Desnuda Bar

(Map p257; ☎718-387-0563; www.desnudawbk.com; 221 S 1st St, btwn Roebling St & Driggs Ave, Williamsburg; raw bar items $16-18, mains $22-24; 🕐6pm-midnight Mon-Thu, to 2am Fri & Sat, 5-11pm Sun; [S]G to Metropolitan Ave, L to Bedford Ave) Slurp down briny oysters, sweet clams, tangy ceviches and well-matched wines at this charming wine bar and *cevicheria,* an outpost of the East Village original. Sitting on 18 seats at the raw bar, diners connect with the chefs tailoring their meal. Come Sunday or Monday for $1 oysters and cheap drinks, or get the same deal from 6pm to 8pm nightly.

Spuyten Duyvil Bar

(Map p257; ☎718-963-4140; www.spuytenduyvilnyc.com; 359 Metropolitan Ave, btwn Havemeyer & Roebling Sts, Williamsburg; 🕐5pm-2am Mon-Fri, noon-3am Sat, to 2am Sun; [S]L to Lorimer St, G to Metropolitan Ave) This low-key Williamsburg bar looks as though it was pieced together from a rummage sale, with red-painted pressed-tin ceilings, medical charts and vintage bikes on the walls, and mismatched thrift-store furniture. But the selection of beer (Belgian especially) is staggering, the mixed-age crowd is sociable and there's a large, leafy backyard that's open in good weather.

Lavender Lake Pub

(Map p256; ☎347-799-2154; www.lavenderlake.com; 383 Carroll St, btwn Bond St & Gowanus Canal, Gowanus; 🕐4pm-midnight Mon-Thu, to 2am Fri, noon-2am Sat, to 10pm Sun; [S]F, G to Carroll St, R to Union St) This gem of a bar – named after the colorfully polluted Gowanus Canal – is set in a former stable and serves carefully selected craft beers and a few seasonal cocktails mixed from ingredients such as jalapeño-infused tequila. The lumber-decked garden is a brilliant spot in summer, and there's always good food (mains $13 to $15). Weekday happy hour runs until 7pm.

June Wine Bar

(Map p256; ☎917-909-0434; www.junebk.com; 231 Court St, btwn Warren & Baltic Sts, Cobble Hill; happy hour 5-7pm Mon-Fri, brunch 11am-4pm Sat & Sun, dinner 5:30pm-midnight Sun-Thu, to 1am Fri & Sat; [S]F, G to Bergen St) Seductive use of curved, polished wood, leadlighting and inviting niches make June a delightful place to linger over interesting natural wines from Europe, America and Australia. Dishes such as raw fluke with apple, kohlrabi, *yuzu* vinaigrette and lemon verbena prove that the food's no afterthought (mains $26 to $28). The doors to a lovely terrace are flung open when it's warm.

Clover Club Cocktail Bar

(Map p256; ☎718-855-7939; www.cloverclubny.com; 210 Smith St, near Baltic St, Cobble Hill; 🕐4pm-2am Mon-Thu, to 4am Fri, 10:30am-4am Sat, to 1am Sun; 🚌B57 to Smith & Douglass Sts, [S]F, G to Bergen St) This delightful cocktail parlor exudes 19th-century elegance with its rich mahogany bar, vintage fixtures and vest-wearing barkeeps. Beautifully prepared cocktails draw in a mostly local crowd, here for lively conversation fueled by creations such as the 'Smash of the Titans' (bourbon, muddled kumquats, lemon, oregano). Clover also serves big weekend brunches matched with excellent Bloody Marys and other 'brunch cocktails.'

SHOWTIME

Music, theater, dance and more

Showtime

Dramatically lit stages, basement jazz joints, high-ceilinged dance halls, and opera houses set for melodramatic tales – for more than a century, New York City has been America's capital of cultural production. It's perhaps best known for its Broadway musicals, presented in lavish early-20th-century theaters that surround Times Square. Beyond Broadway you'll find experimental downtown playhouses, the hallowed concert halls of the Met, and live music joints that pulsate with all manner of melodies, but reserve a special place in their heart for jazz.

In This Section

How to Buy Show Tickets

To purchase tickets for shows, you can either head directly to the venue's box office, or use one of several ticket agencies such as **Telecharge** (www.telecharge.com) or **Ticketmaster** (www.ticketmaster.com). For discounted (up to 50% off) same-day Broadway tickets, visit a **TKTS Booth** (www.tdf.org). For other entertainment (comedy, cabaret, performance art, music, dance and downtown theater), check out **SmartTix** (www.smarttix.com).

OSUGI/SHUTTERSTOCK ©

Village Vanguard (p183)

The Best...

Broadway Shows

Harry Potter and the Cursed Child (p60) Broadway's highest-grossing play of all time.

Book of Mormon (p60) Brilliantly funny, award-winning show by the creators of *South Park*.

Chicago (p60) One of the most scintillating shows on Broadway.

Kinky Boots (p60) Book well ahead to score seats for this over-the-top musical.

Hamilton (p59) If you can't get tickets, try standing in the cancellation line outside the theater.

For Jazz

Jazz at Lincoln Center (p186) Innovative fare under the guidance of jazz luminary Wynton Marsalis.

Village Vanguard (p183) Legendary West Village jazz club.

Smalls (p183) Tiny West Village basement joint that evokes the feel of decades past.

Barbès (p189) Obscure but celebratory rhythms from around the globe in Park Slope.

Birdland (p187) Sleek Midtown lounge that hosts big-band sounds, Afro-Cuban jazz and more.

Financial District & Lower Manhattan

Flea Theater Theater

(Map p246; ☎tickets 212-226-0051; www.theflea.org; 20 Thomas St, btwn Timble Pl & Broadway, Tribeca; tickets from $10; 👪; [S]A/C, 1/2/3 to Chambers St, R/W to City Hall) One of NYC's top off-Off-Broadway venues, Flea is famous for staging innovative and timely new works. It houses three performance spaces, including the 'Siggy,' named for co-founder Sigourney Weaver. The year-round program includes music and dance productions, as well as Sunday shows for young audiences (aged two and up) and SERIALS, a rollicking late-night competition series of 10-minute plays.

Soho Rep Theater

(Soho Repertory Theatre; Map p246; ☎212-941-8632; www.sohorep.org; 46 Walker St, btwn Church St & Broadway, Tribeca; [S]A/C/E to Canal St, 1 to Franklin St) This is one of New York's finest Off-Broadway companies, wowing audiences and critics with its annual trio of sharp, innovative new works. Kathleen Turner, Allison Janney, Ed O'Neill and John C Reilly all made their professional debuts in this 65-seat theater, and the company's productions have garnered more than 20 Obie (Off-Broadway Theater) Awards. Check the website for current or upcoming shows.

SoHo & Chinatown

Joe's Pub Live Music

(Map p246; ☎212-539-8778, tickets 212-967-7555; www.joespub.com; Public Theater, 425 Lafayette St, btwn Astor Pl & 4th St, NoHo; [S]6 to Astor Pl; R/W to 8th St-NYU) Part bar, part cabaret and performance venue, intimate Joe's serves up both emerging acts and top-shelf performers. Past entertainers have included Patti LuPone, Amy Schumer, the late Leonard Cohen and British songstress Adele (in fact, it was right here that Adele gave her very first American performance, back in 2008). Entrance is through the Public Theater.

Film Forum Cinema

(Map p246; ☎212-727-8110; www.filmforum.com; 209 W Houston St, btwn Varick St & Sixth Ave, SoHo; adult/child $15/9; 🕐noon-midnight; [S]1 to Houston St) This nonprofit cinema shows an astounding array of independent films, revivals and career retrospectives from greats such as Orson Welles. Showings often include director talks or other film-themed discussions for hardcore cinephiles. In 2018, the cinema upgraded its theaters to improve the seating, leg room and sight lines, and expanded to add a fourth screen.

East Village & Lower East Side

Metrograph Cinema

(Map p246; ☎212-660-0312; www.metrograph.com; 7 Ludlow St, btwn Canal & Hester Sts, Lower East Side; tickets $15; 🕐11am-midnight Sun-Wed, to 2am Fri & Sat; 📶; [S]F to East Broadway, B/D to Grand St) The Lower East Side hasn't gentrified this far yet, giving the owners of this true movie mecca the chance to acquire a building adequate for their vision. It has two screens, both a state-of-the-art digital projector and an old 35mm reel-to-reel. The expertly curated films often form series on subjects such as Japanese animation studio Ghibli or provocateur Gaspar Noé.

Performance Space New York Theater

(Map p246; ☎212-477-5829; www.performancespacenewyork.org; 150 First Ave, at E 9th St, East Village; [S]L to 1st Ave, 6 to Astor Pl) Founded in 1980 as Performance Space 122, this cutting-edge theater once housed in an abandoned public school now boasts state-of-the-art performance spaces, artist studios, a new lobby and a roof deck. The bones of the former schoolhouse remain, as does its experimental theater bona fides: Eric Bogosian, Meredith Monk, the late Spalding Gray and Elevator Repair Service have all performed here.

Nuyorican Poets Café Live Performance

(Map p246; ☎212-780-9386; www.nuyorican.org; 236 E 3rd St, btwn Aves B & C, East Village; tickets $8-30; [S]F to 2nd Ave) Going strong since 1973, the legendary Nuyorican is home to poetry slams, hip-hop performances, plays, films, dance and music. It's living East Village history but also a vibrant, still-relevant nonprofit arts organization. Check the website for events and buy tickets online for the more popular weekend shows. Or try out your lyrical skills at Monday's open-mic night (9pm; $8).

Slipper Room Live Performance

(Map p246; ☎212-253-7246; www.slipperroom.com; 167 Orchard St, entrance on Stanton St, Lower East Side; from $10; ⏰doors open 1hr before performance; [S]F to 2nd Ave) This two-story club hosts offbeat shows, including some of the city's best burlesque performers in each Friday's 'Slipper Room Show' (9:30pm; $20) and the outrageous romp 'Mr Choade's Upstairs Downstairs,' the city's longest-running variety show (9:30pm Saturday; $20). But whatever mix of acrobatics, sexiness, comedy and music you catch, you won't be disappointed. Event calendar and tickets available online.

Top Five For Laughs

Upright Citizens Brigade Theatre (p187) Hilarious comedy sketches and improv.

Comedy Cellar (p184) A well-loved basement comedy joint in Greenwich Village.

Caroline's on Broadway (Map p252; ☎212-757-4100; www.carolines.com; 1626 Broadway, at 50th St, Midtown West; [S]N/R/W to 49th St; 1, C/E to 50th St) The go-to spot for seeing famous comics perform.

Peoples Improv Theater (p185) Intimate club for top-notch laughs with free Wednesday improv sessions and cheap beer.

Comedy Cellar (p184)

M. STAN REAVES/ALAMY STOCK PHOTO ©

✪ West Village, Chelsea & Meatpacking District

Sleep No More Theater

(Map p250; ☎box office 212-904-1880; www.sleepnomorenyc.com; 530 W 27th St, btwn Tenth & Eleventh Aves, Chelsea; tickets from $100; ⏰sessions begin 4-7pm; [S]1, C/E to 23rd St) One of the most immersive theater experiences ever conceived, *Sleep No More* is a loose, noir retelling of *Macbeth* set inside a series of Chelsea warehouses that have been redesigned to look like the 1930s-era 'McKittrick Hotel' (a nod to Hitchcock's *Vertigo*); the hopping jazz bar, Manderley, is another Hitchcock reference, this time to his adaptation of Daphne du Maurier's *Rebecca*.

Village Vanguard Jazz

(Map p246; ☎212-255-4037; www.villagevanguard.com; 178 Seventh Ave S, btwn W 11th & Perry Sts, West Village; cover around $35; ⏰7:30pm-12:30am; [S]1/2/3 to 14th St, A/C/E, L to 8th Ave-14th St) Possibly NYC's most prestigious jazz club, the Vanguard has hosted virtually every major star of the past 50 years. Starting out in 1935 as a venue for beat poetry and folk music, it occasionally returns to its roots, but most of the time it's just big, bold jazz all night long. The Vanguard Jazz Orchestra has been a Monday-night mainstay since 1966.

Smalls Jazz

(Map p246; ☎646-476-4346; www.smallslive.com; 183 W 10th St, btwn W 4th St & Seventh Ave S, West Village; cover $20; ⏰7pm-3:30am Mon-Fri, from 4pm Sat & Sun; [S]1 to Christopher St-Sheridan

Sq, A/C/E, B/D/F/M to W 4th St-Washington Sq) Living up to its name, this cramped but appealing basement jazz den offers a grab-bag collection of acts who take the stage nightly. Admission includes a come-and-go policy if you need to duck out for a bite, and there's an afternoon jam session on Saturday and Sunday that's not to be missed.

Blue Note Jazz

(Map p246; ☎212-475-8592; www.bluenote.net; 131 W 3rd St, btwn Sixth Ave & MacDougal St, West Village; ⏰box office 10am-7pm, doors open 6pm; [S]A/C/E, B/D/F/M to W 4th St-Washington Sq) With the likes of Sarah Vaughan, Lionel Hampton and Dizzy Gillespie gracing its stage since it opened in 1981, Blue Note is one of NYC's premier jazz clubs. Most shows are $20 to $45 at the bar or $35 to $55 at a table, but prices can rise for the biggest stars. There's also jazz brunch ($40) at 11:30am and 1:30pm Sunday.

IFC Center Cinema

(Map p246; ☎212-924-7771; www.ifccenter.com; 323 Sixth Ave, at W 3rd St, West Village; adult/child tickets $15/11; 📶; [S]A/C/E, B/D/F/M to W 4th St-Washington Sq) This art-house cinema in NYU land has a solidly curated lineup of new indies, cult classics and foreign films. Catch shorts, documentaries, mini festivals, '80s revivals, director-focused series, weekend classics and frequent special series, such as cult favorites *(The Shining, Taxi Driver, Aliens)* at midnight.

LGBT Community Center Arts Center

(Map p246; ☎212-620-7310; www.gaycenter.org; 208 W 13th St, btwn Seventh & Greenwich Aves, West Village; ⏰9am-10pm Mon-Sat, to 9pm Sun; [S]1/2/3 to 14th St, A/C/E, L to 8th Ave-14th St) 'The Center' has been the nexus of LGBT+ culture in the village since 1983. That's because it provides a surrogate home for LGBT+ folks who may not feel so comfortable in their actual one. It's host to endless groups, and you can relax at the community-oriented cafe run by **Think Coffee**.

Comedy Cellar Comedy

(Map p246; ☎212-254-3480; www.comedycellar.com; 117 MacDougal St, btwn W 3rd St & Minetta Lane, West Village; cover $10-24; ⏰11am-3am;

Blue Note

ZOLTAN TARLACZ/SHUTTERSTOCK ©

§A/C/E, B/D/F/M to W 4th St-Washington Sq) This legendary, intimate basement comedy club beneath the Olive Tree cafe in the West Village features a cast of talented regulars (Colin Quinn, Judah Friedlander, Wanda Sykes), plus occasional high-profile drop-ins like Dave Chappelle, Jerry Seinfeld and Amy Schumer. Its success has spawned offspring – locations in Las Vegas and at the **Village Underground**, around the corner at 130 W 3rd St.

Cherry Lane Theatre   Theater
(Map p246; ☏212-989-2020; www.cherrylane theater.org; 38 Commerce St, off Bedford St, West Village; §1 to Christopher St-Sheridan Sq) A little backstreet theater of distinctive charm, Cherry Lane has a long and distinguished history. Started by poet Edna St Vincent Millay in 1924, it has given a voice to numerous playwrights and actors over the years, showcasing the early work of such heavyweights as Harold Pinter and Edward Albee. Readings, plays and spoken-word performances rotate frequently.

Duplex   Cabaret
(Map p246; ☏212-255-5438; www.theduplex. com; 61 Christopher St, at Seventh Ave S, West Village; cover $10-25; ⊙4pm-4am; §1 to Christopher St-Sheridan Sq, A/C/E, B/D/F/M to W 4th St-Washington Sq) Cabaret, comedy and campy dance moves are par for the course at the legendary Duplex, going strong since 1950. Pictures of Joan Rivers line the walls, and performers like to mimic her sassy form of self-deprecation while getting in a few jokes about audience members as well. It's a fun and unpretentious place, but certainly not for the bashful.

✪ Union Square, Flatiron District & Gramercy

Peoples Improv Theater   Comedy
(PIT; Map p250; ☏classes 212-563-7488; www. thepit-nyc.com; 123 E 24th St, btwn Lexington & Park Aves, Gramercy; 🖥; §F/M, N/R, 6 to 23rd St) Aglow in red neon, this bustling comedy club serves up top-notch laughs

🎧 Musical Metropolis

This is the city where jazz players such as Ornette Coleman, Miles Davis and John Coltrane pushed the limits of improvisation in the '50s. It's where various Latin sounds came together to form the hybrid we now call salsa, where folk singers such as Bob Dylan and Joan Baez crooned protest songs in coffeehouses, and where bands such as the New York Dolls and the Ramones tore up the stage in Manhattan's gritty downtown. It was the ground zero of disco. And it was the cultural crucible where hip-hop was nurtured and grew – then exploded. The city remains a magnet for musicians to this day. The local indie-rock scene is especially vibrant: the Yeah Yeah Yeahs, LCD Sound system and Animal Collective all emerged out of NYC. Williamsburg is at the heart of the action, packed with clubs and bars, as well as indie record labels and internet radio stations. The best venues for rock include the Music Hall of Williamsburg and the Brooklyn Bowl, as well as Manhattan's Bowery Ballroom. Harlem, the birthplace of bebop and once the stomping ground of greats like Louis Armstrong, Billie Holiday and Charlie Parker, is still a great place for grassroots jazz: try Silvana (p174), Shrine (p174) and Ginny's Supper Club (p174).

Bowery Ballroom
EMMA SWANN/ALAMY STOCK PHOTO ©

at dirt-cheap prices. The string of nightly acts ranges from stand-up to sketch and musical comedy. On Wednesdays there's

 Attend a TV Taping

Saturday Night Live (www.nbc.com/saturday-night-live)

One of the most popular NYC-based shows – line up by 7am the day of the show on the 48th St side of **Rockefeller Plaza** for standby lottery tickets. You can choose a standby ticket for either the 8pm dress rehearsal or the 11:30pm live broadcast. The tickets are limited to one per person and are issued on a first-come, first-served basis. You will need to bring valid photo ID when the ticket is issued, as well as to the show later that day. Audience members must be 16 or over.

The Daily Show with Trevor Noah

(www.showclix.com/event/thedailyshowwithtrevornoah) Sign up online to catch this popular news parody show. Reservations for shows are released on a gradual basis a few weeks before, so it pays to keep visiting the website. Tapings take place at 6pm and around 7:15pm Monday through Thursday. Check-in begins at 2:30pm, at which time the actual tickets are distributed. Consider arriving early as there is no guarantee of entry. Upon collecting your tickets at the venue you will be given a time to return (usually around 4:30pm). Audience members must be aged 18 or over.

For more show ticket details, visit the websites of individual TV stations, or check out www.nycgo.com/articles/tv-show-tapings.

NBC Studios, Rockefeller Plaza (p83)
JAMES R MARTIN/SHUTTERSTOCK ©

free improv from 7pm; come early to drink in the cheap and cheerful, lipstick-red bar. PIT also runs courses, including three-hour, drop-in improv workshops at its Midtown venue, **Simple Studios** (Map p250; 212-273-9696; http://simplestudiosnyc.com; 134 W 29th St, btwn Sixth & Seventh Aves, Midtown West; 9am-11pm Mon-Fri, to 10pm Sat & Sun; 1, N/R to 28th St).

Midtown

Jazz at Lincoln Center   Jazz

(Map p254; Dizzy's Club Coca-Cola reservations 212-258-9595, Rose Theater & Appel Room tickets 212-721-6500; www.jazz.org; Time Warner Center, 10 Columbus Circle, Broadway at W 59th St; A/C, B/D, 1 to 59th St-Columbus Circle) Perched atop the Time Warner Center, Jazz at Lincoln Center consists of three state-of-the-art venues: the midsized **Rose Theater**; the panoramic, glass-backed **Appel Room**; and the intimate, atmospheric **Dizzy's Club Coca-Cola**. It's the last of these that you're most likely to visit, given its nightly shows (cover charge $20 to $45). The talent is often exceptional, as are the dazzling Central Park views.

Carnegie Hall   Live Music

(Map p252; 212-247-7800; www.carnegiehall.org; 881 Seventh Ave, at W 57th St; tours adult/child $17/12; tours 11:30am, 12:30pm, 2pm & 3pm Mon-Fri, 11:30am & 12:30pm Sat Sep-Jun; N/R/W to 57th St-7th Ave) Few venues are as famous as Carnegie Hall. This legendary music hall may not be the world's biggest, nor its grandest, but it's definitely one of the most acoustically blessed venues around. Opera, jazz and folk greats feature in the **Isaac Stern Auditorium**, with edgier jazz, pop, classical and world music in the popular **Zankel Hall**. The intimate **Weill Recital Hall** hosts chamber-music concerts, debut performances and panel discussions.

Birdland   Jazz

(Map p252; 212-581-3080; www.birdlandjazz.com; 315 W 44th St, btwn Eighth & Ninth Aves; cover $30-50; 5pm-1am; ; A/C/E to 42nd

OSUGI/SHUTTERSTOCK ©

Birdland

St-Port Authority Bus Terminal) This bird's got a slick look, not to mention the legend – its name dates from bebop legend Charlie Parker (aka 'Bird'), who headlined at the previous location on 52nd St, along with Miles, Monk and just about everyone else (you can see their photos on the walls). The 44th St club is intimate; come for the electrifying Big Band session on Fridays at 5:30pm.

Jazz Standard Jazz

(Map p250; ☎212-576-2232; www.jazzstandard.com; 116 E 27th St, btwn Lexington & Park Aves; cover $25-40; 🕒shows 7:30pm & 9:30pm; [S]6 to 28th St) Jazz luminaries like Ravi Coltrane, Roy Haynes and Ron Carter have played at this sophisticated club. The service is impeccable and the Southern food (from Danny Meyer's upstairs Blue Smoke restaurant) is great. The club's artistic director is Seth Abramson, a guy who really knows his jazz. A popular jazz 'Smokestack' brunch ($35) is also an option from 11:30am to 2:30pm on Sunday.

Playwrights Horizons Theater

(Map p250; ☎212-564-1235; www.playwrightshorizons.org; 416 W 42nd St, btwn Ninth & Tenth Aves, Midtown West; [S]A/C/E to 42nd St-Port Authority Bus Terminal) An excellent place to catch what could be the next big thing, this veteran 'writers' theater' is dedicated to fostering contemporary American works. Notable past productions include Kenneth Lonergan's *Lobby Hero*, Bruce Norris' Tony Award–winning *Clybourne Park*, as well as Doug Wright's *I Am My Own Wife* and *Grey Gardens*.

Upright Citizens Brigade Theatre Comedy

(UCB; ☎212-366-9176; www.ucbtheatre.com; 555 W 42nd St, btwn Tenth & Eleventh Aves, Hell's Kitchen; free-$10; 🕒7:30pm-midnight; [S]A/C/E to 42nd St-Port Authority) Comedy sketch shows, improv and variety reign at the new location of the legendary venue, which receives drop-ins from casting directors and often features well-known figures from TV. Entry is cheap, and so are the beer and wine. You'll find quality shows happening

★ **Best Classical Music & Opera**

Metropolitan Opera House (p110)

National Sawdust (p190)

Brooklyn Academy of Music (p189)

Carnegie Hall (p186)

nightly, from about 7:30pm, though the Sunday-night Asssscat Improv session is always a riot.

Magnet Theater
Comedy

(Map p250; ☑tickets 212-244-8824; www.magnettheater.com; 254 W 29th St, btwn Seventh & Eighth Aves, Midtown West; ⓢ1 to 28th St; C/E to 23rd St; 1/2/3 to 34th St-Penn Station) Tons of comedy in several incarnations (mostly improv) lures the crowds at this theater/training-ground for comics. Performances vary weekly, though regular favorites include Megawatt ($7; featuring the theater's resident ensembles) and the Friday Night Sh*w ($10), the latter using the audience's written rants and confessions to drive the evening's shenanigans.

Second Stage Theater
Theater

(Tony Kiser Theater; Map p252; ☑tickets 212-246-4422; www.2st.com; 305 W 43rd St, at Eighth Ave, Midtown West; ⊗box office noon-6pm Sun-Fri, to 7pm Sat; ⓢA/C/E to 42nd St-Port Authority Bus Terminal) This nonprofit theater company is famed for debuting the work of talented emerging writers as well as that of the country's more established names. If you're after well-crafted contemporary American theater, this is a good place to find it. Second Stage operates two theaters – Tony Kiser is the main one and Hayes (nearby on W 44th St) is a recent acquisition.

Don't Tell Mama
Cabaret

(Map p252; ☑212-757-0788; www.donttellmamanyc.com; 343 W 46th St, btwn Eighth & Ninth Aves, Midtown West; ⊗4pm-2:30am Sun-Thu, to 3:30am Fri & Sat; ⓢN/Q/R, S, 1/2/3, 7 to Times Sq-42nd St) Piano bar and cabaret venue extraordinaire, Don't Tell Mama is an unpretentious little spot that's been around

for more than 30 years and has the talent to prove it. Its regular roster of performers aren't big names, but true lovers of cabaret who give each show their all, and singing waitstaff add to the fun.

😊 Upper East Side

Café Carlyle
Jazz

(Map p254; ☑212-744-1600; www.thecarlyle.com; Carlyle Hotel, 35 E 76th St, at Madison Ave; cover $120-215, food & drink minimum $25-75; ⊗shows 8:45pm & 10:45pm; ⓢ6 to 77th St) This swanky spot at the Carlyle Hotel draws top-shelf talent. Bring mucho bucks: the cover charge ($120 to $215 per person) doesn't include food or drinks, and there's a minimum spend. The dress code is 'chic' – gentlemen, wear a jacket.

Frick Collection Concerts
Classical Music

(Map p254; ☑212-547-0715; www.frick.org/programs/concerts; 1 E 70th St, at Fifth Ave; $45; ⓢ6 to 68th St-Hunter College) Every two to four weeks, the opulent Frick collection mansion-museum (p51) hosts a Sunday 5pm concert that brings in world-renowned performers, such as cellist Yehuda Hanani and violinist Thomas Zehetmair: check the website for the schedule. Ticket holders can browse the museum for no extra charge for up to one hour before the concerts.

😊 Upper West Side & Central Park

Film Society of Lincoln Center
Cinema

(Map p254; ☑212-875-5610; www.filmlinc.com; Lincoln Center; ⓢ1 to 66th St-Lincoln Center) The Film Society is one of New York's cinematic gems, providing an invaluable platform for a wide gamut of documentary, feature, independent, foreign and avant-garde art pictures. Films screen in one of two facilities at Lincoln Center: the **Elinor Bunin Munroe Film Center** (Map p254; ☑212-875-5232; www.filmlinc.com; 144 W 65th St, btwn Broadway &

Amsterdam Ave; adult/student $15/12; [S]1 to 66 St-Lincoln Center), a more intimate, experimental venue, or the **Walter Reade Theater** (Map p254; ☎212-875-5601; www.filmlinc.com; 165 W 65th St, btwn Broadway & Amsterdam Ave; [S]1 to 66th St-Lincoln Center), with wonderfully wide, screening room–style seats.

✪ Harlem & Upper Manhattan

Marjorie Eliot's Parlor Jazz Jazz

(☎212-781-6595; 555 Edgecombe Ave, Apartment 3F, at 160th St, Washington Heights; donations appreciated; ⏰3:30pm Sun; [S]A/C to 163rd St-Amsterdam Ave; 1 to 157th St) Each Sunday the charming Ms Eliot provides one of New York's most magical experiences: free, intimate jazz jams in her own apartment. Dedicated to her two deceased sons, the informal concerts feature a revolving lineup of talented musicians, enchanting guests from all over the globe. Go early, as this event is popular (there's usually a line by 2:45pm).

✪ Brooklyn

Brooklyn Academy of Music Performing Arts

(BAM; Map p256; ☎718-636-4100; www.bam.org; 30 Lafayette Ave, at Ashland Pl, Fort Greene; 📶; [S]B/D, N/Q/R, 2/3, 4/5 to Atlantic Ave-Barclays Center) Founded in 1861 (the year the Civil War erupted), BAM is the country's oldest performing-arts center. Spanning several venues in the Fort Greene area, the complex offers innovative and edgier works of opera, modern dance, music, cinema and theater – everything from 'retro-modern' Mark Morris Group ballets and Laurie Anderson multimedia shows to avant-garde Shakespeare productions, comedy and kids' shows.

Barbès Live Music

(Map p256; ☎347-422-0248; www.barbesbrooklyn.com; 376 9th St, at Sixth Ave, Park Slope; requested donation for live music $10; ⏰5pm-2am Mon-Thu, 2pm-4am Fri & Sat, to 2am Sun; [S]F, G to 7th Ave, R to 4th Ave-9th St) This compact bar and performance space,

Brooklyn Academy of Music

OSUGI/SHUTTERSTOCK ©

Kings Theatre

named after a North African neighborhood in Paris, is owned by French musician (and longtime Brooklyn resident) Olivier Conan, who sometimes plays here with his Latin-themed band, Las Rubias del Norte. There's live music all night, every night: an impressively eclectic lineup including Afro-Peruvian grooves, West African funk, gypsy swing, and other diverse sounds.

National Sawdust   Live Performance
(Map p257; ☏646-779-8455; www.nationalsaw dust.org; 80 N 6th St, at Wythe Ave, Williamsburg; ⏰10am-midnight; 👶; 🚌B32 to Wythe Ave-N 6th St, 🚇L to Bedford Ave) Covered in wildly hued murals, this cutting-edge space for classical and new music has come a long way since its days as a sawdust factory. The angular, high-tech interior stages contemporary opera with multimedia projections, electro-acoustic big-band jazz and concerts by experimental composers, alongside less commonly encountered genres – perhaps Inuit throat singing, African tribal funk or sung Icelandic sagas.

St Ann's Warehouse   Theater
(Map p256; ☏718-254-8779; www.stannsware house.org; 45 Water St, at Old Dock St, Dumbo; 🚌B25 to Water/Main Sts, 🚇A/C to High St, F to York St) This handsome red-brick building, a Civil War–era tobacco warehouse, is the first permanent home of avant-garde performance company St Ann's. The 'ware-house' – a high-tech, flexible 320-seat theater – is ideal for staging genre-bending theater, music, dance and puppet performances.

Bell House   Live Performance
(Map p256; ☏718-643-6510; www.thebellhouse ny.com; 149 7th St, btwn Second & Third Aves, Gowanus; ⏰5pm-late; 📶; 🚇F, G, R to 4th Ave-9th St) This 1920s warehouse in the light-industrial grid of Gowanus showcases high-profile live music and variety, spanning indie rockers, DJ nights, comedy shows, burlesque parties and more. The handsomely converted performance area holds up to 500 beneath its timber rafters, and the friendly little Front Lounge has flickering

candles, leather armchairs and plenty of beers behind the long oak bar.

Nitehawk Cinema Cinema

(Map p257; ☎718-782-8370; www.nitehawkcinema.com; 136 Metropolitan Ave, btwn Berry & Wythe Sts, Williamsburg; tickets adult/child $12/9; 👪; [S]L to Bedford Ave) This indie triplex has a fine lineup of first-run and repertory films, a good sound system and comfy seats...but the best part is that you can dine and drink throughout the movie. Munch on hummus plates, sweet-potato risotto balls or crispy quail on black lentils. Pair your food with matched drafts, wines and cocktails, if you fancy going all out.

Jalopy Live Music

(Map p256; ☎718-395-3214; http://jalopytheatre.org; 315 Columbia St, btwn Hamilton Ave & Woodhull St, Columbia St Waterfront District; ⏰4-9pm Mon, noon-midnight Tue-Sun; 👪; 🚌B61 to Columbia & Carroll Sts, [S]F, G to Carroll St) This tavern, and music and teaching space at the fringes of Carroll Gardens and Red Hook is a fun, DIY kind of affair, where the beer's cold and you can usually catch a bluegrass, country, klezmer or ukulele show. There's no charge for feel-good Roots 'n' Ruckus shows every Wednesday at 9pm; check the website for what else is on.

Kings Theatre Theater

(☎box office 718-856-5464; www.kingstheatre.com; 1027 Flatbush Ave, at Tilden Ave, Flatbush; ⏰box office noon-5:30pm Mon-Sat; [S]2, 5, Q to Beverly Rd) This dream palace from the twilight of cinema's pre-Depression heyday is a gorgeous reminder of the past – and a top-notch concert venue to boot. Allowed to fall derelict after closing for unpaid taxes in the 1970s, it was sensitively restored in 2015. Today, the gold-and-red lobby, elaborately painted ceiling and plush chairs are gloriously reborn.

Music Hall of Williamsburg Live Music

(Map p257; ☎718-486-5400; www.musichallofwilliamsburg.com; 66 N 6th St, btwn Wythe & Kent Aves, Williamsburg; tickets $10-65; [S]L to Bedford Ave) This popular venue is *the* place to see indie bands in Brooklyn – everyone from They Might Be Giants to Teenage Fanclub and Kendrick Lamar has played here. (For many groups playing New York, this is their one and only spot.) It's got an intimate feel (capacity is 550) and typically programs several interesting shows a week.

ACTIVE NEW YORK CITY

Sports, biking, tours and more

Active New York City

Although hailing cabs in New York City can feel like a blood sport, and waiting on subway platforms in summer heat is steamier than a sauna, New Yorkers still love to stay active in their spare time. And considering how limited the green spaces are in the city, it's surprising for some visitors just how active the locals can be.

For those who prefer their sport sitting down, there's a packed calendar of over half a dozen pro teams playing within the metropolitan area. Football, basketball, baseball, hockey, tennis – there's lots of excitement right on your doorstep.

In This Section

Sports Seasons

In the US, the football (NFL) season generally runs from September to January; basketball (NBA) from October through May; ice hockey (NHL) from October to April; and major-league baseball from April to October. The US Open, America's biggest tennis tournament, takes place in late August/early September.

SOLEPSIZM/SHUTTERSTOCK ©

Prospect Park (p98)

The Best...

Parks for Stretching Legs

Central Park (p36) The city's play-ground has forested paths, tennis courts and cycling tours.

Governors Island (p105) Car-free island just a quick hop from Lower Manhattan or Brooklyn.

Brooklyn Bridge Park (p102) This beautifully designed waterfront green space is Brooklyn's pride and joy.

Prospect Park (p98) Escape the crowds at Brooklyn's gorgeous park, with trails, hills, a canal, lake and meadows.

Inwood Hill Park Serene setting of forest and salt marsh in Upper Manhattan.

Pro Sports Teams

New York Yankees The legendary base-ball team battles it out in the Bronx.

New York Giants Football powerhouse that plays in New Jersey.

New York Knicks See the Knicks at Madison Square Garden.

Brooklyn Nets The hot new NBA team call Brooklyn's Barclays Center home.

Brooklyn Cyclones See a Minor League Baseball game near Coney Island's boardwalk.

New York Mets NYC's other baseball team play their games at Citi Field in Queens.

⊙ Sports Arenas

Yankee Stadium   Stadium
(📞212-926-5337; www.mlb.com/yankees; 1 E
161st St, at River Ave; tours $20; S B/D, 4 to
161st St-Yankee Stadium) The Boston Red Sox
like to talk about their record of nine World
Series championships in the last 90 years...
well, the Yankees have won 27 in that
period. The team's magic appeared to have
moved with them across 161st St to the
new Yankee Stadium, where they played
their first season in 2009 – winning the
World Series there in a six-game slugfest
against the Phillies. The Yankees play from
April to October.

Madison
Square Garden   Live Performance
(MSG, 'the Garden'; Map p250; www.thegarden.
com; 4 Pennsylvania Plaza, Seventh Ave, btwn
31st & 33rd Sts; S A/C/E, 1/2/3 to 34th St-Penn
Station) NYC's major performance venue
– part of the massive complex housing
Penn Station – hosts big-arena performers,
from Kanye West to Madonna. It's also a
sports arena, with **New York Knicks** (www.
nba.com/knicks) and **New York Liberty**
(https://liberty.wnba.com) basketball
games and **New York Rangers** (www.nhl.
com/rangers) hockey games, as well as
boxing and events like the Annual Westmin-
ster Kennel Club Dog Show.

Barclays
Center   Stadium
(Map p256; 📞917-618-6100; www.barclays
center.com; cnr Flatbush & Atlantic Aves,
Prospect Heights; S B/D, N/Q/R, 2/3, 4/5 to
Atlantic Ave-Barclays Center) The Dodgers
still play baseball in Los Angeles, but the
Brooklyn Nets in the NBA (formerly
the New Jersey Nets) now hold court at
this high-tech stadium. Basketball aside,
Barclays also stages boxing, professional
wrestling, major concerts and big shows:
Ariana Grande, Bruce Springsteen, Justin
Bieber, Cher, Cirque de Soleil and even
Disney on Ice.

Madison Square Garden

EQROY/SHUTTERSTOCK © ARCHITECT: CHARLES LUCKMAN

Activities & Fitness

Jump into the Light VR Amusement Park
(Map p246; ☎646-590-1172; www.jumpintothe light.nyc; 180 Orchard St, btwn E Houston & Stanton Sts, East Village; 10min/day $10/30; ⏰1-11pm Mon-Thu, to midnight Fri, 11am-midnight Sat, to 11pm Sun; [S]F to 2nd Ave) Ready to jump off a skyscraper, climb a mountain, parachute from a plane and kill a whole bunch of zombies? Then head to this incredible, first-of-its-kind virtual-reality arcade, where you can explore all the different activities and, best of all, start to understand how cool VR is going to be. Interactive artwork and other futuristic tech are also on display.

Chelsea Piers Complex Health & Fitness
(Map p250; ☎212-336-6666; www.chelsea piers.com; Pier 62, at W 23rd St, Chelsea; ⏰5:30am-11pm Mon-Fri, 8am-9pm Sat & Sun; 👪; 🚌M23 to 12th Ave-W 23 St, [S]1, C/E to 23rd St) This massive waterfront sports center caters to the athlete in everyone. You can hit endless golf balls at the four-level driving range, skate on an indoor ice rink or rack up strikes in a jazzy bowling alley. There's basketball at Hoop City, a sailing school for kids, batting cages, a huge gym and covered swimming pool, and indoor rock climbing.

Central Park Tennis Center Tennis
(Map p254; ☎212-316-0800; www.centralpark tenniscenter.com; Central Park, btwn W 94th & 96th Sts; ⏰7am-dusk Apr-Nov; [S]B, C to 96th St) This daylight-hours-only facility has 26 clay courts for public use and four hard courts for lessons. You can buy single-play tickets ($15; cash only) here, and can reserve a court if you pick up a $15 permit at **Arsenal** (Map p254; ☎gallery 212-360-8163; www.nycgovparks.org; Central Park, at Fifth Ave & E 64th St; ⏰9am-5pm Mon-Fri; [S]N/R/W to 5th Ave-59th St) [FREE]. The least busy times are roughly from noon to 4pm weekdays. Closest park entrance is Central Park West and 96th St.

Biking the Big Apple

NYC has taken enormous strides in making the city more bike-friendly, adding hundreds of miles of bike lanes in recent years. That said, we recommend that the uninitiated stick to the less hectic trails in the parks and along the waterways, such as Central Park, Prospect Park, the Manhattan Waterfront Greenway and the Brooklyn Waterfront Greenway. Citi Bike (www.citibikenyc.com) is handy for quick jaunts, but for longer rides, you'll want a proper rental. Biking tours let you cover a lot of ground and are worth considering. Try Bike & Roll (p200) or Central Park Bike Tours (p200).

Park Row, Financial District

JJFARQ/SHUTTERSTOCK ©

New York Trapeze School Health & Fitness
(Map p246; ☎212-242-8769; www.newyork. trapezeschool.com; Pier 40, at West Side Hwy, West Village; per class $40-75; ⏰May-Oct; [S]1 to Houston St) Fulfill your circus dreams on the flying trapeze in this open-air tent by the river, open from May to October and located atop Pier 40. The school also has an indoor facility in South Williamsburg, Brooklyn, that's open year-round. Call or check the website for daily class times. There's a one-time registration fee ($10).

Spas & Baths

Great Jones Spa Spa
(Map p246; ☎212-505-3185; www.gjspa.com; 29 Great Jones St, btwn Lafayette St & Bowery,

Useful Websites

NYC Parks (www.nycgovparks.org) Details on park services, including free pools and basketball courts, plus borough biking maps.

New York Road Runners Club (www.nyrr.org) Organizes weekend runs and races citywide.

Central Park (www.centralparknyc.org) Lists myriad activities and events held at NYC's best-loved green space.

NYC (www.nycgo.com/sports) Lists all the major sporting events and activities happening in town.

Central Park (p36)

WINSTON TAN/SHUTTERSTOCK ©

NoHo; ⏰9am-10pm; [S]6 to Bleecker St; B/D/F/M to Broadway-Lafayette St) Don't skimp on the services at this downtown feng shui–designed place, whose offerings include blood-orange salt scrubs and stem-cell facials. If you spend over $100 per person (not difficult: hour-long massages/facials start at $150/135), you get access to the water lounge with thermal hot tub, sauna, steam room and cold plunge pool (swimwear required). There's even a three-story indoor waterfall.

Russian & Turkish Baths Bathhouse

(Map p246; ☎212-674-9250; www.russianturkishbaths.com; 268 E 10th St, btwn First Ave & Ave A, East Village; 1 visit $48; ⏰noon-10pm Mon, Tue, Thu & Fri, from 10am Wed, from 9am Sat, from 8am Sun; [S]L to 1st Ave, 6 to Astor Pl) Since 1892 this cramped, grungy downtown spa has been drawing a polyglot and eclectic mix: actors, students, frisky couples, singles on the make, Russian regulars and old-school locals, who strip down to their skivvies (or the roomy cotton shorts provided) and rotate between steam baths, an ice-cold plunge pool, a sauna and the sun deck.

Ice Skating

Wollman Skating Rink Skating

(Map p254; ☎212-439-6900; www.wollmanskatingrink.com; Central Park, btwn E 62nd & 63rd Sts; adult Mon-Thu $12, Fri-Sun $19, child $6, skate rentals $10; ⏰10am-2:30pm Mon & Tue, to 10pm Wed & Thu, to 11pm Fri & Sat, to 9pm Sun late Oct-early Apr; 👪; [S]F to 57 St; N/R/W to 5th Ave-59th St) This rink is much larger than the Rockefeller Center skating rink, and not only does it allow all-day skating, its position at the southeastern edge of Central Park offers magical views. There's locker rental for $5 and a spectator fee of $5. Cash only.

Rink at Rockefeller Center Ice Skating

(Map p252; ☎212-332-7654; www.therinkatrockcenter.com; Rockefeller Center, Fifth Ave, btwn W 49th & 50th Sts; adult $25-33, child $15, skate rental $13; ⏰8:30am-midnight mid-Oct–Apr; 👪; [S]B/D/F/M to 47th-50th Sts-Rockefeller Center) From mid-October to April, Rockefeller Plaza is home to New York's most famous ice-skating rink. Carved out of a recessed oval with the 70-story art-deco Rockefeller Center (p225) towering above, plus a massive Christmas tree during the holiday season, it's incomparably magical. It's also undeniably small and crowded. Opt for the first skating period of the day (8:30am) to avoid a long wait.

LeFrak Center at Lakeside Boating

(Map p256; ☎718-462-0010; www.lakesideprospectpark.com; 171 East Dr, near Ocean & Parkside Aves, Prospect Park; skating $7.25-10, skate rental $7, boat rental per hour $16-36, bike rental per hour $13-38; ⏰hours vary; 👪; [S]Q to Parkside Ave) The most significant addition to Prospect Park (p98) since its creation, the LeFrak is a 26-acre ecofriendly playground. In winter there's ice-skating, in summer there's roller-skating and a sprinkler-filled water-play area for kids to splash about in. Pedal boats and kayaks are also available when it's warm, and a variety of bikes can be rented to ride around the park.

🌀 Water Activities

Staten Island Ferry   Cruise
(Map p244; www.siferry.com; Whitehall Terminal, 4 Whitehall St, at South St, Lower Manhattan; ⏱24hr; ⓢ1 to South Ferry, R/W to Whitehall St, 4/5 to Bowling Green) **FREE** Staten Islanders know these hulking orange ferries as commuter vehicles, while Manhattanites think of them as their secret, romantic vessels for a spring-day escape. Yet many tourists are also wise to the charms of the Staten Island Ferry, whose 25-minute, 5.2-mile journey between Lower Manhattan and the Staten Island neighborhood of St George is one of NYC's finest free adventures.

Loeb Boathouse   Boating
(Map p254; ☎212-517-2233; www.thecentralpark boathouse.com; Central Park, btwn 74th & 75th Sts; boating per hr $15; ⏱10am-6:30pm; ♿; ⓢB, C to 72nd St; 6 to 77th St) Central Park's boathouse has a fleet of 100 rowboats, as well as a Venetian-style gondola that you can reserve for up to six people if you'd rather someone else do the paddling ($45 for 30 minutes). Rentals include life jackets and require ID and a $20 deposit. Cash only.

Rentals are weather permitting and available virtually all year as long as the temperature is above about 50°F (10°C).

Downtown Boathouse   Kayaking
(Map p246; www.downtownboathouse.org; Pier 26, Hudson River Greenway, near N Moore St, Tribeca; ⏱9am-5pm Sat & Sun mid-May–mid-Oct, plus 5-7:30pm Tue-Thu mid-Jun–mid-Sep; ♿; ⓢ1 to Canal St) **FREE** This active public boathouse on Pier 26 offers free, walk-up, 20-minute kayaking sessions (including equipment) on the Hudson River on weekends and some weekday evenings. For more activities here and at Piers 84 and 96 – kayaking trips,

🏀 Running in New York City

Central Park's loop roads are best during traffic-free hours, though you'll be in the company of many cyclists and in-line skaters. The 1.6-mile path surrounding the Jacqueline Kennedy Onassis Reservoir (where Jackie O used to run) is for runners and walkers only; access it between 86th and 96th Sts. Running along the Hudson River is a popular path, best from about 30th St to Battery Park in Lower Manhattan. The Upper East Side has a path that runs along FDR Dr and the East River (from 63rd St to 115th St). Brooklyn's Prospect Park has plenty of paths (and a 3-mile loop), while 1.3-mile-long Brooklyn Bridge Park has incredible views of Manhattan (reach it via Brooklyn Bridge to up the mileage). The New York Road Runners Club (www.nyrr.org) organizes weekend runs citywide, including the New York City Marathon.

New York City Marathon
DARIUSZ GRYCZKA/SHUTTERSTOCK ©

stand-up paddle boarding and classes – check out www.hudsonriverpark.org. There are also free lessons on Wednesday evenings and a summer-only location on Governors Island (p105).

Manhattan Community Boathouse   Kayaking
(www.manhattancommunityboathouse.org; Pier 96, at 56th St, Hudson River Park; ⏱10am-6pm Sat & Sun Jun-early Oct, plus 5:30-7:30pm Mon-Wed Jun-Aug; ♿; ☒M12 to 12th Ave/56th St, ⓢA/C, B/D, 1 to 59th St-Columbus Circle) **FREE** Fancy a quick glide on the mighty Hudson? This

Roller Derby in New York

NYC's only all-female and skater-operated roller derby league, the **Gotham Girls** (www.gothamgirlsrollerderby.com; tickets from $30; 🕒Mar-Aug; 👪), has four borough-inspired home teams: the Bronx Gridlock, Brooklyn Bombshells, Manhattan Mayhem and Queens of Pain. These are some of the highest-level players of the sport you're likely to see: their top travel team, the All-Stars, are five-time world champions – including a recent undefeated stretch for four years running. The teams play at various locations around NYC during the season; check the website for information.

Gotham Girls

PEOPLE/ALAMY STOCK PHOTOS ©

volunteer-run boathouse offers free kayaking on summer weekends. No reservations: it's first-come, first-served. It also offers free classes in kayaking technique and safety.

Family Activities

Bike & Roll Cycling

(Map p254; ☎212-260-0400; www.bikeandrollnyc.com; 451 Columbus Ave, btwn 81st & 82nd Sts; bike rentals per hr/day adult from $10/45, child $6/30, e-bike per hr/day $20/100; 🕒9am-6pm; 👪; [S]B, C to 81st St-Museum of Natural History; 1 to 79th St) Located a block from Central Park, this friendly outfit rents bicycles for adults and kids, with helmet, U-lock, handlebar bag, rear storage rack and a free cycling map. Baby seats are available too. It also offers two- to three-hour guided tours (adult $40 to $50, child $25 to $35) of just Central Park or the park plus the car-free Hudson River Greenway.

E-bikes are also now available for rentals or tours – good for those who need a bit of extra wind in their sails on the hills in Central Park.

Belvedere Castle Bird-watching

(Map p254; ☎212-772-0288; www.centralparknyc.org; Central Park, at W 79th St; 🕒10am-4pm; 👪; [S]1/2/3, B, C to 72nd St) For a DIY birding expedition with kids, borrow a 'Discovery Kit' at Belvedere Castle in Central Park, which comes with binoculars, a bird book, colored pencils and paper – a perfect way to get the kids excited about birds. Picture ID is required.

Brooklyn Bowl Bowling

(Map p257; ☎718-963-3369; www.brooklynbowl.com; 61 Wythe Ave, btwn N 11th & N 12th Sts, Williamsburg; lane rental per 30min $25, shoe rental $5; 🕒6pm-late Mon-Fri, from 11am Sat & Sun; 👪; [S]L to Bedford Ave, G to Nassau Ave) This incredible alley is housed in the 23,000-sq-ft former Hecla Iron Works, which provided ornamentation for several NYC landmarks at the turn of the 20th century. There are 16 lanes surrounded by cushy sofas and exposed brick walls. In addition to bowling, Brooklyn Bowl hosts **concerts** throughout the week, and there's always good food on hand.

Saturdays from 11am to 5pm and Sundays to 6pm are all-ages Family Bowl hours. (Nighttime bowling is for ages 21 and over only.)

Tours

Central Park Bike Tours Cycling

(Map p254; ☎212-541-8759; www.centralparkbiketours.com; 203 W 58th St, at Seventh Ave; rentals per 2hr/day $20/40, 2hr tours adult/child $49/35; 🕒rentals 8am-9pm Apr-Oct, to 6pm Nov-Mar, tours 9am, 10am, 1pm & 4pm; [S]A/C, B/D, 1 to 59th St-Columbus Circle) This place rents out good bikes (helmets, locks and bike map included) and leads two-hour guided tours of Central Park and the

Belvedere Castle, Central Park (p36)

Brooklyn Bridge area. If you book through its website, tours are discounted by 30%.

Museum Hack Walking

(☏347-282-5001; www.museumhack.com; 2hr tour adult/student from $69/59) For a fascinating, alternative perspective of the Metropolitan Museum of Art (p48), sign up for a tour with Museum Hack. Knowledgeable but delightfully irreverent guides take on topics like 'Badass Bitches' (a look at paradigm-shifting feminist artists), an unofficial 'Boy Wizard' magic tour for witches, squibs and muggles, and an 'Un-Highlights Tour'

that will take you to corners of the museum few visitors know about.

Big Apple Greeter Walking

(☏212-669-8159; www.bigapplegreeter.org) FREE For an inside take on NYC, book a walking tour in the neighborhood of your choice led by an enthusiastic local volunteer. You'll be matched with a guide who suits your needs, whether that means speaking Spanish, knowing American Sign Language, or where to find the best wheelchair-accessible spots in the city. Reserve four weeks in advance.

REST YOUR HEAD

Top tips for the best accommodations

Rest Your Head

New York's accommodations scene is eye-wateringly expensive, but there are dozens of top-class, gorgeous hotels for visitors prepared to splash the cash. Creative minds have descended upon the city to engineer memorable spaces for weary visitors, so even though the city 'never sleeps,' you certainly can. What the city lacks (and desperately needs) is decent options for budget travelers – NYC's hostels are certainly not world class, and those on a budget may find themselves pushed to the fringes of the city to get a bargain. Prices are driven by demand: book well ahead to score a good deal on a room in the best-located midrange hotels.

In This Section

Prices & Tipping

A 'budget hotel' in NYC generally costs up to $200 for a standard double room. For a midrange option, plan on spending $200 to $350. Luxury options run $350 and higher. Breakfast isn't usually included as standard and will cost extra.

Tip the hotel housekeeper $3 to $5 per night, tip porters around $2 per bag. Staff providing service (hailing cabs, room service, concierge help) should be tipped accordingly.

Previous page: View of the Empire State Building (p66) from Park Ave
KOLDERAL/GETTY IMAGES ©

Reservations

Reservations are essential – walk-ins are practically impossible and prices will steadily increase until the absolute last minute (like, 24 hours before check-in). Reserve your room as early as possible and make sure you understand your hotel's cancellation policy. Expect check-in to always be in the middle of the afternoon and check-out in the late morning. Early check-ins are rare, though high-end establishments can often accommodate with advance notice.

Booking Services

NYC (www.nycgo.com/hotels) Loads of listings from the NYC Official Guide.

Newyorkhotels.org (www.newyork hotels.org) Easy-to-navigate site affiliated with Booking.com.

Lonely Planet (lonelyplanet.com/usa/new-york-city/hotels) Accommodation reviews and online booking service.

Renting Rooms & Apartments Online

More and more travelers are bypassing hotels and staying in private apartments listed online through companies such as Airbnb. The wealth of options is staggering, with more than 25,000 listings per night scattered in every corner of New York City. If you want a more local, neighborhood-oriented experience (or are traveling as a family), then this can be a great way to go.

There are a few things, however, to keep in mind. First off: many listings are actually illegal. Laws in NYC dictate that apartments can be rented out for less than 30 days only if the occupants are present. Effects on the immediate community are another issue, with some neighbors complaining about noise, security risks and the unexpected transformation of their residence into a hotel of sorts. There are also the larger impacts on the housing market: some landlords are cashing in, knowing they can earn more from holiday rentals than with long-term tenants. Taking thousands of possible rentals off the market is only driving rental prices for NYC residents ever higher.

Booking Tips & Room Rates

Pricing is hard to pin down in NYC because virtually all hotels run a dynamic pricing model, which means prices fluctuate based on availability and are guaranteed to skyrocket during periods of high demand (such as December and summer, and during popular city events/festivals). With more than 60 million visitors a year, New York is well set up to cater to tourist traffic and you'll always find a bed. That said, decent-priced hotels in Manhattan do sell out – especially in the weeks leading up to Christmas – and it pays to book well ahead.

If you're looking to find the best room rates, then flexibility is key – weekdays are often cheaper, and you'll generally find that accommodations offer significant discounts for stays from January to March. If you are visiting over a weekend, try for a business hotel in the Financial District – these tend to empty out at weekends. Occasionally you'll get better deals through booking websites, but hotels will usually price-match if you book direct and may throw in extra perks.

Accommodation Types

B&Bs & Family-Style Guesthouses

Offer homely furnishings, more personal attention and some serious savings (if you don't mind eating breakfast communally).

Boutique Hotels

Usually have tiny rooms with fantastic amenities and at least one celebrity-filled basement bar, rooftop bar or hip, flashy restaurant on-site.

Classic Hotels

Typified by old-fashioned European-style grandeur; these usually cost the same as boutiques; rooms may be larger but interiors are often tired-looking.

Luxury Hotels

Bells-and-whistles properties that see a lot of wealthy jetsetters; expect impeccable service, designer furnishings, in-house spas, restaurants run by celebrity chefs.

Business Hotels

No-nonsense, contemporary spaces that often offer discounts on weekends and make up for lack of character with functionality.

Hostels

Functional dorms (bunk beds and bare walls) that are nonetheless communal and friendly. Many have a backyard garden, kitchen and a pretty lounge that make up for the soulless rooms and often out-of-the-way locations.

Upper West Side & Central Park

Upper East Side

Midtown

West Village, Chelsea & Meatpacking District

Union Square, Flatiron District & Gramercy

SoHo & Chinatown

East Village & Lower East Side

Financial District & Lower Manhattan

Brooklyn

Neighborhood	For	Against
Financial District & Lower Manhattan	Convenient to Tribeca's nightlife and ferries. Cheap weekend rates at business hotels.	The southernmost areas can feel impersonal, though Tribeca has some great dining options.
SoHo & Chinatown	Shop to your heart's content right on your doorstep. Excellent dining options and a thriving nightlife.	Crowds (mostly tourists) swarm the streets of SoHo almost any time of day. Expensive.
East Village & Lower East Side	Funky and fun, the area feels the most quintessentially 'New York' to visitors and Manhattanites alike.	Options skew toward very pricey or bare-bones basic, with not much in the middle.
West Village, Chelsea & Meatpacking District	Brilliantly close-to-everything feel in a thriving, picturesque part of town that has an almost European flavor.	Prices soar for traditional hotels, but remain reasonable for B&Bs.
Union Square, Flatiron District & Gramercy	Subway access to anywhere in the city. Close to the Village and Midtown; good dining options.	Prices are high and there's not much in the way of neighborhood flavor.
Midtown	In the heart of the postcard's version of NYC: skyscrapers, museums, shopping and shows.	One of the most expensive areas; expect small rooms. Touristy and impersonal. Lackluster dining scene.
Upper East Side	Near top-notch museums and Central Park. Designer shops on Park Ave.	Fewer options, and wallet-busting prices; not particularly central.
Upper West Side & Central Park	Great for Central Park, Lincoln Center and the Museum of Natural History.	More family style than lively scene.
Harlem & Upper Manhattan	Great neighborhood vibe, better prices. Stellar live music.	Long subway rides to the action downtown and in Brooklyn.
Brooklyn	Better prices; great for exploring the most creative neighborhoods.	It can be a long commute to Midtown and points north.

Brooklyn Bridge (p46)

In Focus

Passengers on the subway

MATIAS HONKAMAA/SHUTTERSTOCK ©

New York City Today

New York remains an economic dynamo with record-low unemployment, overflowing city coffers and a building boom across the five boroughs. Beneath the veneer, however, are plenty of challenges, including an aging transit system, rising homelessness and the ongoing threat of terrorism. This city, however, takes everything in its stride. As former president Barack Obama once said, 'New Yorkers are as tough as they come.'

Tale of Two Cities

In many ways, New York is becoming ever more divided between the haves and the have-nots. Staggering development projects and high-priced apartments litter the landscape, from the $4.5-billion Hudson Yards to 432 Park, the Rafael Viñoly–designed superslim tower that in 2018 became the single best-selling building in NYC, with luxury condo sales topping $2 billion.

Meanwhile, the ranks of the homeless continue to grow. Today, there are more than 70,000 homeless people in the city, the highest level since the Great Depression of the 1930s. From 2010 to 2017, the median NYC rent rose by around 33% to over $3000 a month. Annually, rents during that period increased more than twice as fast as wages.

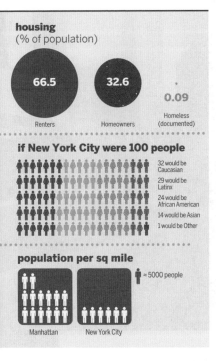

housing
(% of population)

66.5 — Renters

32.6 — Homeowners

0.09 — Homeless (documented)

if New York City were 100 people

32 would be Caucasian

29 would be Latinx

24 would be African American

14 would be Asian

1 would be Other

population per sq mile

♦ ≈ 5000 people

Manhattan   New York City

Most New Yorkers live between the two extremes, though the lack of affordable housing has placed a huge strain on residents. On average residents pay nearly 60% of their income on rent. It's no wonder that of the families living in NYC's homeless shelters, one-third of the adults have a job. Increasingly, young professionals and families are being forced to move further out to new frontiers like Jersey City, where the resident population has risen almost 10% since 2010.

A Progressive Mayor

Politically, New Yorkers are a liberal bunch (look out for the President Trump–bating on church billboards and in retail stores around town). Democrat mayor Bill de Blasio came into office in 2014 aiming to address the egregious inequalities in New York. One of his big early successes was the creation of free universal pre-kindergarten for all New Yorkers. In 2015 and 2016, under De Blasio, the city also instituted a rent-freeze, which benefited more than two million people living in rent-controlled apartments.

Creating affordable housing was another central goal of his agenda – envisioning the creation or preservation of 200,000 units of affordable housing by 2024. By the end of his first term in 2017, the mayor trumpeted the creation of 77,000 affordable housing units. In the realm of wages, he gave all 50,000 city workers a raise, increasing the minimum wage to $15 an hour, which went into effect at the end of 2018. Under the mayor, unemployment also reached record lows of 4% – its lowest in nearly 40 years. The city has also seen record-low crime rates under De Blasio.

Given his many successes, De Blasio coasted to victory during his bid for reelection, winning handily his second term as the head of America's largest city in 2017.

Subway Blues

One of the big challenges New York faces is maintaining its transit system. The century-old subway has been much afflicted lately, with a host of problems. Severely overcrowded trains and the increasing frequency of train breakdowns have led to much public resentment toward the Metropolitan Transit Authority (MTA). The trains themselves, along with the platforms and stations, are woeful compared with those in other world cities such as London. According to MTA officials, updating the system would take decades and cost billions of dollars.

Adding to many New Yorkers' troubles is the shutdown of the L train for much-needed repairs in April 2019. This key Manhattan–Brooklyn line provided service for some 225,000 riders daily who now have to find alternate means of transport for at least 15 months while works are carried out.

National September 11 Memorial & Museum (p86)

MATTHEW T CARROLL/GETTY IMAGES ©

History

This is the tale of a city that never sleeps, of a kingdom where tycoons and world leaders converge, of a place that's seen the highest highs and the most devastating lows. Yet through it all, it continues to reach for the sky (both figuratively and literally). And to think it all started with $24 and a pile of beads...

c AD 1500

About 15,000 Native Americans live in 80 sites around the island. The groups include the feuding Iroquois and Algonquins.

1625–26

The Dutch West India Company imports slaves from Africa to work in the fur trade and construction.

1646

The Dutch found the village of Breuckelen (Brooklyn) on the eastern shore of Long Island, naming it after Breukelen in the Netherlands.

Lower Manhattan

ELO|_OMELLA/GETTY IMAGES ©

Buying Manhattan

The Dutch West India Company sent 110 settlers to begin a trading post here in 1624. They settled in Lower Manhattan and called their colony New Amsterdam, touching off bloody battles with the unshakable Lenape, a people who had roots on the island dating back 11,000 years. It all came to a head in 1626, when the colony's first governor, Peter Minuit, became the city's first (but certainly not the last) unscrupulous real estate agent by purchasing Manhattan's 14,000 acres from the Lenape for 60 guilders ($24) and some glass beads.

By the time peg-legged Peter Stuyvesant arrived to govern the colony in 1647, the Lenape population had dwindled to about 700. In 1664 the English arrived in battleships; Stuyvesant avoided bloodshed by surrendering without a shot. King Charles II renamed the colony after his brother the Duke of York. New York became a prosperous British port and the population rose to 11,000 by the mid-1700s; however, colonists started to become resentful of British taxation.

1784	**1811**	**1863**
Alexander Hamilton founds America's first bank, the Bank of New York, with holdings of $500,000.	Manhattan's grid plan is developed by Mayor DeWitt Clinton, reshaping the city and laying plans for the future.	Civil War draft riots erupt, lasting for three days; order is restored by the Federal Army.

Revolution & War

By the 18th century the economy was so robust that the locals were improvising ways to avoid sharing the wealth with London, and New York became the stage for the fatal confrontation with King George III. Revolutionary battles began in August of 1776, when General George Washington's army lost about a quarter of its men in just a few days. The general retreated, and fire engulfed much of the colony. But soon the British left and Washington's army reclaimed their city. In 1789 the retired general found himself addressing crowds at Federal Hall, gathered to witness his presidential inauguration. Alexander Hamilton, as Washington's secretary of the treasury, began rebuilding New York and working to establish the New York Stock Exchange.

Population Bust, Infrastructure Boom

There were setbacks in the 19th century: the bloody Draft Riots of 1863, cholera epidemics, tensions among 'old' and 'new' immigrants, and poverty and crime in Five Points, the city's first slum. But the city prospered and found resources for mighty public works. Begun in 1855, Central Park was a vision of green reform and a boon to real-estate speculation. It also offered work relief when the Panic of 1857 shattered the nation's finance system. Another vision was realized by German-born engineer John Roebling, who designed the Brooklyn Bridge, spanning the East River and connecting lower Manhattan and Brooklyn.

The Burgeoning Metropolis

By the start of the 20th century, elevated trains carried a million people a day in and out of the city. Rapid transit opened up areas of the Bronx and Upper Manhattan. Tenements were overflowing with immigrants arriving from southern Italy and Eastern Europe, who increased the metropolis to about three million. Newly wealthy folks – boosted by an economy jump-started by financier JP Morgan – built splendid mansions on Fifth Ave. Reporter and photographer Jacob Riis illuminated the widening gap between the classes, leading the city to pass much-needed housing reforms.

Rights for Women & Workers

Wretched factory conditions – low pay, long hours, abusive employers – in the early 20th century were highlighted by a tragic event in 1911. The infamous Triangle Shirtwaist Company fire saw rapidly spreading flames catch onto the factory's piles of fabrics, killing 146 of the 500 female workers who were trapped behind locked doors. The event led to sweeping labor reforms after 20,000 female garment workers marched to City Hall. Nurse and midwife Margaret Sanger opened the first birth-control clinic in Brooklyn and suffragists held rallies to obtain the vote for women.

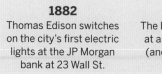

1882
Thomas Edison switches on the city's first electric lights at the JP Morgan bank at 23 Wall St.

1883
The Brooklyn Bridge, built at a cost of $15.5 million (and 27 lives), opens on 24 May.

1904
The city's first subway line opens, carrying 150,000 on its first day in operation.

The Jazz Age

The 1920s saw the dawning of the Jazz Age, when Prohibition outlawed the sale of alcohol, encouraging bootlegging and speakeasies, as well as organized crime. Congenial mayor James Walker was elected in 1925, Babe Ruth reigned at Yankee Stadium and the Great Migration from the South led to the Harlem Renaissance, when the neighborhood became a center of African American culture and society. Harlem's nightlife attracted the flappers and gin-soaked revelers that marked the complete failure of Prohibition.

Hard Times

The stock market crashed in 1929 and the city dealt with the Great Depression through grit, endurance, rent parties, militancy and public works projects. Texas-born, Yiddish-speaking mayor Fiorello La Guardia worked to bring relief in the form of New Deal–funded projects. WWII brought troops to the city, ready to party in Times Square before shipping off to Europe. Converted to war industries, factories hummed, staffed by women and African Americans who had rarely before had access to good, unionized jobs. With few evident controls on business, Midtown bulked up with skyscrapers after the war.

Move to the Beats

The 1960s ushered in an era of legendary creativity and anti-establishment expression, with many of its creators centered right downtown in Greenwich Village. One movement was abstract expressionism, a large-scale outbreak of American painters – Mark Rothko, Jackson Pollock, Lee Krasner, Helen Frankenthaler and Willem de Kooning among them – who offended and intrigued with incomprehensible squiggles and blotches and exuberant energy. Then there were the writers, such as Beat poets Allen Ginsberg and Jack Kerouac and novelist/playwright Jane Bowles. They gathered in Village coffeehouses to exchange ideas and find inspiration, which was often discovered in the form of folk music from burgeoning big names, such as Bob Dylan.

Enter Robert Moses

Working with Mayor La Guardia to usher the city into the modern age was Robert Moses, an urban planner who would influence the physical shape of the city more than anyone else in the 20th century. He was the mastermind behind the Triborough Bridge (now the Robert F Kennedy Bridge), Jones Beach State Park, the Verrazano–Narrows Bridge, the West Side Hwy and the Long Island parkway system – not to mention endless highways, tunnels and bridges, which shifted this mass-transit area into one largely dependent on the automobile.

1939	1969	1977
The World's Fair opens in Queens. With the future as its theme, the exposition invites visitors to take a look at 'the world of tomorrow.'	Police officers raid the gay friendly Stonewall Inn, sparking days of rioting and the birth of the modern gay-rights movement.	A summer blackout leaves New Yorkers in the dark for 24 sweltering hours, which leads to rioting around the city.

★ **Best Places to Learn About NYC History**

Ellis Island (p42)

Lower East Side Tenement Museum (p94)

Museum of Chinese in America (p74)

National September 11 Memorial Museum (p87)

Museum of Chinese in America (p74)

RANDY DUCHAINE/ALAMY STOCK PHOTO ©

'Drop Dead'

By the early 1970s deficits had created a fiscal crisis. President Gerald Ford refused to lend federal aid – summed up by the *Daily News* headline 'Ford to City, Drop Dead!' Massive layoffs decimated the working class; untended bridges, roads and parks reeked of hard times. The traumatic '70s – which reached a low point in 1977 with a citywide blackout and the terror caused by serial killer Son of Sam – drove down rents, helping to nourish an alternative culture that transformed the former industrial precincts of SoHo and Tribeca into energized nightlife districts.

Out of the Ashes

While the stock market boomed for much of the 1980s, neighborhoods struggled with the spread of crack cocaine; the city reeled from the impact of addiction, crime and AIDS. Squatters in the East Village fought back when police tried to clear a big homeless encampment, leading to the Tompkins Square Park riots of 1988. In South Bronx, a wave of arson reduced blocks of apartments to cinders. But amid the smoke, an influential hip-hop culture was born there and in Brooklyn.

Still convalescing from the real-estate crash of the late 1980s, the city faced crumbling infrastructure, jobs leaking south and Fortune 500 companies leaving for suburbia. Then the dot-com market roared in, turning the New York Stock Exchange into a speculator's fun park, and the city launched a frenzy of building and partying unparalleled since the 1920s.

With pro-business, law-and-order Rudy Giuliani as mayor, the dingy and destitute were swept from Manhattan's yuppified streets to the outer boroughs, leaving room for the well-off to live the high life. Giuliani grabbed headlines with his campaign to stamp out crime, even kicking the sex shops off notoriously seedy 42nd St.

● **1988**
Squatters riot when cops attempt to remove them from their de facto home in the East Village's Tompkins Square Park.

● **2001**
On September 11, terrorist hijackers fly two planes into the Twin Towers, destroying the World Trade Center and killing nearly 3000 people.

● **2008–9**
The stock market crashes due to mismanagement by major American financial institutions.

The New Millennium

The 10 years after September 11, 2001 were a period of rebuilding – both physically and emotionally. In 2002 mayor Michael Bloomberg began the task of picking up the pieces of a shattered city. New York did see a great deal of renovation and reconstruction, especially after the city hit its stride with spiking tourist numbers in 2005. By the latter part of Bloomberg's second term as mayor, the entire city seemed to be under construction, with luxury high-rise condos sprouting up in every neighborhood.

But soon the economy buckled under its own weight in what has largely become known as the Global Financial Crisis. The city was paralyzed as the cornerstones of the business world were forced to close shop. Although hit less badly than many pockets of the country, NYC still saw a significant dip in real-estate prices and many cranes turned to frozen monuments of a broken economy.

In 2011 the city commemorated the 10th anniversary of the September 11 attacks with the opening of a remembrance center, while the half-built Freedom Tower – a new corporate behemoth – loomed overhead.

September 11

On September 11, 2001, terrorists flew two hijacked planes into the World Trade Center's Twin Towers, turning the whole complex to dust and rubble and killing nearly 3000 people. Downtown Manhattan took months to recover from the ghastly fumes wafting from the ruins as forlorn missing-person posters grew ragged on brick walls. While the city mourned its dead and recovery crews coughed their way through the debris, residents braved constant terrorist alerts and an anthrax scare. Shock and grief drew people together, uniting the often-fractious citizenry in an effort not to succumb to despair.

Storms & Political Change

New York's resilience would be tested again in 2012 by superstorm Hurricane Sandy. On October 29, cyclonic winds and drenching rain pounded the city, causing severe flooding and property damage in all five boroughs, including to the NYC subway system, the Hugh L Carey Tunnel to Brooklyn and the World Trade Center site. A major power blackout plunged much of Lower Manhattan into surreal darkness, while trading at the New York Stock Exchange was suspended for two days in its first weather-related closure since 1888. In the neighborhood of Breezy Point, Queens, a devastating storm surge hindered the efforts of firefighters confronted with a blaze that reduced over 125 homes to ashes. The fire went down as one of the worst in NYC's history, while the storm itself claimed 44 lives in the city alone.

The winds of political change swept through the city in November 2013, when Bill de Blasio, a self-proclaimed progressive, became the city's first Democrat mayor since 1989. The 52-year-old also became the first white mayor of NYC with an African American spouse, Chirlane McCray. He was re-elected in 2017.

2012	2016	2017
Superstorm Sandy hits NYC in October, cutting power and causing major flooding and property damage.	Architect Santiago Calatrava's landmark World Trade Center Transportation Hub officially opens in Lower Manhattan.	Massive projects continue, with ongoing work on the 28-acre Hudson Yards, and the opening of the Second Ave subway line.

IAC Building (far left; p221) on the High Line (p52)

Art & Architecture

Peel back the concrete urban landscape, and you discover one of the world's great artistic centers. The city has been a showcase for talents great and small, who have added their mark to the city's canvas – both on its gallery walls and on its gritty streets in the form of architectural icons that soar above the crowded sidewalks.

An Artistic Heavyweight

That New York claims some of the world's mightiest art museums attests to its enviable artistic pedigree. From Pollock and Rothko to Warhol and Rauschenberg, the city has nourished many of America's greatest artists and artistic movements.

The Birth of an Arts Hub

In almost all facets of the arts, New York really got its sea legs in the early 20th century, when the city attracted and retained a critical mass of thinkers, artists, writers and poets. It was at this time that the homegrown art scene began to take shape. In 1905, photographer (and husband of Georgia O'Keeffe) Alfred Stieglitz opened 'Gallery 291,' a Fifth Ave space that provided a vital platform for American artists and helped establish photography as a credible art form.

In the 1940s, an influx of cultural figures fleeing the carnage of WWII saturated the city with fresh ideas – and New York became an important cultural hub. Peggy Guggenheim established the Art of this Century gallery on 57th St, a space that helped launch the careers of painters such as Jackson Pollock, Willem de Kooning and Robert Motherwell. These Manhattan-based artists came to form the core of the abstract expressionist movement (also known as the New York School), creating an explosive and rugged form of painting that changed the course of modern art as we know it.

An American Avant-Garde

The abstract expressionists helped establish New York as a global arts center. Another generation of artists then carried the baton. In the 1950s and '60s Robert Rauschenberg, Jasper Johns and Lee Bontecou turned paintings into off-the-wall sculptural constructions that included everything from welded steel to taxidermy goats. By the mid-60s, pop art – a movement that utilized the imagery and production techniques of popular culture – had taken hold, with Andy Warhol at the helm.

Graffiti & Street Art

Contemporary graffiti as we know it was cultivated in NYC. In the 1970s, the graffiti-covered subway train became a potent symbol of the city, and work by figures such as Dondi, Blade and Lady Pink became known around the world. In addition, fine artists such as Jean-Michel Basquiat, Kenny Scharf and Keith Haring began incorporating elements of graffiti into their work.

The movement received new life in the late 1990s when a new generation of artists – many with art-school pedigrees – began using materials such as cut paper and sculptural elements. Well-known New York City artists working in this vein include John Fekner, Stephen 'Espo' Powers, Swoon, the twin-brother duo Skewville and Shepard Fairey, who later went on to create the Obama 'Hope' poster. These days, spray-can and stencil hot spots include the Brooklyn side of the Williamsburg Bridge and the corner of Troutman St and St Nicholas Ave in Bushwick, also in Brooklyn.

By the '60s and '70s, when New York's economy was in the dumps and much of SoHo lay in a state of decay, the city became a hotbed of conceptual and performance art. Gordon Matta-Clark sliced up abandoned buildings with chainsaws and the artists of Fluxus staged happenings on downtown streets. Carolee Schneemann organized performances that utilized the human body. At one famous 1964 event, she had a crew of nude dancers roll around in an unappetizing mix of paint, sausages and dead fish in the theater of a Greenwich Village church.

Art Today

New York remains the world's gallery capital, with more than 800 spaces showcasing all kinds of art all over the city. The major institutions – the Metropolitan Museum of Art, the Museum of Modern Art, the Whitney Museum of American Art, the Guggenheim Museum, the Met Breuer and the Brooklyn Museum – deliver major retrospectives covering everything from Renaissance portraiture to contemporary installation. But art lovers should also try the small fringe galleries – Chelsea is a hot spot for blue-chip dealers such as David Zwirner. Galleries that showcase emerging and midcareer artists dot the Lower East Side, while emerging and experimental scenes are concentrated around the Brooklyn neighborhoods of Bushwick, Greenpoint, Clinton Hill and Bedford-Stuyvesant (Bed-Stuy).

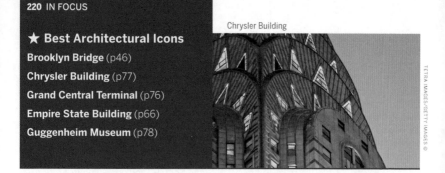

Chrysler Building

Architecture

New York's architectural history is a layer cake of ideas and styles – one that is literally written on the city's streets. There are the revivals (Greek, Gothic, Romanesque and Renaissance) and the unadorned forms of the International style. But if there is one style associated with New York beyond all others it is art deco, which was fused onto the cityscape in the 1930s. Today, icons like the Chrysler and Empire State are decadent reminders of that defining era.

Beaux-Arts Blockbusters

At the turn of the 20th century, New York entered a gilded age. Industrialists such as JP Morgan, Henry Clay Frick and John D Rockefeller – awash in steel and oil money – built themselves lavish manses. Public buildings grew ever more extravagant in scale and ornamentation. Architects, many of whom trained in France, came back with European design ideals. Gleaming white limestone began to replace all the brownstone, first stories were elevated to allow for dramatic staircase entrances, and buildings were adorned with sculptured keystones and Corinthian columns.

McKim, Mead and White's Villard Houses, from 1884 (now the Palace Hotel), show the movement's early roots. Loosely based on Rome's Palazzo della Cancelleria, they channeled the symmetry and elegance of the Italian Renaissance. Other classics include the central branch of the New York Public Library (1911), designed by Carrère and Hastings; the 1902 extension of the Metropolitan Museum of Art, by Richard Morris Hunt; and Warren and Wetmore's stunning Grand Central Terminal (1913), which is capped by a statue of Mercury, the god of commerce.

Reaching Skyward

By the time New York settled into the 20th century, elevators and steel-frame engineering had allowed the city to grow up – literally. This period saw a building boom of skyscrapers, starting with Cass Gilbert's neo-Gothic 60-story Woolworth Building (1913), which was the world's tallest building for almost two decades.

Others soon followed. In 1930, the Chrysler Building, the 77-story art-deco masterpiece designed by William Van Alen, trumped the Woolworth as the world's tallest structure. The following year, the record was broken by the Empire State Building, a clean-lined moderne monolith crafted from Indiana limestone with a beautiful art-deco interior. Its spire was meant to be used as a mooring mast for dirigibles (airships) – an idea that made for good publicity, but which proved to be impractical and unfeasible.

The influx of displaced European architects and other thinkers who had resettled in New York by the end of WWII fostered a lively dialogue between American and European architects. This was a period when urban planner Robert Moses furiously rebuilt vast swaths of New York – to the detriment of many neighborhoods – and designers and artists became obsessed with the clean, unadorned lines of the International style.

The city's greatest emblem of this architectural era is the controversial inverted ziggurat of the Guggenheim Museum, which was completed in 1959 but conceived more than a decade earlier.

The New Guard

By the late 20th century, numerous architects began to rebel against the hard-edged, unornamented nature of modernist design. Among them was Philip Johnson. His pink-granite AT&T Building (now Sony Tower; 1984) – topped by a scrolled, neo-Georgian pediment – has become a postmodern icon of the Midtown skyline.

What never became an icon was Daniel Libeskind's twisting, angular design for the One World Trade Center (2013) tower, replaced by a boxier architecture-by-committee glass obelisk. On the same site, budget blowouts led to tweaks of Santiago Calatrava's luminous design for the World Trade Center Transportation Hub (2016). According to critics, what should have looked like a dove in flight now resembles a winged dinosaur. The original Norman Foster design for Two World Trade Center was scrapped for one by Danish firm Bjarke Ingels Group (BIG). According to the chief operating officer of 21st Century Fox, James Murdoch, Foster's design was too conventional for what will become the media company's new base. BIG responded with its trademark unconventionalism: a tower of giant, differently sized boxes, soaring playfully into the sky.

Not that Foster can't do cutting-edge style. The British architect's Hearst Tower (2006) – a glass skyscraper zigzagging its

Starchitects on the Line

Frank Gehry's 2007 IAC Building – a billowing, white-glass structure often compared to a wedding cake – is one of a growing number of 'starchitect' creations appearing around railway-turned-urban-park, the High Line. The most significant of these is Renzo Piano's new Whitney Museum (2015), dramatically asymmetrical and clad in blue-gray steel. Turning heads eight blocks to the north is 100 Eleventh Ave (2010) by French architect Jean Nouvel, an exuberant arrangement of angled windows that is nothing short of mesmerizing. In 2017 the area also welcomed Iraqi-British architect Zaha Hadid's apartment complex at 520 West 28th St. Its voluptuous, sci-fi curves are complemented by a 2500-sq-ft sculpture deck showcasing art presented by Friends of the High Line.

Next on the agenda is a redevelopment of the Hudson Yards area to connect with the northern end of the High Line. This dramatic 11-hectare project is the largest development in NYC since the Rockefeller Center, and is transforming Midtown's underutilized west side with an entirely new neighborhood of shops, restaurants and apartments.

At its heart, a huge public space is anchored by the Vessel – an Escher-like steel structure by Heatherwick Studio rising skywards in the shape of a vase, with 2500 steps fashioned into a series of interlocking walkways and staircases designed for climbing. The development also includes an outdoor observation deck on the 100th floor of 30 Hudson Yards that, at 1100ft above ground, is the highest of its kind in the Western Hemisphere.

way out of a 1920s sandstone structure – remains a Midtown trailblazer. The building is one of numerous daring 21st-century additions to the city's architectural portfolio, among them Brooklyn's sci-fi arena Barclays Center (2012), Thom Mayne's folded-and-slashed 41 Cooper Square (2009) in the East Village, and Frank Gehry's rippling, 76-story apartment tower New York by Gehry (2011) in the Financial District.

Drag queen outside the Stonewall Inn

LOTTIE DAVIES/LONELY PLANET ©

LGBT+ New York City

New York City is out and damn proud. It was here that the Stonewall Riots took place, that the modern gay rights movement bloomed and that America's first Pride march hit the streets. Yet even before the days of 'Gay Lib,' the city had a knack for all things queer and fabulous, from Bowery sex saloons and Village Sapphic poetry to drag balls in Harlem.

Subversion in the Villages

In the 1890s New York City's rough-and-ready Lower East Side established quite a reputation for being home to venues offering everything from cross-dressing spectaculars to back rooms for same-sex shenanigans. As New York strode into the 20th century, free-thinking bohemians began stepping into Greenwich Village. A number of LGBT-owned businesses lined MacDougal St, among them the legendary Eve's Hangout at number 129, which was famous for two things: poetry readings and a sign on the door that read 'Men allowed but not welcome.' There would have been little chance of welcome drinks when police raided the place in June 1926, charging the owner, Polish Jewish immigrant Eva Kotchever (Eve Addams), with 'obscenity' for penning her Lesbian Love anthology, and deporting her back to Europe.

Divas, Drag & Harlem

While Times Square had developed a reputation for attracting gay men – many of them working in the district's theaters, restaurants and speakeasy bars – the hottest gay scene in the 1920s was found further north in Harlem, where the drag balls were a hit with both gay and straight New Yorkers. The biggest of the lot was the Hamilton Lodge Ball, held annually at the swank Rockland Palace on 155th St. Commonly dubbed the 'Faggots' Ball', it was a chance for both gay men and women to (legally) cross-dress and steal a same-sex dance, and for fashionable 'normals' to indulge in a little voyeuristic titillation. It was attended by everyone from prostitutes to high-society families, including the Astors and the Vanderbilts. Even the papers covered the extravaganza, with its outrageous frocks the talk of the town.

The Stonewall Revolution

The relative transgression of the early 20th century was replaced with a new conservatism in the following decades, as the Great Depression, WWII and the Cold War took their toll. Conservatism was helped along by Senator Joseph McCarthy, who declared that homosexuals in the State Department threatened America's security and children. Tougher policing aimed to eradicate LGBT+ visibility in the public sphere, forcing the scene further underground in the 1940s and '50s. Yet on June 28, 1969, when eight police officers raided the Stonewall Inn – a gay-friendly watering hole in Greenwich Village – patrons did the unthinkable: they revolted. They began bombarding the officers with coins, bottles, bricks and chants of 'gay power' and 'we shall overcome.' The cops were also met by a line of high-kicking drag queens. Their collective anger and solidarity was a turning point, igniting intense and passionate debate about discrimination and forming the catalyst for the modern gay rights movement, not just in New York, but across the US and in countries from the Netherlands to Australia. In June 2019 New York hosted the international WorldPride celebration for the 50th anniversary of the Stonewall riots, which led to the march's inception.

In the Shadow of AIDS

LGBT+ activism intensified as HIV and AIDS hit world headlines in the early 1980s. Faced with ignorance, fear and the moral indignation of those who saw AIDS as a 'gay cancer,' activists such as writer Larry Kramer set about tackling what was quickly becoming an epidemic. Out of his efforts was born ACT UP (AIDS Coalition to Unleash Power) in 1987. The epidemic itself had a significant impact on New York's artistic community. Among its most high-profile victims were artist Keith Haring, photographer Robert Mapplethorpe and fashion designer Halston. Yet out of this loss grew a tide of powerful AIDS-related plays and musicals that would become part of America's mainstream cultural canon. Among these are Tony Kushner's political epic *Angels in America* and Jonathan Larson's rock musical *Rent*. Both works would win Tony Awards and the Pulitzer Prize.

Marriage & Politics

The LGBT+ fight for complete equality took two massive steps forward in 2011. On September 20, a federal law banning LGBT+ military personnel from serving openly – the so-called 'Don't Ask, Don't Tell' policy – was repealed after years of intense lobbying. Three months earlier persistence had led to an even greater victory – the right to marry. The New York State Assembly passed the Marriage Equality Act, and it was signed into law on June 24, the very eve of New York City Gay Pride. State victory became a national one on June 26, 2015, when the US Supreme Court ruled that same-sex marriage is a legal right across the country, striking down the remaining marriage bans in 13 US states.

New York Public Library (p69)

MICHAEL LEE/GETTY IMAGES ©

NYC on Screen

New York City has a long and storied life on screen. It was on these streets that a bumbling Woody Allen fell for Diane Keaton in Annie Hall, that Meg Ryan faked her orgasm in When Harry Met Sally, and that Sarah Jessica Parker philosophized about the finer points of dating and Jimmy Choos in Sex & the City. To fans, traversing the city can feel like one big déjà vu of memorable scenes, characters and one-liners.

Landmarks on Screen

It's not surprising that NYC feels strangely familiar to many first-time visitors – the city itself has racked up more screen time than most Hollywood divas put together, and many of its landmarks are as much a part of American screen culture as its red-carpet celebrities. Take the **Staten Island Ferry** (p199), which takes bullied secretary Melanie Griffith from suburbia to Wall St in *Working Girl* (1988); **Battery Park** (www.nycgovparks.org; Broadway, at Battery Pl, Financial District; ⏰6am-1am; [S]4/5 to Bowling Green, R/W to Whitehall St, 1 to South Ferry), where Madonna bewitches Aidan Quinn and Rosanna Arquette in *Desperately Seeking Susan* (1985); or the New York County Courthouse, where villains get what they deserve in *Wall Street* (1987) and *Goodfellas* (1990), as well as in small-screen classics such as *Cagney & Lacey*, *NYPD Blue* and *Law & Order*. The latter show, famous for showcasing New

York and its characters, is honored with its own road – Law & Order Way – that leads to Pier 62 at Chelsea Piers.

Few landmarks can claim as much screen time as the **Empire State Building** (p66), famed for its spire-clinging ape in *King Kong* (1933, 2005), as well as for the countless romantic encounters on its observation decks. One of its most famous scenes is Meg Ryan and Tom Hanks' after-hours encounter in *Sleepless in Seattle* (1993). The sequence – which uses the real lobby but a studio-replica deck – is a tribute of sorts to *An Affair to Remember* (1957), which sees Cary Grant and Deborah Kerr make a pact to meet and (hopefully) seal their love atop the skyscraper.

Sarah Jessica Parker is less lucky in *Sex & the City* (2008), when a nervous Mr Big jilts her and her Vivienne Westwood wedding dress at the **New York Public Library** (p69). Perhaps he'd seen *Ghostbusters* (1984) a few too many times, its opening scenes featuring the haunted library's iconic marble lions and Rose Main Reading Room. The library's foyer sneakily stands in for the Metropolitan Museum of Art in *The Thomas Crown Affair* (1999), in which thieving playboy Pierce Brosnan meets his match in sultry detective Rene Russo. It's at the fountain in adjacent Bryant Park that DIY sleuth Diane Keaton debriefs husband Woody Allen about their supposedly bloodthirsty elderly neighbor in *Manhattan Murder Mystery* (1993).

Across **Central Park** (p36) – whose own countless scenes include Barbra Streisand and Robert Redford rowing on its lake in clutch-a-tissue *The Way We Were* (1973) – stands the Dakota Building, used in the classic thriller *Rosemary's Baby* (1968). The Upper West Side is also home to Tom's Restaurant, whose facade was used regularly in *Seinfeld*. Another neighborhood star is the elegant **Lincoln Center** (p108), where Natalie Portman slowly loses her mind in the psychological thriller *Black Swan* (2010), and where love-struck Brooklynites Cher and Nicolas Cage meet for a date in *Moonstruck* (1987).

The more recent Oscar-winner *Birdman* (2014) shines the spotlight on Midtown's glittering Theater District, in which a long-suffering Michael Keaton tries to stage a Broadway adaptation at the St James Theatre on W44th St.

Hollywood Roots & Rivals

Believe it or not, America's film industry is an East Coast native. Fox, Universal, Metro, Selznick and Goldwyn all originated here in the early 20th century, and long before Westerns were shot in California and Colorado, they were filmed in the (now former) wilds of New Jersey. Even after Hollywood's year-round sunshine lured the bulk of the business west by the 1920s, 'Lights, Camera, Action' remained a common call in Gotham. The heart of the local scene was Queens' still-kicking Kaufman Astoria Studios.

Dancing in the Street

In the cult musical *Fame* (1980), New York High School of Performing Arts students do little for the city's traffic woes by dancing on Midtown's streets. The film's graphic content was too much for the city's Board of Education, who banned shooting at the real High School of Performing Arts, then located at 120 W 46th St. Consequently, filmmakers used the doorway of a disused church on the opposite side of the street for the school's entrance, and Haaren Hall (Tenth Ave and 59th St) for interior scenes.

Fame is not alone in turning Gotham into a pop-up dance floor. In *On the Town* (1949), starstruck sailors Frank Sinatra, Gene Kelly and Jules Munshin look straight off a Pride float as they skip, hop and sing their way across this 'wonderful town,' from the base of **Lady Liberty** (p40) to **Rockefeller Plaza** (p83) and the **Brooklyn Bridge** (p46). Another

NYC on TV

Over 70 TV shows are filmed in NYC, from hit series such as *Law & Order: Special Victims Unit* and *The Good Fight* and quirky comedies like *The Marvelous Mrs Maisel* to long-standing classics including *The Tonight Show Starring Jimmy Fallon* and *Saturday Night Live*. Combined, the city's TV and film industries spend over $8 billion on production annually and support 130,000 jobs. More than a third of professional actors in the US are based here.

wave of campness hits the bridge when Diana Ross and Michael Jackson cross it in *The Wiz* (1978), a bizarre take on *The Wizard of Oz*, complete with munchkins in Flushing Meadows Corona Park and an Emerald City at the base of the WTC Twin Towers. The previous year, the bridge provided a rite of passage for a bell-bottomed John Travolta in *Saturday Night Fever* (1977), who leaves the comforts of his adolescent Brooklyn for the bigger, brighter mirror balls of Manhattan. Topping them all, however, is the closing scene in Terry Gilliam's *The Fisher King* (1991), which sees **Grand Central Terminal's Main Concourse** (p77) turned into a ballroom of waltzing commuters.

NYC on Film

It would take volumes to cover all the films tied to Gotham, so fire up your imagination with the following celluloid hits:

Taxi Driver (Martin Scorsese, 1976) Robert de Niro plays a mentally unstable Vietnam War vet whose violent urges are heightened by the city's tensions.

Manhattan (Woody Allen, 1979) A divorced New Yorker dating a high-school student falls for his best friend's mistress in what is essentially a love letter to NYC. Catch romantic views of the Queensboro Bridge and the Upper East Side.

Desperately Seeking Susan (Susan Seidelman, 1985) A case of mistaken identity leads a bored New Jersey housewife on a wild adventure through Manhattan's subcultural wonderland. Relive mid-1980s East Village and long-gone nightclub Danceteria.

Summer of Sam (Spike Lee, 1999) Spike Lee puts NYC's summer of 1977 in historical context by weaving together the Son of Sam murders, the blackout, racial tensions and the misadventures of one disco-dancing Brooklyn couple, including scenes at CBGB and Studio 54.

Angels in America (Mike Nichols, 2003) This movie version of Tony Kushner's Broadway play recalls 1985 Manhattan: crumbling relationships, AIDS out of control and a closeted Roy Cohn – adviser to President Ronald Reagan – doing nothing about it except falling ill himself. Follow characters from Brooklyn to Lower Manhattan to Central Park.

Party Monster (Fenton Bailey, 2003) Starring Macaulay Culkin, who plays the notorious club kid and killer Michael Alig, this is a disturbing look into the drug-fueled downtown clubbing culture of the late '80s. The former Limelight club is featured prominently.

Precious (Lee Daniels, 2009) This unflinching tale of an obese, illiterate teenager who is abused by her parents takes place in Harlem, offering plenty of streetscapes and New York–ghetto 'tude.

Birdman (Alejandro G Iñárritu, 2014) Oscar-winning black-comedy/drama *Birdman* documents the struggles of a has-been Hollywood actor trying to mount a Broadway show.

Ghostbusters (Paul Feig, 2016) The reboot of the original 1984 film received mixed reviews but broke new ground with its all-female leads.

The Greatest Showman (Michael Gracey, 2017) Musical starring Hugh Jackman, Michelle Williams and Zac Efron. Inspired by the story of PT Barnum, who established the first circus and freak show in 19th-century Manhattan.

Times Square (p62)

LUCIANO MORTULA-S/SHUTTERSTOCK ©

Survival Guide

Directory A–Z

Accessible Travel

Much of the city is accessible, with curb cuts for wheelchair users. All the major sites (the Met museum, the Guggenheim and Lincoln Center) are also accessible. Some, but not all, Broadway theaters are accessible.

Unfortunately, only about 100 of New York's 468 subway stations are fully wheelchair accessible. In general, the bigger stations have access, such as 14th St-Union Sq, 34th St-Penn Station, 42nd St-Port Authority Terminal, 59th St-Columbus Circle and 66th St-Lincoln Center. For a complete list of accessible subway stations, visit http://web.mta.info/accessibility/stations.htm. Also visit www.nycgo.com/accessibility. All of NYC's MTA buses are wheelchair accessible, and are often a better option than negotiating cramped subway stations.

You can order an accessible taxi through Accessible Dispatch (☏646-599-9999; http://accessible-dispatch.org); there's also an app that allows you to request the nearest available service.

Another excellent resource is the **Big Apple Greeter** (☏212-669-8198; www.bigapplegreeter.org) **FREE** program, which has more than 50 volunteers on staff with physical disabilities who are happy to show off their corner of the city.

Download Lonely Planet's free *Accessible Travel* guides from http://lptravel.to/AccessibleTravel.

Book Your Stay Online

For more accommodation reviews by Lonely Planet authors, check out http://hotels.lonelyplanet.com/new-york. You'll find independent reviews, as well as recommendations on the best places to stay. Best of all, you can book online.

Customs Regulations

US Customs allows each person over the age of 21 to bring 1L of liquor and 200 cigarettes into the US duty free. Agricultural items including meat, fruits, vegetables, plants and soil are prohibited. US citizens are allowed to import, duty free, up to $800 worth of gifts from abroad, while non-US citizens are allowed to import $100 worth. For updates, check www.cbp.gov.

Discount Cards

If you plan on blitzing the major sights, consider buying one of the numerous multi-attraction passes (see www.nycgo.com/attraction-passes). Getting one of these discount cards will save you a wad of cash. Go online for more details, and to purchase these passes.

New York CityPASS (www.citypass.com)

The New York Pass (www.newyorkpass.com)

Downtown Culture Pass (www.downtownculturepass.org)

Explorer Pass (www.smartdestinations.com)

Electricity

The US electric current is 110V to 115V, 60Hz AC. Outlets are made for flat two-prong plugs (which often have a third, rounded prong for grounding). If your appliance is made for another electrical system (eg 220V), you'll need a step-down converter, which can be bought at hardware stores and drugstores. Most electronic devices (laptops, camera-battery chargers etc) are built for dual-voltage use, however, and will only need a plug adapter.

Type A
120V/60Hz

Type B
120V/60Hz

Health

Emergency services can be stress-inducing and slow (unless your medical condition is absolutely dire); a visit should be avoided if other medical services can be provided to mitigate the situation.

Travel MD (212-737-1212; www.travelmd.com) Offers 24-hour medical advice for visitors to NYC, and appointments for hotel visits can be made.

Bellevue Hospital Center (☎212-562-4141; www.nychealthandhospitals.org/bellevue; 462 First Ave, at 27th St, Midtown East; [S]6 to 28th St)

Tisch Hospital (New York University Langone Medical Center; ☎212-263-5800; www.nyulangone.org/locations/tisch-hospital; 550 First Ave; ⏰24hr)

Lenox Hill Hospital (☎212-434-2000; www.northwell.edu/find-care/locations/lenox-hill-hospital; 100 E 77th St, at Lexington Ave; ⏰24hr; [S]6 to 77th St)

Insurance

Before traveling, contact your health-insurance provider to find out what types of medical care will be covered outside your hometown (or home country). Overseas visitors should acquire travel insurance that covers medical situations in the US, as nonemergency care for uninsured patients can be very expensive. For non-emergency appointments at hospitals, you'll need proof of insurance or cash.

Even with insurance, you'll most likely have to pay up front for nonemergency care and then wrangle with your insurance company afterward in order to get your money reimbursed.

Internet Access

Most public parks in the city now offer free wi-fi. Some prominent ones include the High Line, Bryant Park, Battery Park, City Hall Park, Madison Square Park, Tompkins Square Park and Union Square Park (Brooklyn is also well covered). Note that although Central Park is technically covered, connectivity is poor. For other locations, check out www.nycgovparks.org/facilities/wifi.

Museums also often offer free wi-fi, as do underground subway stations. LinkNYC (www.link.nyc) has installed free internet-connected kiosks, replete with charging stations and wi-fi access. The network aims to install some 7500 of these structures throughout the five boroughs. Coverage is widespread in Midtown Manhattan, but gets increasingly spotty the further north or south you go, particularly in SoHo and the Lower East Side.

It's rare to find accommodations in New York City that don't offer free wi-fi these days. Most cafes offer wi-fi for customers (though they may not always advertise it), as do the ubiquitous Starbucks around town.

Tipping

Tipping is *not* optional; only withhold tips in cases of outrageously bad service.

Restaurant servers 18–20%, unless a gratuity is already charged on the bill (usually only for groups of five or more).

Bartenders 15–20% per round, minimum per drink $1 for standard drinks, and $2 per specialty cocktail.

Taxi drivers 10–15%, rounded up to the next dollar.

Airport & hotel porters $2 per bag, minimum per cart $5.

Hotel maids $2–4 per night, left in envelope or under the card provided.

Legal Matters

If you're arrested, you have the right to remain silent. There is no legal reason to speak to a police officer if you don't wish to – especially since anything you say 'can and will be used against you' – but never walk away from an officer until given permission. All persons who are arrested have the legal right to make one phone call. If you don't have a lawyer or family member to help you, call your consulate. The police will give you the number upon request.

LGBT+ Travelers

One of the largest centers of its kind in the world, the **LGBT Community Center** (☎212-620-7310; www.gaycenter.org; 208 W 13th St, btwn Seventh & Greenwich Aves, West Village; ⏰9am-10pm Mon-Sat, to 9pm Sun; [S]1/2/3 to 14th St, A/C/E, L to 8th Ave-14th St) provides a ton of regional publications about LGBT+ events and nightlife, and hosts frequent special events – dance parties, art exhibits, Broadway-caliber performances, readings and political panels. Plus it's home to the National Archive for Lesbian, Gay, Bisexual & Transgender History (accessible to researchers by appointment); a community-oriented cafe; a small exhibition space, the Campbell-Soady Gallery; and a cyber center.

Money

ATMs

ATMs are on practically every corner. Try to withdraw cash from ones attached to banks – usually in a 24-hour-access lobby, filled with up to a dozen monitors at major branches. The other option is private ATMs that sit in delis, restaurants, bars and grocery stores. Beware: these lone wolves charge fierce service fees of $3 to $5.

Changing Money

Banks and moneychangers, found all over New York City (including all three major airports), will give you US currency based on the current exchange rate. Travelex (www.travelex.com) has a branch in Times Square.

Credit Cards

Major credit cards are accepted at most hotels, restaurants and shops throughout New York City. In fact, you'll find it difficult to perform certain transactions, such as purchasing tickets to performances and renting a car, without one.

Opening Hours

Standard business hours are as follows:

Banks 9am to 6pm Monday to Friday, some also 9am to noon Saturday

Bars 5pm to 4am

Businesses 9am to 5pm Monday to Friday

Clubs 10pm to 4am

Restaurants Breakfast 6am to 11am, lunch noon to around 3pm, and dinner 5pm to 11pm. Weekend brunch 10am to 4pm.

Shops 10am to around 7pm weekdays, 11am to around 8pm Saturday, and Sunday can be variable – some stores stay closed, while others keep weekday hours. Stores tend to stay open later in the neighborhoods downtown, such as SoHo.

Public Holidays

Major NYC holidays and special events may force the closure of many businesses or attract crowds, making dining and accommodations reservations difficult.

New Year's Day January 1

Martin Luther King Day Third Monday in January

Presidents' Day Third Monday in February

Easter March/April

Memorial Day Late May

Gay Pride Last Sunday in June

Independence Day July 4

Labor Day Early September

Rosh Hashanah and Yom Kippur Mid-September to mid-October

Halloween October 31

Thanksgiving Fourth Thursday in November

Christmas Day December 25

New Year's Eve December 31

Safe Travel

New York City is one of the safest cities in the USA – in 2017 homicides fell to a record low of fewer than 300 and overall violent-crime statistics declined for the 27th straight year. Still, it's best to take a common-sense approach to the city.

• Don't walk around alone at night in unfamiliar, sparsely populated areas.

• Be aware of pickpockets, particularly in mobbed areas such as Times Square or Penn Station at rush hour.

• While it's generally safe to ride the subway after midnight, you may want to skip going underground and take a taxi instead, especially if traveling alone.

Taxes & Refunds

Restaurants and retailers never include the sales tax – 8.875% – in their prices, so beware of ordering the $14.99 lunch special when you only have $15 to your name. Hotel rooms in New York City are subject to a 14.75% tax, plus a flat $3.50 occupancy tax per

Practicalities

Newspapers

New York Post (www.nypost.com) The *Post* is known for screaming headlines, conservative political views and its popular Page Six gossip column.

New York Times (www.nytimes.com) 'The gray lady' is far from staid, with hard-hitting political coverage, and sections on technology, the arts and dining out.

Magazines

New York Magazine (www.nymag.com) A biweekly magazine with feature stories and great listings about anything and everything in NYC, plus an indispensable website.

New Yorker (www.newyorker.com) This highbrow weekly covers politics and culture through its famously lengthy works of reportage; it also publishes fiction and poetry.

Time Out New York (www.timeout.com/newyork) A biweekly magazine with event listings and restaurant and nightlife roundups.

Radio

WNYC (820AM and 93.9FM; www.wnyc.org), NYC's public radio station, is the local NPR affiliate and offers a blend of national and local talk and interview shows.

Smoking

Strictly forbidden in any location that's considered a public place, including subway stations, restaurants, bars, taxis and parks.

night. Since the US has no nationwide value-added tax (VAT), foreign visitors cannot make 'tax-free' purchases.

Telephone

Phone numbers within the US consist of a three-digit area code followed by a seven-digit local number. In NYC, you will always dial 10 numbers: 1 + the three-digit area code + the seven-digit number. To make an international call from NYC, call 011 + country code + area code + number. When calling Canada, there is no need to use the 011.

Cell Phones

International travelers can use local SIM cards in a smartphone provided it is unlocked. Alternatively, you can buy a cheap US phone and load it with prepaid minutes. Some phone carriers also offer free international data roaming so check your package before leaving home.

Emergency & Important Numbers

Local directory	411
Municipal offices & NYC information	311
National directory information	212-555-1212
Fire, police & ambulance	911

Toilets

Considering the number of pedestrians, there's a noticeable lack of public restrooms around the city. You'll find spots to relieve yourself in Grand Central Terminal, Penn Station and Port Authority Bus Terminal, and in parks, including Madison Square Park, Battery Park, Tompkins Square Park, Washington Square Park and Columbus Park in Chinatown, plus several places scattered around Central Park – check www.nycgovparks.org/facilities/bathrooms for a full list of locations. A good bet, though, is to pop into a Starbucks (there's one about every three blocks), or a department store (Macy's, Century 21, Bloomingdale's).

Tourist Information

There are infinite online resources to get up-to-the-minute information about New York. In person, try one of the official branches of **NYC Information Center** (www.nycgo.com) such as the ones in **Times Square** (212-484-1222; www.nycgo.com; Broadway Plaza, btwn W 43rd & 44th Sts; 8am-8pm; N/Q/R/W, S, 1/2/3, 7, A/C/E to Times Sq-42nd St) or **Macy's Herald Square**

(212-484-1222; www.nycgo.com; Macy's, 151 W 34th St, at Broadway; 10am-10pm Mon-Sat, to 9pm Sun; B/D/F/M, N/Q/R/W to 34th St-Herald Sq).

Visas

The US Visa Waiver Program (VWP) allows nationals of 38 countries to enter the US without a visa, but you must have a machine-readable passport to qualify and must fill out an ESTA (Electronic System for Travel Authorization) application before departing. ESTA costs $14 and lasts for two years. Visit www.cbp.gov/travel/international-visitors/esta to apply.

Transport

Getting There & Away

With its three busy airports, two main train stations and a monolithic bus terminal, New York City rolls out the welcome mat for millions of visitors who come to take a bite out of the Big Apple each year.

Direct flights are possible from most major American and international cities. Figure six hours from Los

Angeles, seven hours from London and Amsterdam, and 14 hours from Tokyo. If you're visiting from within the US, consider getting here by train instead of car or plane to enjoy a mix of bucolic and urban scenery en route, without unnecessary traffic hassles, security checks and excess carbon emissions.

Flights, cars and tours can be booked online at lonelyplanet.com/bookings.

Air

JFK

John F Kennedy International Airport (JFK; ☎718-244-4444; www.jfkairport.com; [S]A to Howard Beach, E, J/Z to Sutphin Blvd-Archer Ave then Airtrain), 15 miles from Midtown in southeastern Queens, has six working terminals, serves more than 59 million passengers annually and hosts flights coming and going from all corners of the globe. You can use the AirTrain (free within the airport) to move from one terminal to another.

Taxi

A yellow taxi from Manhattan to the airport will use the meter; prices (often about $60) depend on traffic. Expect the ride to take 45 to 60 minutes. From JFK, taxis charge a flat rate of $52 to any destination in Manhattan (not including tolls or tip). To/from a destination in Brooklyn, the metered fare should be about $45 (Coney Island) to $62 (downtown Brooklyn). Fares for ridesharing apps like Lyft and Uber change depending on the time of day.

Shuttles & Car Services

Shared vans, like those offered by **Super Shuttle Manhattan** (www.supershuttle.com), cost around $20 to $26 per person, depending on the destination. If traveling to the airport from NYC, car services have set fares from around $50.

Express Bus

The **NYC Express Bus** (formerly called the NYC Airporter bus; www.nycairporter.com) runs to Grand Central Terminal or the Port Authority Bus Terminal from JFK between 11am and 7pm. The one-way fare is $19.

Subway

The subway is the cheapest but slowest way of reaching Manhattan. From the airport, hop on the AirTrain ($5, payable as you exit) to Sutphin Blvd-Archer Ave (Jamaica Station) to reach the E, J or Z line (or the Long Island Rail Road). To take the A line instead, ride the AirTrain to Howard Beach station. The E train to Midtown has the fewest stops. Expect the journey to take a little over an hour to Midtown.

Long Island Railroad (LIRR)

This is by far the most relaxing way to arrive in the city. From the airport, take the AirTrain ($5, as you exit) to Jamaica Station. From there, LIRR trains go frequently to Penn Station in Manhattan or to Atlantic Terminal in Brooklyn (near Fort Greene, Boerum Hill and the Barclay Center). It's about a 20-minute journey from station to station. One-way fares to either Penn Station or Atlantic Terminal cost $10.25 ($7.50 at off-peak times).

LaGuardia Airport

Used mainly for domestic flights, **LaGuardia** (LGA; ☎718-533-3400; www.laguardiaairport.com; 🚌M60, Q70) is smaller than JFK but only 8 miles from midtown Manhattan; it sees nearly 30 million passengers per year. A much-needed $4 billion overhaul of its terminal facilities has begun and is expected to be finished in 2021.

Taxi

A taxi to/from Manhattan costs about $42 for the approximately half-hour ride; it's metered, no set fare. Fares for ride-hailing apps like Lyft and Uber vary.

Car Service

A car service to LaGuardia costs from around $44. The airport's website lists companies that ply this route.

Express Bus

The **NYC Express Bus** costs $16 and goes to/from Grand Central and the Port Authority Bus Terminal.

Public Transportation

It's less convenient to get to LaGuardia by public transportation than the other airports. The best subway link is the 74 St-Broadway station (7 line, or the E, F, M and R lines at the connecting Jackson Heights-Roosevelt Ave station) in Queens, where you can pick up the Q70 Express Bus to the airport (about 10 minutes to the airport). Or you can catch the M60 bus from several subway stops in upper Manhattan and Harlem or from the Astoria Blvd station (Hoyt Ave at 31st St) on the N/W subway lines.

Newark Liberty International Airport

Don't write off New Jersey when looking for airfares to New York. About the same distance from Midtown as JFK (16 miles), **Newark** (EWR; ☑973-961-6000; www. newarkairport.com) is used by many New Yorkers (there are some 36 million passengers annually) and is a hub for United Airlines. A $2.4 billion redevelopment of Terminal A is scheduled to be completed in 2022.

Car Service

A car service runs about $50 to $70 for the 45-minute ride from Midtown – a taxi is roughly the same. You'll have to pay a whopping $15 to get into NYC through the Lincoln (at 42nd St) and Holland (at Canal St) Tunnels and, further north, the George Washington Bridge, though there's no charge going back through to NJ. There are a couple of cheap tolls on New Jersey highways, too, unless you ask your driver to take Hwy 1 or 9.

Subway & Train

NJ Transit (www.njtransit. com) runs a rail service (with a $5.50 AirTrain connection) between Newark airport (EWR) and New York's Penn Station for $13 each way. The trip takes 25 minutes and runs every 20 or 30 minutes from 4:20am to about 1:40am. Hold onto your ticket, which you must show upon exiting at the airport.

Express Bus

The **Newark Liberty Airport Express** (www. newarkairportexpress.com) has a bus service between the airport and Port Authority Bus Terminal, Bryant Park and Grand Central Terminal in Midtown ($17 one-way). The 45-minute ride goes every 20 minutes from 6:45am to 11:15pm and every half-hour from 4:15am to 9am and 11pm to 2:20am.

Getting Around

Check the Metropolitan Transportation Authority website (www.mta.info) for public transportation information (buses and subway), a route planner and notifications of delays and alternate travel routes during frequent maintenance.

Bicycle

Hundreds of miles of designated bike lanes have been added over the past decade. Add to this the excellent bike-sharing network **Citi Bike** (www. citibikenyc.com), and you

---

Climate Change & Travel

Every form of transport that relies on carbon-based fuel generates CO_2, the main cause of human-induced climate change. Modern travel is dependent on airplanes, which might use less fuel per mile per person than most cars but travel much greater distances. The altitude at which aircraft emit gases (including CO_2) and particles also contributes to their climate change impact. Many websites offer 'carbon calculators' that allow people to estimate the carbon emissions generated by their journey and, for those who wish to do so, to offset the impact of the greenhouse gases emitted with contributions to portfolios of climate-friendly initiatives throughout the world. Lonely Planet offsets the carbon footprint of all staff and author travel.

have the makings for a surprisingly bike-friendly city. There are hundreds of Citi Bike stations spread across Manhattan and parts of Brooklyn, housing the iconic bright-blue and very sturdy bicycles. Rates are reasonable for short-term users and there are an estimated 12,000 bikes in the system.

Tourists can either pay for a single ride ($3), or buy a pass (24-hour/three-day passes $12/24 including tax) at any Citi Bike station. You will then be given a five-digit code to unlock a bike. Return the bike to any station within 30 minutes to avoid incurring extra fees. Reinsert your credit card (you won't be charged) and follow the prompts to check out a bike again. If you buy a pass, you can make an unlimited number of 30-minute checkouts during the time period you've paid for. Helmets aren't required by law, but strongly recommended (you'll need to bring your own).

Boat

NYC Ferry (www.ferry.nyc; one-way $2.75) Operating in the East River since May 2017 (the company replaced the former East River Ferry service), these boats link Manhattan, Brooklyn, Queens and the Bronx. At only $2.75 a ride ($1 more to bring a bicycle on board) and with charging stations and mini convenience stores on board, it's an altogether more pleasurable commute than being stuck underground on the subway. It has become a popular and scenic way to reach beach spots in Rockaway, Queens.

NY Water Taxi (www.nywatertaxi.com) Has a fleet of zippy yellow boats that provide hop-on, hop-off services with a few stops around Manhattan (Pier 83 at W 42nd St; Battery Park; Pier 16 near Wall St) and Brooklyn (Pier 1 in Dumbo). At $37 for an all-day pass, though, it's priced more like a sightseeing cruise than practical transport.

Staten Island Ferry (www.siferry.com; Whitehall Terminal, 4 Whitehall St, at South St, Lower Manhattan; 🕒24hr; [S]1 to South Ferry, R/W to Whitehall St, 4/5 to Bowling Green) [FREE] Bright orange and large, this free commuter-oriented ferry to Staten Island makes constant journeys across New York Harbor. Even if you simply turn around to reboard in Staten Island, the views of lower Manhattan and the Statue of Liberty make this a great sightseeing experience and one of the cheapest romantic dates in the city.

Bus

Buses can be a handy way to cross town or to cover short distances when you don't want to bother going underground. Rides cost the same as subway ($2.75 per ride), and you can use your MetroCard or pay in cash (exact change in coins required) when entering the bus. If you pay with a MetroCard, you get one free transfer from bus to subway, bus to bus, or subway to bus within a two-hour window. If you pay in cash, ask for a transfer (good only for a bus-to-bus transfer) from the bus driver when paying.

Car & Motorcycle

Unless you plan to explore far-flung corners of the outer boroughs, it's a bad idea to have a car in NYC. Parking garages can be quite expensive, and finding street parking can be maddeningly difficult. If you drive in from New Jersey, you'll also have to contend with high tolls. Unlike in most other parts of the US, turning right on a red light is not legal here.

Subway

The New York subway system, run by the Metropolitan Transportation Authority (www.mta.info), is iconic, cheap ($2.75 per ride, regardless of the distance traveled), round-the-clock and often the fastest and most reliable way to get around the city. It's also safer and (a bit) cleaner than it used to be. Free wi-fi is available in all underground stations. A 7-Day Unlimited Pass costs $32.

It's a good idea to grab a free map from a station attendant. If you have a smartphone, download a useful app (like the free Citymapper), with subway map and alerts of service outages.

Taxi

Hailing and riding in a cab, once rites of passage in New York, are being replaced by the ubiquity of ride-hailing app services like Lyft and Uber. Most taxis in NYC are clean and, compared to those in many international cities, pretty cheap.

It's $2.50 for the initial charge (first one-fifth of a mile), 50¢ for each additional one-fifth mile as well as per 60 seconds in slow/non-moving traffic, $1 peak surcharge (weekdays 4pm to 8pm), and a 50¢ night surcharge (8pm to 6am), plus an MTA State surcharge of 50¢ per ride. Passengers must pay all bridge and tunnel toll charges. Tips are expected to be 10% to 15%, but give less if you feel in any way mistreated; be sure to ask for a receipt and use it to note the driver's license number. See www.nyc.gov/taxi for more information.

Boro Taxis

Green Boro Taxis operate in the outer boroughs and Upper Manhattan. These allow folks to hail a taxi on the street in neighborhoods where yellow taxis rarely roam. They have the same fares and features as yellow cabs, and are a good way to get around the outer boroughs (from, say, Astoria to Williamsburg, or Park Slope to Red Hook). Drivers are reluctant (but legally obligated) to take passengers into Manhattan as they aren't legally allowed to take fares going out of Manhattan south of 96th St.

Behind the Scenes

Acknowledgements

Cover photograph: Brooklyn Bridge, Antonino Bartuccio/4Corners ©

This Book

This 4th edition of Lonely Planet's *Best of New York City* guidebook was curated by Lorna Parkes, and researched and written by Lorna, Hugh McNaughtan and Regis St Louis. The previous edition was curated by Ali Lemer, and researched and written by Ali, Robert Balkovich, Ray Bartlett and Regis. This guidebook was produced by the following:

Destination Editors Evan Godt, Trisha Ping

Senior Product Editor Martine Power

Regional Senior Cartographer Alison Lyall

Product Editor Ronan Abayawickrema

Book Designer Fergal Condon

Assisting Editors Sarah Bailey, Katie Connolly, Amy Lynch, Monique Perrin, Claire Rourke, Sam Wheeler

Cover Researcher Brendan Dempsey-Spencer

Thanks to Mikki Brammer, Gwen Cotter, Liz Heynes, Sandie Kestell, Virginia Moreno, Jenna Myers, Genna Patterson

Send Us Your Feedback

We love to hear from travelers – your comments keep us on our toes and help make our books better. Our well-traveled team reads every word on what you loved or loathed about this book. Although we cannot reply individually to postal submissions, we always guarantee that your feedback goes straight to the appropriate authors, in time for the next edition. Each person who sends us information is thanked in the next edition, the most useful submissions are rewarded with a selection of digital PDF chapters.

Visit lonelyplanet.com/contact to submit your updates and suggestions or to ask for help. Our award-winning website also features inspirational travel stories, news and discussions.

Note: We may edit, reproduce and incorporate your comments in Lonely Planet products such as guidebooks, websites and digital products, so let us know if you don't want your comments reproduced or your name acknowledged. For a copy of our privacy policy visit lonelyplanet.com/privacy.

Index

A

B

000 Map pages

C

D

E

    accommodations 207

    drinking 168-9

    entertainment 182-3

    food 128-30

    nightlife 168-9

    shopping 151, 153

economy 210-11

electricity 228-9

Ellis Island 42-5

emergency numbers 232

Empire Fulton Ferry State Park Park 47

Empire State Building 66-9

entertainment 179-91, see also individual neighborhoods

    Broadway shows 181

    comedy clubs 183

Symbols & Map Key

Look for these symbols to quickly identify listings:

- ◉ Sights
- ✪ Activities
- ✪ Courses
- ✪ Tours
- ✪ Festivals & Events
- ✪ Eating
- ✪ Drinking
- ✪ Entertainment
- ✪ Shopping
- ✪ Information & Transport

These symbols and abbreviations give vital information for each listing:

- ✿ Sustainable or green recommendation
- **FREE** No payment required

- ☎ Telephone number
- ◷ Opening hours
- Ⓟ Parking
- ☺ Nonsmoking
- ✱ Air-conditioning
- @ Internet access
- ☎ Wi-fi access
- ⚲ Swimming pool

- ☒ Bus
- ☒ Ferry
- ☒ Tram
- ☒ Train
- ☒ English-language menu
- ✎ Vegetarian selection
- ☒ Family-friendly

Find your best experiences with these Great For... icons.

- Art & Culture
- Beaches
- Budget
- Cafe/Coffee
- Cycling
- Detour
- Drinking
- Entertainment
- Events
- Family Travel
- Food & Drink
- History
- Local Life
- Nature & Wildlife
- Photo Op
- Scenery
- Shopping
- Short Trip
- Sport
- Walking
- Winter Travel

Sights

- ⊕ Beach
- ⊕ Bird Sanctuary
- ⊕ Buddhist
- ⊕ Castle/Palace
- ⊕ Christian
- ⊕ Confucian
- ⊕ Hindu
- ⊕ Islamic
- ⊕ Jain
- ⊕ Jewish
- ⊕ Monument
- ⊕ Museum/Gallery/ Historic Building
- ⊕ Ruin
- ⊕ Shinto
- ⊕ Sikh
- ⊕ Taoist
- ⊕ Winery/Vineyard
- ⊕ Zoo/Wildlife Sanctuary
- ⊚ Other Sight

Points of Interest

- ◎ Bodysurfing
- ◎ Camping
- ◎ Cafe
- ◎ Canoeing/Kayaking
- • Course/Tour
- ◎ Diving
- ◎ Drinking & Nightlife
- ◎ Eating
- ◎ Entertainment
- ◎ Sento Hot Baths/ Onsen
- ◎ Shopping
- ◎ Skiing
- ◎ Sleeping
- ◎ Snorkelling
- ◎ Surfing
- ◎ Swimming/Pool
- ◎ Walking
- ◎ Windsurfing
- ◎ Other Activity

Information

- ⑤ Bank
- ⑥ Embassy/Consulate
- ⊕ Hospital/Medical
- @ Internet
- ⊚ Police
- ⊚ Post Office
- ⊕ Telephone
- ⊕ Toilet
- ⊕ Tourist Information
- • Other Information

Geographic

- ⊕ Beach
- ⊷ Gate
- ⊕ Hut/Shelter
- ⊕ Lighthouse
- ⊚ Lookout
- ▲ Mountain/Volcano
- ⊚ Oasis
- ⊕ Park
-)(Pass
- ⊕ Picnic Area
- ⊕ Waterfall

Transport

- ⊕ Airport
- Ⓑ BART station
- ⊗ Border crossing
- Ⓣ Boston T station
- Ⓑ Bus
- ⊷⊕⊷ Cable car/Funicular
- ⊸⊛⊸ Cycling
- ⊸⊕⊸ Ferry
- Ⓜ Metro/MRT station
- ⊸⊕⊸ Monorail
- Ⓟ Parking
- ⊕ Petrol station
- ⑤ Subway/S-Bahn/ Skytrain station
- ⊚ Taxi
- ⊷⊕⊷ Train station/Railway
- ⨯⨯⨯⨯ Tram
- Ⓤ Underground/ U-Bahn station
- • Other Transport

Cyclists in Central Park (p36)

CDRIN/SHUTTERSTOCK ©

New York City Maps

Lower Manhattan

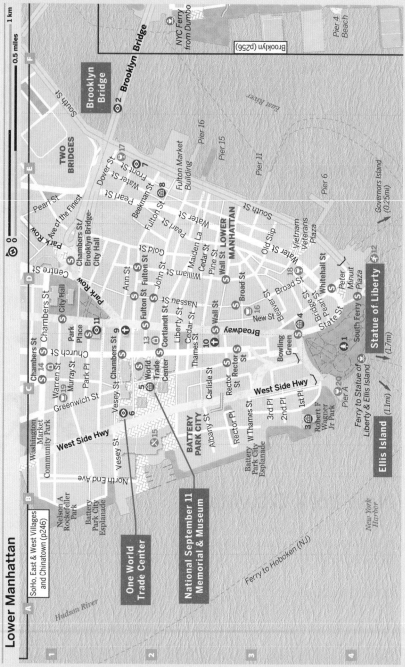

SoHo, East & West Villages and Chinatown (p246)

One World Trade Center

National September 11 Memorial & Museum

Brooklyn Bridge

Statue of Liberty

Ellis Island

TWO BRIDGES

LOWER MANHATTAN

BATTERY PARK CITY

Brooklyn (p256)

NYC Ferry from Dumbo

Ferry to Statue of Liberty & Ellis Island

Ferry to Hoboken (NJ)

Hudson River

New York Harbor

East River

Governors Island (0.25mi)

West Side Hwy

West Side Hwy

West Side Hwy

Broadway

0.5 miles
1 km

Pier 4 Beach
Pier 16
Pier 15
Pier 11
Pier 6
Fulton Market Building
South St
South St
Vietnam Veterans Plaza
Old Slip
Pine St
Cedar St
Maiden La
Water St
William St
Gold St
Fulton St
John St
Nassau St
Ann St
Beekman St
Pearl St
Front St
Water St
Dover St
Pearl St
Ave of the Finest
Park Row
Centre St
Park Row
Chambers St/
Brooklyn Bridge-
City Hall
City Hall
Chambers St
Warren St
Murray St
Park Pl
Park Place
Greenwich St
Church St
Vesey St
Vesey St
North End Ave
Battery Park City Esplanade
Albany St
Rector Pl
Carlisle St
Thames St
Cedar St
Liberty St
Cortlandt St
Fulton St
World Trade Center
3rd Pl
2nd Pl
1st Pl
W Thames St
Battery Pl
Rector St
Rector St
Robert F Wagner Jr Park
Pier A
South Ferry
Peter Minuit Plaza
State St
Whitehall St
Pearl St
Bridge St
Broad St
Broad St
Beaver St
New St
Wall St
Wall St
Bowling Green
Washington Market Community Park
Nelson A Rockefeller Park

Lower Manhattan

◉ Sights
1 Battery Park C4
2 Brooklyn Bridge F2
3 Museum of Jewish Heritage..................... C4
4 National Museum of the American
   Indian.. D3
5 National September 11 Memorial
   Museum C2
   One World Observatory..................... (see 6)
6 One World Trade Center........................... C2
7 South Street Seaport District................... E2
8 South Street Seaport Museum................. E2
9 St Paul's Chapel... D2
10 Trinity Church C3
11 Woolworth Building..................................... D1

⊕ Activities, Courses & Tours
12 Staten Island Ferry..................................... D4

⊕ Shopping
13 Century 21.. C2
14 Philip Williams Posters............................... C1

⊗ Eating
15 Brookfield Place C2
   Hudson Eats....................................... (see 15)
   Le District.. (see 15)

⊙ Drinking & Nightlife
16 Bluestone Lane... D3
17 Cowgirl SeaHorse E2
18 Dead Rabbit D3
19 Kaffe 1668 South.. C1
20 Pier A Harbor House................................... C4

SoHo, East & West Villages and Chinatown

A · B · C · D

W 14th St
83
Little W 12th St
93
3
9

High Line

46
8th Ave-14th St
31

14th St
14th St

6th Ave-14th St

14th St-Union Sq

WEST VILLAGE
103
76
W 13th St
W 12th St

Greenwich Ave

Fifth Ave

Gansevoort St
Horatio St
Jane St
W 12th St

65
110
29

Bank St
W 4th St

61

W 11th St
W 10th St
W 9th St

58
E 11th St

GREENWICH VILLAGE

MEATPACKING DISTRICT
35
38

Whitney Museum of American Art

Bleecker Playground
108

Waverly Pl

Sixth Ave (Avenue of the Americas)

E 8th St

51

Christopher St-Sheridan Sq
7
98
85

Washington Sq W

39

8

Hudson River Park

Bank St
W 11th St
Perry St
Charles St
W 10th St
Christopher St
Barrow St
Morton St
Leroy St
Clarkson St

West Side Hwy

Greenwich St
Hudson St

60
78
19
52

74
Grove St
43
Commerce St
96

Seventh Ave

Bedford St

Bleecker St
Cornelia St

W 4th St-Washington Sq

94
101
21

97

MacDougal St
Sullivan St
Thompson St
LaGuardia Pl

W 3rd St

Bleecker St

New York University

87

James J Walker Park

Houston St
99

W Houston St
King St
Charlton St
Vandam St
Spring St
Dominick St

W Houston St

44
Prince St

Spring St

SOHO

26

Mercer St

13

77

Watts St

Broome St

Canal St
Watts St

Grand St

Wooster St
Greene St

Hudson River Park

Hudson St

Canal St

Canal St
Canal St

Lispenard St
109

Holland Tunnel

Vestry St
Laight St

Hudson Square

73

25
White St

TRIBECA
10

West Side Hwy

N Moore St

Greenwich St

91
54
32

Hudson St

Franklin St
Franklin St
Leonard St

Broadway

Washington Market Community Park

56
Reade St

36
Thomas St
64
Worth St
100
Duane St

Hudson River

Lower Manhattan (p244)

0 | 1 km
0 | 0.5 miles

E   **F**   **G**   **H**

14th St-Union Sq
3rd Ave
86   1st Ave
Midtown Manhattan (p250)
E 14th St

E 13th St
88
23
E 13th St

33

E 12th St
89

Third Ave
Second Ave
Ave A
Ave C
Ave D

E 11th St
57
106 14
E 10th St
E 10th St
81
E 9th St
Tompkins Square Park
E 9th St

8th St-NYU
E 9th St
16
St Marks Pl
First Ave
E 8th St

Astor Pl
55
E 7th St
69
Ave B
E 7th St

ALPHABET CITY

Broadway
Lafayette St
Fourth Ave
102
75
E 6th St
E 6th St

E 5th St
67
E 5th St
E 5th St

NOHO
EAST VILLAGE
E 4th St

Great Jones St
37
New York City Marble Cemetery
E 3rd St
105

11 27 49
E 2nd St

Bleecker St
80
72
E Houston St

Broadway-Lafayette St
84
2nd Ave
E Houston St
Hamilton Fish Park

18
42 45
NOLITA
28
71
Essex St
Norfolk St
Suffolk St
Clinton St
50
Stanton St
LOWER EAST SIDE

20
Prince St
Elizabeth St
Bowery
6
107
12
Orchard St
Allen St
63
Rivington St

53
22
Forsyth St
Eldridge St
62
Delancey-Essex Sts

66
95
Delancey St
Lower East Side Tenement Museum

Spring St
92
40
Bowery
4
34
Columbia St

17
Kenmare St
90
Sara D Roosevelt Park
Broome St
15

30
82
47
Mott St
79
Grand St

24 41
5
48
LITTLE ITALY
Hester St
104
E Broadway
Henry St
Madison St

Canal St
Hester St
Canal St
WH Seward Park
East Broadway

CHINATOWN
Bowery
Confucius Plaza
Pike St
Monroe St
Cherry St

68
2
59
Doyers St
E Broadway
Madison St
Market St
Manhattan Bridge
Rutgers Park
South St

70
Catherine St

Federal Plaza
1
Park Row

SoHo, East & West Villages and Chinatown

Midtown Manhattan

SoHo, East & West Villages and Chinatown (p246)

Midtown Manhattan

⊙ Sights
1	Chelsea Market	B4
2	Empire State Building	D2
3	Madison Square Park	D3
4	New York Public Library	D1
5	Union Square Greenmarket	D4

⊕ Activities, Courses & Tours
6	Chelsea Piers Complex	A4
7	Simple Studios	C3

⊟ Shopping
8	192 Books	B4
9	ABC Carpet & Home	D4
10	Bedford Cheese Shop	E4
11	Fishs Eddy	D4
12	Hell's Kitchen Flea Market	B1
13	Housing Works Thrift Shop	C4
14	Macy's	C2
15	Nepenthes New York	B1

⊗ Eating
16	Big Daddy's	D4
	Chelsea Market	(see 1)
17	Cookshop	B4
18	Craft	D4
19	Eataly	D3
20	Eleven Madison Park	D3
21	Foragers Table	B4
22	Gramercy Tavern	D4
23	Hangawi	D2
24	Maialino	E4
25	O-ya	E3
26	Sons of Thunder	E1

⊜ Drinking & Nightlife
27	Bathtub Gin	B4
	Birreria	(see 19)
28	Eagle NYC	A3
29	Lillie's Victorian Establishment	D4
30	Old Town Bar & Restaurant	D4
31	Pier 66 Maritime	A3
32	Raines Law Room	D4
33	Stumptown Coffee Roasters	D3
34	Top of the Strand	D1

⊛ Entertainment
35	Jazz Standard	E3
36	Madison Square Garden	C2
37	Magnet Theater	C3
38	New Amsterdam Theatre	C1
39	Peoples Improv Theater	E3
40	Playwrights Horizons	B1
41	Sleep No More	A3

Times Square

Central Park & Uptown

Central Park & Uptown

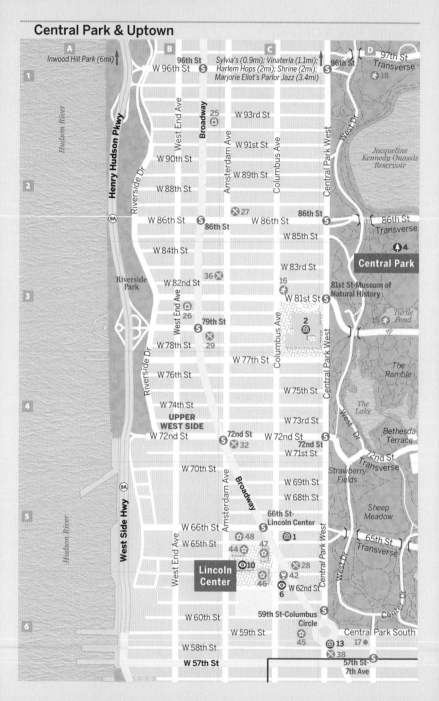

Inwood Hill Park (6mi)

Hudson River

Henry Hudson Pkwy

Riverside Dr

West End Ave

Broadway

Amsterdam Ave

Columbus Ave

Central Park West

96th St
W 96th St

Sylvia's (0.9mi); Vinatería (1.1mi);
Harlem Hops (2mi); Shrine (2mi);
Marjorie Eliot's Parlor Jazz (3.4mi)

96th St

97th St Transverse

18

W 93rd St

25

W 91st St

W 90th St

W 89th St

W 88th St

27

Jacqueline Kennedy Onassis Reservoir

W 86th St

86th St

W 86th St

86th St

W 85th St

86th St Transverse

4

W 84th St

Central Park

Riverside Park

W 83rd St

W 82nd St

36

16

81st St-Museum of Natural History

W 81st St

15

Turtle Pond

West End Ave

26

79th St

2

W 78th St

29

W 77th St

The Ramble

W 76th St

W 75th St

The Lake

W 74th St

UPPER WEST SIDE

W 73rd St

Bethesda Terrace

W 72nd St

72nd St

32

W 72nd St

72nd St

W 71st St

72nd St Transverse

W 70th St

Strawberry Fields

Amsterdam Ave

Broadway

W 69th St

W 68th St

Sheep Meadow

66th St-Lincoln Center

W 66th St

1

65th St Transverse

West End Ave

W 65th St

48

44

47

Lincoln Center

10

28

42

46

6

W 62nd St

West Dr

Center Dr

59th St-Columbus Circle

W 60th St

W 59th St

45

Central Park South

17

Hudson River

West Side Hwy

W 58th St

13

38

W 57th St

57th St-7th Ave

0 1 km
0 0.5 miles

E

Harlem Haberdashery (1.5mi);
Ginny's Supper Club (1.6mi);
Red Rooster (1.6mi);
Sylvia's (1.7mi)

F
Yankee Stadium
(3.8mi)
E 96th St
96th St

G
96th St
E 95th St

H
Mill Rock
Island
1

East River

Franklin D Roosevelt Dr

E 94th St

E 93rd St

9
E 92nd St

E 91st St

5 31

8 **Guggenheim Museum**

43
**UPPER
EAST SIDE**

Carl
Schurz
Park
2

E 89th St

E 87th St

E 86th St
35
86th St
E 86th St

14
86th St
E 85th St

24
E 84th St

E 83rd St

40
E 82nd St
E 81st St

12 **Metropolitan
Museum of Art**

41

E 80th St

E 79th St
E 79th St

E 78th St

39
77th St
E 77th St

30
E 76th St

E 75th St

11
E 74th St
33
E 73rd St
37

Franklin D Roosevelt Dr

3

Roosevelt
Island
4

E 72nd St
E 72nd St
72nd St

7
E 71st St

E 70th St

E 69th St
Rockefeller
University

East River

5

68th St-
Hunter College
E 68th St

E 67th St

E 66th St

3
E 65th St
E 65th St

Roosevelt
Island
5

Lexington Ave-
63rd St

West Rd

5th Ave-
59th St
Lexington Ave-
59th St
21
23
Roosevelt Island Tramway

Ed Koch Queensboro Bridge
6

22
E 59th St
59th St
E 59th St

E 58th St

57th St
Times Square (p252)
E 57th St

The
Mall

Literary
Walk

The
Dairy

The
Pond

Conservatory
Water

Fifth Ave
Madison Ave
Park Ave
Lexington Ave
Second Ave
First Ave
York Ave

Third Ave

East Dr

Brooklyn

◉ Sights
1 Brooklyn Botanic Garden D2
2 Brooklyn Bridge Park A1
3 Brooklyn Heights Promenade.................... A1
4 Brooklyn Museum D2
5 Empire Stores & Tobacco Warehouse A1
6 Jane's Carousel A1
7 Lefferts Historic House............................. D3
8 Prospect Park C3
9 Prospect Park Zoo D3

◉ Activities, Courses & Tours
10 LeFrak Center at Lakeside........................ D3

◉ Shopping
11 Brooklyn Flea... A1
12 Dellapietras.. A2
13 Twisted Lily... B2

◉ Eating
14 Ample Hills Creamery B2

15 Berg'n D2
16 Fornino at Pier 6 .... A2
17 Four & Twenty Blackbirds......................... B3
18 Juliana's... A1
19 Olmsted C2
20 One Girl Cookies.. A1

◉ Drinking & Nightlife
21 Clover Club... B2
22 June.. B2
23 Lavender Lake B3
24 Montero Bar & Grill A2

◉ Entertainment
25 Barbès C3
26 Barclays Center.. C2
27 Bell House B3
28 Brooklyn Academy of Music...................... B2
29 Jalopy... A3
30 St Ann's Warehouse A1

Williamsburg

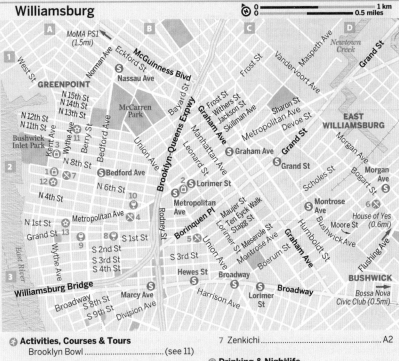

Our Story

A beat-up old car, a few dollars in the pocket and a sense of adventure. In 1972 that's all Tony and Maureen Wheeler needed for the trip of a lifetime – across Europe and Asia overland to Australia. It took several months, and at the end – broke but inspired – they sat at their kitchen table writing and stapling together their first travel guide, *Across Asia on the Cheap*. Within a week they'd sold 1500 copies. Lonely Planet was born.

Today, Lonely Planet has offices in Franklin, London, Melbourne, Oakland, Dublin, Beijing, and Delhi, with more than 600 staff and writers. We share Tony's belief that 'a great guidebook should do three things: inform, educate and amuse'.

Our Writers

Lorna Parkes

A Londoner by birth, Melburnian by palate and ex-Lonely Planet staffer in both cities, Lorna has contributed to numerous Lonely Planet books and magazines. She's discovered she writes best on planes, and is most content when researching food and booze. Wineries and the tropics are her go-to happy places (not at the same time!), but Yorkshire will always be special to her. Follow her on Twitter @Lorna_Explorer.

Hugh McNaughtan

A former English lecturer, Hugh swapped grant applications for visa applications, and turned his love of travel into a full-time thing. Having done a bit of restaurant-reviewing in his home town (Melbourne) he's now eaten his way across four continents. He's never happier than when on the road with his two daughters. Except perhaps on the cricket field...

Regis St Louis

Regis grew up in a small town in the American Midwest. He spent his formative years learning Russian and a handful of Romance languages, which has served him well on journeys across much of the globe. Regis has contributed to more than 50 Lonely Planet titles, covering destinations across six continents. When not on the road, he lives in New Orleans.

STAY IN TOUCH LONELYPLANET.COM/CONTACT

AUSTRALIA The Malt Store, Level 3, 551 Swanston St, Carlton, Victoria 3053
☎ 03 8379 8000,
fax 03 8379 8111

IRELAND Digital Depot, Roe Lane (off Thomas St), Digital Hub, Dublin 8, D08 TCV4, Ireland

USA 124 Linden Street, Oakland, CA 94607
☎ 510 250 6400,
toll free 800 275 8555,
fax 510 893 8572

UK 240 Blackfriars Road, London SE1 8NW
☎ 020 3771 5100,
fax 020 3771 5101

twitter.com/
lonelyplanet

facebook.com/
lonelyplanet

instagram.com/
lonelyplanet

youtube.com/
lonelyplanet

lonelyplanet.com/
newsletter